Our Violent World

To the memory of Dora Clemencia Azmitia Dorantes. Known to her friends as 'Menchy', she was involved in indigenous and urban education projects in her country, Guatemala. On 21 September 1981, when she was 23 years old and three months' pregnant, she was taken by a death squad.

Our Violent World

Terrorism in Society

Kevin McDonald

First published 2013 by
PALGRAVE MACMILLAN

Palgrave Macmillan in the UK is an imprint of Macmillan Publishers Limited, registered in England, company number 785998, of Houndmills, Basingstoke, Hampshire RG21 6XS.

Palgrave Macmillan in the US is a division of St Martin's Press LLC, 175 Fifth Avenue, New York, NY 10010.

Palgrave Macmillan is the global academic imprint of the above companies and has companies and representatives throughout the world.

Palgrave® and Macmillan® are registered trademarks in the United States, the United Kingdom, Europe and other countries

ISBN 978–0–230–22473–5 hardback
ISBN 978–0–230–22474–2 paperback

This book is printed on paper suitable for recycling and made from fully managed and sustained forest sources. Logging, pulping and manufacturing processes are expected to conform to the environmental regulations of the country of origin.

A catalogue record for this book is available from the British Library.

A catalog record for this book is available from the Library of Congress.

10 9 8 7 6 5 4 3 2 1
22 21 20 19 18 17 16 15 14 13

Printed and bound in Great Britain by
CPI Antony Rowe, Chippenham and Eastbourne

Contents

Preface and Acknowledgements

A book is the product of exchanges and experiences, often too numerous to adequately acknowledge, and this is certainly the case with this one. Its origins lie in teaching I was undertaking while at the University of Melbourne. It draws heavily on research undertaken while I was a Marie Curie International Fellow at Goldsmiths College, London, while also benefiting from the critical engagement of members of a doctoral seminar I taught at the École des Hautes Études en Sciences Sociales in Paris. At Goldsmiths, Les Back, Celia Lury, Caroline Knowles and Bev Skegs offered me a supportive and challenging environment, in both the Department of Sociology and the Centre for Urban and Community Research, while sections of the book draw on research undertaken with Mohammed Ilyas, and greatly benefited from the support of Jane Offerman. In Paris, the Centre d'Analyse et d'Intervention Sociologiques at the EHESS offered me a stimulating environment to explore the experience of violence, made possible by the generous support of Philippe Bataille, and the reader may recognize the extent of my debt to exchanges with Michel Wieviorka, Farhad Khosrokhavar, François Dubet, Geoffrey Pleyers, Yvon le Bot, Antimo Farro and Alain Touraine. In Melbourne I have greatly benefited from the support of Victoria University, and in particular its Centre for Cultural Diversity and Wellbeing. This book draws heavily on two publicly funded research projects: a Marie Curie International Fellowship supported by the European Union, and a Discovery Project supported by the Australian Research Council. Without the support of such public funding bodies, research into critical social transformations would no longer be possible.

A book is also a product of exchange and discussion with editors, and in this case exchanges with Anna Marie Reeve and her predecessors at Palgrave Macmillan played a key role in shaping this book. It sets out to explore the contribution that the social sciences might make to understanding and responding to the violence that has played such a role in reshaping societies over the past decade. In particular, it sets out to explore violence as experience, not simply as an idea or a concept. This has not been easy. Discussing actual violence needs considerable care, in part because violence is disturbing. In writing this book I did not want to amplify the impact of violence nor contribute to forms of trauma and shock. But it has sought to engage with experiential dimensions of violence, attempting to explore violence as a form of agency, one that is embodied, shaped by an imaginary extending beyond the boundaries of day-to-day experience. This has meant trying to reconstruct dimensions of the experience of people who have engaged in violence, not to demonise them, nor in any way to justify them, but above all not to reduce them to easily understood caricatures. This is an ethical as well as an intellectual position. In working through these questions, discussions with my editors, together with the generous comments of anonymous reviewers, have proved invaluable.

I was in central London using the transport system on the day of the attacks of 7 July 2005, and experienced the resulting close-down of the city, and I have been involved with the Council for Assisting Refugee Academics (CARA) working with Iraqi academics coping with a society and universities smashed by the War on Terror. These personal experiences, even though very much on the edges of some of the events discussed in this book, have alerted me to the responsibility we take on when writing about actions that have led to death, suffering and destruction. It means avoiding a breathless tone that some academic analyses embrace, while not skirting away from violence as an event, in particular in the contemporary world where violence increasingly seeks to kill.

The questions this book explores are critical for the social sciences, Sociology in particular. But they are also questions we confront and live as people. While we academics are often protected by libraries and university life, the research that shapes this book has involved moving beyond those walls, from interviewing supporters of jihad to exploring the increasing importance of extreme violence and its search for death. At times this has not been easy, and the support I have received from my wife Lorna Payne, together with that of our children Sarah, Lynne and Gabriel, has been a constant reminder of the hope, mess and wonder of life.

KEVIN McDONALD

Centre for Cultural Diversity and Wellbeing
Victoria University, Melbourne
Centre d'Analyse et d'Intervention Sociologiques,
École des Hautes Études en Sciences Sociales, Paris

Also by Kevin McDonald

STRUGGLES FOR SUBJECTIVITY: Identity, Action and Youth Experience
GLOBAL MOVEMENTS: Action and Culture

1

The Return of Violence

The early years of the twenty-first century have been shaped by an accelerating shift of social life from national societies to a new global reality. The signs are widespread: the increasing integration of economic and financial systems, population flows and mobility, a new awareness of shared realities, from global films to fashions, the pervasive presence of the Internet and the increasing mediatization of social life, new global risks such as climate change, epidemics and global crime. This new reality brings with it extraordinary possibilities, opening up exchanges, industries and creative flows, evident in the rise of social media and a cluster of practices around new forms of social connection. But at the same time, increased levels of complexity and integration bring with them new types of vulnerability and global shock waves, evident in the reverberations and amplifications of financial crises, flows of disease or the dislocations associated with climate change.

Among the most significant of these changes are transformations in forms of social and political violence, the kinds of violence recently described by the philosopher Charles Taylor as 'categorial', directed towards people whom the protagonists do not personally know (2011). Often such violence is contrasted to the violence that takes place within personal relationships, but as we will see as this book develops, this distinction is not as clear as it once may have been. The chapters that follow attempt to explore a context that has become increasingly evident, as violence that once appeared to be 'contained' by key dimensions of modern society is now much more fluid, increasingly part of the flows making up a global world (Urry 2005). But such violence is not a 'thing' or an object. It is a form of agency, an embodied relationship and human experience. As such, it is a critical lens through which to explore wider transformations of social life. On the other hand, to separate violence from such transformations profoundly limits our capacity to understand, and respond to, one of the most urgent questions shaping the twenty-first century.

The Surveillance Society

Most of us are aware of changing forms or potentials of violence through the growth of security and surveillance (Crelinsten 2009). Some developments are obvious, such as airport security. Others are less so, such as passport tracking systems, internment camps, control orders and detention without trial, or erosion of the distinction between immigration policy and security policy (Connolly 2005: 54). Some receive extensive debate in the press and social media, while other developments are less discussed. Over recent years, for example, states as different as Iran, Saudi Arabia, Israel and the United States have been engaged in the construction of thousands of kilometres of walls along national borders, a development that the political scientist Wendy Brown calls 'walling', something she contends is driven by 'waning sovereignty' (2010). Global military expenditure, which had declined in the years following the end of the Cold War in 1989, expanded rapidly over the first decade of the new century, increasing by some 49 per cent to reach US$1.53 trillion in 2009 (Stockholm International Peace Research Institute 2011). New types of public surveillance involve pervasive but ambiguous categories of 'pre-crime' as public policy seeks to identify groups and individuals 'at risk' of committing criminal acts (Zedner 2007). The changing role of the criminal justice system has become evident in the relentless increase in the number of people imprisoned in the world, a figure that reached some 10.65 million in 2009 (Walmsley 2010).

Political theorists in particular have been aware of the ways these transformations 'resonate', mutually amplifying each other (Connolly 2005: 54). Brian Massumi (2007) argues that we are witnessing the emergence of a new type of governance in complex societies, one shaped by a shift from a model of *prevention*, which operates in an 'objectively knowable world', to a model of *pre-emption*, which involves the attempt to wield power in a world based on uncertainty. Brad Evans (2010) points to the rise of 'consequentialist ethics' involved in this development, where forms of moral judgement framed in terms of 'right' and 'wrong' are becoming redefined as calculations to determine whether a situation is to be judged better or worse as a result of a course of action. These are not minor transformations. The OECD argues that 'security' has become a major area of economic activity, a driver of modern economies (OECD 2004), while the sociologist David Lyon traces the contours of a surveillance society increasingly based on digital technologies (Lyon 2004). The political philosopher William Connolly argues that this new social and political model involves an increasing mobilization of the population against 'unspecified enemies' (2005: 54).

The Blurring of War and Peace

One way to think about this transformation is in terms of a changing relationship between peace and war. The historical sociologist Charles Tilly argues that the emergence of modern societies from the seventeenth century to the Second World War saw violence moving in two directions: increasingly deadly inter-state confrontations and increasingly peaceful domestic societies, evident in the disarming of populations and the rise of peaceful forms of protest and conflict (Tilly 2002, 2003). This constituted an increasingly clear separation between zones of war and zones of peace, a separation that for the philosopher Immanuel Kant constituted the very basis of modern society (Kleingold 2006: ix). This account of the birth of modernity locates violence beyond the borders of increasingly peaceful societies, and to a significant extent has established itself as a structure of thought preventing any significant exploration of the violence at the heart of modern societies, in particular the violence present in colonial expansion, or in the extent of atrocities and extreme violence undertaken by the colonizers in the process of decolonization (Bennett 2011). Within this modern self-understanding, the capacity for extreme violence has always been associated with 'the other', with modern society, by definition, understood as being inherently peaceful.

The securitization we have referred to above signals two related transformations: the separation between war and peace is becoming less and less clear, while the state's monopoly of violence is becoming less and less certain. Rather than war being an external event, the cultural geographer Nigel Thrift argues that contemporary, globalizing societies have entered an 'era of permanent and pervasive war' (2011: 11), with war no longer understood as taking place beyond borders, but across all areas of social life. This shift seems particularly evident when we look at urban design, where we encounter not simply the increasing integration of blast proofing and other defensive systems into buildings, but the actual militarization of urban space, evident in particular in contemporary military theory where older conceptions of 'battlefield' are giving way to new models of 'battle space' (see Graham 2012) where the space of warfare becomes 'coterminus...with the space of civil society itself' (Dillon and Reid 2009: 128). This pattern is evident in the extent that conceptions of urban security developed in a warzone such as post-2003 Baghdad have established themselves as paradigms for policing and security in the cities of North American and Europe (Graham 2010).

War, from this perspective, rather than being an activity beyond the borders of modern society, becomes instead a lens with which to conceive of the core organization of such societies. The rise of war as a lens to frame social life has been particularly evident in military theory. William Lind, for example, argues that the world has entered an age of 'fourth generation war', characterized by the loss of the state's monopoly over the exercise of war. Today states find themselves at war with non-state opponents, wars he argues that states are losing. Writing in a respected journal, Lind argues 'invasion by immigration can be at least as dangerous as invasion by a state army' (2004: 14). We do not need to embrace this type of argument to recognize that the twenty-first century has been shaped by an awareness of a new vulnerability.

The New Vulnerability

The period immediately following the collapse of the Berlin Wall in 1989 was one of celebration of the end of the dangers of the Cold War. This sense of liberation played an important role in the way journalists, politicians and scholars enthusiastically embraced the concept of globalization in the 1990s, installing it as a new 'master narrative' to make sense of transformations reshaping the world, closely linked with the development of what the sociologist Manuel Castells (2001) called the 'internet galaxy'. Observers of this transformation highlighted the potential of new global social movements (McDonald 2006), non-governmental organizations (Tarrow 2005), and celebrated the potential of what increasingly came to be called 'global civil society' (Keane 2003).

But there was also a darker narrative. One influential example was articulated by the American journalist Robert Kaplan (1994), who argued that the end of the Cold War would bring with it an unconstrained expansion of violent conflicts exacerbated by population explosion, and economic and environmental collapse, which would set in motion massive flows of refugees and the proliferation of 'small wars'. This was not a 'global civil society', but a world threatened by chaos, violence and, ultimately, the collapse of the system of international regulation that had been forged by the major powers in the years following the Second World War. Kaplan was not alone. He was joined by the political scientist Samuel Huntington (1996), who argued that the political conflicts of the Cold War period, shaped by opposing ideologies, were giving way to a new type of conflict that he described as a 'clash of civilizations'.

The terms of this debate were transformed by the attacks of 11 September 2001. The attacks not only killed some 3,000 people, they also set in motion a series of shockwaves that are still resonating over a decade later. The United States became militarily engaged in Afghanistan, in what would become the longest war in its history. The attacks highlighted the vulnerability of complex systems, when a small group of people armed with box cutters and fake bombs could succeed in bringing down structures at the centre of world financial and symbolic power (Urry 2005). The period that followed underlined that these attacks were not an isolated event, but signalled the emergence of a movement that manifested its existence essentially through violence. In October 2002, bomb blasts in the nightclub district in Bali, Indonesia, killed over 200 people (Koschade 2006). In March 2004, four massive explosions ripped apart crowded commuter trains in Madrid, Spain, killing 191 people and injuring over 1,000 (Moghadam 2006). In that same month in the United Kingdom a group of men were arrested in possession of some 600 kilograms of ammonium nitrate, later being convicted of planning to blow up a shopping centre and a night club (Scolino and Grey 2006). The following year, in July 2005, four young men blew themselves up on London's transport system, killing themselves and 52 others, while two weeks later another group attempted a similar action (Pape 2006). In Germany in 2006, suitcases filled with powerful explosives failed to detonate on high-speed trains (Khosrokhavar 2009), while in Australia in 2008 a group of men were convicted under anti-terrorism legislation of planning mass murder at a sporting event (Lentini 2008). In November of that same year a group of ten young men launched an attack on Mumbai, India's financial capital, using high-powered rifles and explosives, killing some 170 people over three days (Shekhar 2009). In May 2010, a man attempted to detonate an incendiary bomb in a car parked near New York's Times Square on a busy Saturday night (United States Attorney, New York Southern District New York 2010). In the United Kingdom in February 2012 a group of men pleaded guilty to planning to detonate a bomb at the London Stock Exchange (Burns and Cowell 2012), while in March of that year in the French town of Toulouse a young man went on a killing spree, murdering seven people, including three children and their father at a Jewish school, reportedly filming the killings and claiming links to international networks (Ramadan 2012). Throughout the decade, recurring attempts were made to destroy planes on transatlantic flights, with attempts to conceal explosives in shoes, underwear and soft-drink bottles, leading to worldwide security protocols reminding travellers of the potential for catastrophic violence each time they board an aeroplane (Khosrokhavar 2009).

At the same time, other cases of extreme violence emerged. In Norway in 2011 a young man exploded a car bomb in the capital, Oslo, after which he drove to a youth political camp being held on an island, killing 77 people in total with high-powered weapons, claiming to be fighting against cultural diversity and to having been inspired by the World Trade Center attacks as well as the 1995 destruction of the Federal Building in Oklahoma City in the United States, an attack which killed 169 people (Kellner 2012).

In November 2009 a major in the US Army killed 13 people and wounded 30 on an army base after a period of email contact with a self-styled radical cleric (Chen 2010). In 2007 a student at an American university killed 32 people and wounded another 25 on campus, posting a video to the Internet likening himself to Jesus Christ and condemning his victims before committing suicide (Kao 2012).

These attacks all exhibit a desire to kill as many people as possible. Many were associated with communications technologies, from final testaments posted to the Internet to the perpetrators filming themselves in the act of killing. None of them involved the types of telephone warnings often associated with attacks undertaken by armed groups such as the Irish Republican Army in the 1970s (Clutterbuck 2004). In several cases the people involved in these attacks appeared to be acting alone, or connected with friends in loose networks. What was striking was the lack of the kinds of organization that had characterized violence from earlier periods. In several cases the mental health of those involved became an issue that courts were asked to determine, given the extremity of the violence (Pantucci 2011).

Understanding what is at stake in such violence has emerged as a major challenge confronting complex societies in the twenty-first century. As we might expect, analyses diverge widely. One approach remains framed by the modern self-understanding introduced above, regarding such violence as essentially a product of 'the other', and has been a major factor reshaping immigration and refugee policy across a range of countries (Tumlin 2004). An influential current within this approach looks to religion as a source of violence, an analysis popularized by Huntington's (1996) 'clash of civilization' thesis. Other approaches emphasize that this violence needs to be understood fundamentally in political terms, primarily as a response to Western hegemony and global power (Jackson 2005). We will explore these different approaches in the chapters that follow. But what does seem clear is that in the current context of securitization, potential and actual violence merge, with violence becoming a potential that threatens one of the core dimensions of modern societies – the fact that we live with strangers. It is this shift that means that violence and the vulnerability increasingly associated with it have become a central question for the social sciences, Sociology in particular.

Sociology and Violence

To what extent can a discipline like Sociology help us understand transformations in contemporary violence? To begin to explore this we need to recognize that the relationship between Sociology and violence has been problematic. The origins of what would become Sociology lie in the years leading up to the First World War when, as Hans Joas (2003) observes, war and violence were major issues within the culture of the time. This is reflected in Sociology's founders. Max Weber, the German thinker central to the emergence of the discipline, attached great importance to the historical emergence of armies and the culture of discipline they produced. He argued that war played a critical role in the historical shift from tribal and community-based forms of social organization to states and their societies. The key process for Weber was not the development of technologies of warfare, but the creation of military discipline (Weber 2005: 261; van Krieken 1990). This was critical to the emergence and eventual triumph of state-based societies. For Weber, military discipline gives birth to all discipline; it was at the centre of the emergence and eventual triumph of state-organized societies.

Writing in France, Weber's contemporary Emile Durkheim was equally alert to the question of violence. However, Durkheim associated violence with what he considered to be primitive and impulsive. He regarded violence as disruptive, affirming that it was through ritual and, ultimately, social organization that its disruptive power was contained. Durkheim did not approach violence within a theory of the rationalization of societies, but instead framed it in terms of 'effervescence', of assemblies of dancing people generating enthusiasm as 'electricity', one where 'natural violence' is concentrated and passions unleashed, social norms smashed, and in the process a state of 'exaltation' reached where people find themselves possessed and led by what is experienced as an external power. For Durkheim, this power is society at work, but experienced as the world of the sacred (Durkheim 2001: 163–4). Within Durkheim's work we encounter an account where violence is a path that allows the actor to access a world of the extraordinary. Hans Joas (2003) underlines just how important this conception of *generative* violence was in the period leading up to the Great War of 1914–18. He points to it in the work of thinkers such as the Marxist intellectual Georges Sorel (1908/1999) in France, who argued that workers discover their authentic selves through violence; or in the work of sociologists such as Sombart and Simmel in Germany, who considered violence and war as a means through which societies could free themselves from the deadening routines of modern industrial society. Violence, from this perspective, is understood as a source of regeneration of life (Joas 2003).

Sociology largely constituted itself as a discipline in the period following the Second World War, when there was no consensus regarding these diverging approaches to violence. Indeed, at the time, sociologists largely embraced a model of social change understood as modernization, where violence was either understood as part of an older, dying world, or as an expression of deviance, the failure of the society to integrate certain of its members into the dominant non-violent values and practices. Sociology in a sense had 'moved on', embracing the optimism of the post-1945 period (Joas 2003: 31). Where it did emerge, violence was regarded as a sign of failure or the absence of the social, certainly not its product. Violence became relegated to Sociology's margins (Joas 2003; Malešević 2010), which understood itself as discipline setting out to understand the development of modern, peaceful, societies (Ray 2011). Indeed, in the second half of the twentieth century, the most significant theorizations of violence developed by sociologists, such as Norbert Elias' (1976, 1983) theory of civilizing process, an analysis of self-restraint and of the historical shift from a warrior to a court society, set out to explain what was considered by post-war sociologists as axiomatic, namely the long-term decline in the levels and significance of violence accompanying the birth of modern society (Ray 2011). Elias developed a theory of the decline of violence based on European history, proposing a transition from a more violent Middle Ages to more peaceful court societies. The core of this transition was the development of absolutist monarchies that disarmed the nobility and came to exercise a monopoly over violence. Elias argues that, to the extent that nobles could no longer rely upon violence to achieve their objectives, a culture of courtesy gradually developed, ultimately leading to transformation in personality structure emphasizing self-control and the avoidance of violence (Elias 1976 320–5).

The idea that the state was defined by its monopoly over the means of violence, and that this was central to the creation of modernity, established itself as a proposition widely shared by sociologists. Elias' thesis formed the core of Anthony Giddens' (1987) influential theory of the place of violence in the constitution of modernity (Giddens having taught at Leicester University, where Sociology had been created by Elias). For Giddens, the pacification of societies and the concentration of the means of violence in the hands of the state were two sides of the same process, the 'centralisation of violence' in the state was one of the four dynamics constituting modernity, of importance equal to capitalism, industrialism and the development of capacities of surveillance and administration (Held and Thompson 1989).

Well before the events of September 11 this understanding of modern society was becoming contested. The Balkan wars of the mid-1990s had generated violence and massacres of such horrific proportions that observers had begun to develop theories of 'new wars' (Kaldor 2001) making a radical break with Kantian optimism. Historians noted that the twentieth century had been the most murderous of human history, with some 110 million deaths resulting directly from war (Eckhardt 1992: 272). This meant that 22 times more people had been killed in war during the twentieth century than in the previous 4,900 years of human history (Malešević 2010: 118).

Not only was the scale of violence and killing an increasingly pressing question. Violence seemed less and less contained by professional armies fighting in isolated battlefields. One estimate suggested that civilian deaths resulting from war had risen dramatically over the twentieth century, from 10 per cent of those killed in the First World War, to 50 per cent in the Second World War, and making up 90 per cent of those killed in the wars of the 1990s (Chesterman 2001). While later work by demographers and population scientists would call into question these initial figures (Lacina and Gleditsch 2005), the overall direction is clear. Rather than isolated battlefields, over the twentieth century war came to be fought in cities and suburbs. And rather than a monopoly of states acting through organized armies, the protagonists were increasingly militias, crime groups, families, friends, networks, even individuals. War seemed to be spilling out from the systems and structures established to contain it. It was no longer clear that modern society had 'solved' the problem of violence. Just as were citizens throughout the world, the social sciences were confronting its return.

Violence, Culture and Modern Society: Obedience

While Sociology may have regarded violence as a sign of the failure or absence of society, there have none the less been times when violence has posed questions about the nature of the modern world that have been taken up by sociologists. In the post-war period the most important of these debates focused on the Nazi attempt to destroy Europe's Jewish population, with sociologists joining others in attempting to understand what made such violence possible. This debate took place well after the events themselves, at a time when the term 'Holocaust' emerged in the early 1960s, the period corresponding with the trial of Albert Eichmann, a senior Nazi administrator who had played a central role in organizing the deportation of Jews and others in what came to be known as the Final Solution. In his trial in Jerusalem in 1961, Eichmann set out to defend himself, arguing that he was not responsible for his actions because he was following orders. This argument was explored by the political philosopher Hannah Arendt, who reported on the trial for *The New York Times*, coining the term 'the banality of evil' in response to Eichmann's defence (Arendt 1963).

Eichmann's defence spoke to questions that had been emerging across the social sciences, in Sociology in particular. This was the concern that modern, mass society was generating types of people lacking an inner moral core, happy to conform to the expectations placed upon them. Writing in the same year as Eichmann's trial, the Yale sociologist David Riesman (Riesman *et al.* 1961) coined the term 'outer-directed' to explore the type of personality associated with the 'lonely crowd' of modern industrial society, a type of person who would seek to conform to the demands of authority no matter what form they took. This concern was equally central to the work of the psychologist Stanley Milgram (1961), who, in an experiment we will explore, set out to test whether new social expectations of conformity and obedience could be linked to a new readiness to undertake violence. The prominent social thinker Zygmunt Bauman (1989) was one of a number of sociologists arguing that the cultural patterns of modern society, focused on bureaucratization, were at the origins of the violence unleashed in the Holocaust. This debate posed questions about the very nature of the modern world, framed above all in terms of *obedience*. This was not only a question of the organization and structures of society, but also opened out the issue that Riesman called 'character' and what today we might call subjectivity or agency – a cluster of questions about the way we act in the world and about the moral imagination that sustains that action.

These analyses are very important, to the extent that they link culture, agency and violence with major social patterns. In a way similar to the early 1960s, violence has emerged once again as an issue that confronts us with questions about social organization and moral imagination. But there is a sense that the terms of the 1960s debate, with its focus on conformism and obedience, fails to capture some new dynamic that is at work today. Rather than obedience, a cluster of new questions are emerging, associated with forms of violence that appear increasingly fluid, no longer contained by the institutions that have shaped modern societies. And arguably the most fluid of these is the violence widely referred to as terrorism.

Terrorism?

As we saw above, early sociological accounts of violence were structured in two quite different ways. One was shaped by a Weberian tradition emphasizing discipline and specialization, its paradigm being the emergence of what would become the rationalized army. The other was shaped by a Durkheimian emphasis on violence as fusion into something larger, an access to an extraordinary realm, experienced as the sacred. These contrasting approaches have important echoes today. One product of analyses frames violence in terms of intention and strategy, considering it the product of a 'rational actor'. The other approaches violence in terms of loss of control and fusion, a model conceptualized in terms of the 'fanatical actor'. As we will see, these two accounts of violence recur across a wide range of analyses, where the more extreme the violence, the more the analysis is located at one or the other end of this polarity. This is particularly the case with terrorism, where analysis is polarized between two models: the fanatic who is outside any appeal to rationality, and the calculating actor who lacks any capacity for human empathy.

Despite it being widely used in political debate and public policy, many social scientists are reluctant to use the term 'terrorism'. There are a number of issues involved. Perhaps the principal one is pointed to by the sociologist Austin Turk, who underlines that terrorism is not an unambiguous 'given' of the real world, but a social construction involving an interpretation of events. Both the construction of *what* constitutes terror and *who* is a terrorist are embedded within broader dynamics of conflict, where 'ideological warfare to cast the enemy as an evildoer is a dimension of the struggle to win support for one's own cause' (Turk 2004). Turk is pointing to the truism that 'one person's terrorist is another person's freedom fighter', evident in the extent that people previously reviled as terrorists may later come to be regarded as national heroes and statesmen. A second problem with the term 'terrorism' refers to its intellectual and organizational location. Institutionally, research on terrorism has often been marginal within universities, more likely to be located in strategic think tanks and institutes than in academic departments. As a result, a significant number of those involved in terrorism studies have backgrounds in security services or the armed forces, often claiming privileged access to 'insider knowledge'. This has led to a field shaped more by experts and expertise rather than the debates and research programmes characterizing other academic areas (Ranstorp 2006).

This reliance on expertise is central to one of the dimensions of 'terrorism studies' pointed to by Martha Crenshaw, namely its lack of theoretical development, evident in the extent to which the field consists largely of collections of descriptive work (2000: 405). The absence of theoretical debates that could structure research programmes may explain the extraordinary importance that debates about definitions of terrorism play in this area, with one recent study pointing to over 100 'definitions' of terrorism being offered in key journals (Schmid 2004). The seemingly never-ending debates about definitions clearly reflect the lack of theoretical models and the difficulty of producing ongoing research programmes. But they alert us to something else as well: the extent to which much of the discussion of terrorism is in fact coded argument about whether a particular actor or struggle can be regarded as legitimate or not.

The close alignment between terrorism research and national security priorities has also tended to determine when the term is used. Official histories tend to either eclipse the role of violence in national histories, or transform it into a heroic enterprise. There are few national histories that make explicit reference to the role of terrorist violence in the birth of the nation. Equally, there is a wide consensus in the academic literature that terrorism never succeeds (Hoffman 2011), but to a significant extent this may be because if it succeeds, violence once considered terrorist comes to be redefined as a struggle for national liberation. From this perspective, the only violence labelled as terrorist is violence that has failed.

Virtuous Violence

The origins of the modern use of the term 'terrorism' date from the French Revolution, when 'terror' was used to describe the revolutionary violence carried out by the Committee of Public Safety in 1794. In this case we encounter violence that is loaded with meaning, clearly part of a wider cultural as much as social and political context. Under the leadership of Maximilien de Robespierre, terror was unleashed not simply as a tactic to deal with opponents, but as a form of government. For Robespierre, terror was closely associated with the sovereignty of the new revolutionary state: in a time of peace, the basis of this sovereignty was the virtue of the people; but in a time of war, the rule of the people required terror. For Robespierre, terror was fundamentally concerned with virtue and what he called 'great things'. In his report to the National Convention, Robespierre articulates what amounts to key dimensions of an 'imaginary of terror', calling for policies that would 'excite love of the homeland, the purification of morals, the lifting up of souls', which would free the French people from 'the abjection of the personal self, everything that encourages interest in small things and the contempt of great things' (Robespierre 1794). For Robespierre, terror was much more than a policy of intimidation. It was violence that understood itself as an expression of virtue, capable of freeing the population from the 'abjection of the personal' and opening them to the encounter with 'great things'.

The association of violence with virtue was not only central to politics at this time; it also played an important role within the culture of the time. The relationship between violence, virtue and citizenship was central to a contemporary of Robespierre, the author and libertine D. A. F. de Sade. De Sade was outside the new moral order created by the primacy of the virtuous collective, a world he describes and explores in his writing through turning it on its head. For de Sade, virtue is a form of repression, focused above all on sexual repression, something that must be overcome through desire. But for de Sade, desire is realized through violence, most notably in his novel *Justine* (de Sade 1787/2010), the story of a woman who is kidnapped, tortured and raped, but who through this violence comes to discover the extent to which she is trapped by virtue, ultimately experiencing freedom through de Sade's (and the reader's) symbolic fulfilment of the fantasy of 'profaning and martyring a saint' (Seybert 1995: 56). De Sade turns Robespierre's world on its head, as law and virtue are abolished in the world of the libertine. For both Robespierre and de Sade, as Isabelle Sommier perceptively observes, violence becomes 'an instrument of communion with a principle of a higher order' (in these cases, virtue and its opposite, desire), 'in whose name it becomes justified' (Sommier 2002: 475). Here we see echoes of Durkheim's understanding of violence as a path to an experience of fusion with something greater, something beyond. Violence here allows the person to transcend the mundane, day-to-day world. This kind of violence has been described by the German sociologist Bernd Weisbrod (2002) as 'redemptive violence', as violence that not only transforms but 'saves'. This alerts us to the ways that terror as a form of violence is charged with meaning.

It is important to recognize that the violence unleashed during the Terror was not only charged with themes of virtue and grandeur, it was public violence. The executions undertaken by the Committee of Public Safety took place not within the prison walls, but at the centre of the vast Place de la Révolution (later renamed Place de la Concorde), watched by thousands of people, where the act of killing became associated with a new type of sacred power (Hunt 1990). The public nature of this violence alerts us to a crucial dimension of terrorism: it involves not only perpetrators and victims, but also involves witnesses, and this clearly distinguishes it from other forms of violence. Terror is fundamentally a form of *communicative* violence, one that constructs a public experience.

War and the Violence of States

The association of the term 'terrorism' with what we might broadly regard as a 'security paradigm' has meant that such cultural and communicative dimensions of terrorist violence have tended to be marginalized from analysis. Equally, the violence of states has also been largely excluded from the study of terror: terrorism is instead conceptualized as something to which states must respond (Schinkel 2010). As a result, not only does much research on terrorism focus on debates about definitions, but many of these definitions analytically separate terrorism from the action of states. The United States Department of State defines terrorism as 'premeditated, politically motivated violence perpetrated against noncombatant targets by subnational groups or clandestine agents, usually intended to influence an audience' (US Department of State 2003: xiii). This influential definition restricts terrorism to the action of subnational, non-state groups, and has promoted polemic responses from critical researchers who point to the terrorist actions of states, ranging from the execution of opponents to forms of warfare that increasingly appear directed at terrorizing populations. For critics of American policy, such as Noam Chomsky, low-intensity conflict, where military action is directed primarily at civilians and irregular forces rather than at other armies, amounts to what he calls 'state terrorism' (2011: 376).

There are important issues here, but perhaps best approached by side-stepping the debate about 'who is a terrorist'. A better approach may be to frame the issues in terms of transformations in contemporary warfare. The political scientist Mary Kaldor (2001) highlights the increasing role of non-state actors in war, from organized crime to ethnic groups, highlighting the end of states' monopoly of the prosecution of war. Kaldor argues that there is strong evidence that the purpose and target of violence in war is changing. In classical war, the goal is to capture territory, and the principal means through which this is pursued is the battle. She notes that guerrilla warfare maintained the objective of controlling territory, but sought to do so through controlling populations rather than winning battles, which were avoided. Protagonists of 'new wars', she asserts, no longer seek to 'win hearts and minds' as did classical guerrilla forces, but instead seek to control the population by instilling terror, which she sees as directed towards 'getting rid of everyone of different identity' (2001: 8). Kaldor argues that today war no longer takes place through battles, but through mass killing and forcible expulsion, involving political, psychological and economic techniques of intimidation, illustrated by the killings of civilians in Iraq or Darfur. This shift, she argues, explains the expansion in civilian casualties and numbers of displaced people and refugees in contemporary war. This is not as a result of stray bullets or the confusion of non-combatants for fighters. Instead, killing and terrorizing civilian populations has become one of the principal means through which war is prosecuted.

This account involves a significant break with the dominant sociological models of warfare, which have emphasized discipline, professionalization and specialization. Giddens, for example, when discussing the development of modern armies, highlights the importance of the introduction of uniforms, which help 'strip individuals of those traits that might interfere with routinized patterns of obedience' (1987: 230). For Giddens, this is part of a modernization process involving the 'industrialisation of war', one through which the soldier becomes 'a specialist purveyor of the means of violence' (Giddens 1987: 230). This Weberian account is echoed in the recent analysis of Siniša Malešević, who describes the emergence of the modern military in the following terms:

> From now on the military is run by highly specialised professionals that undergo long institutionalised training, that are separated from the rest of society, have a fixed system of promotion based on skills and experience, follow a consistent

system of abstract rules, obey an impersonalised hierarchical order ... the modern
military is the epitome of Weberian bureaucracy.

(Malešević 2010: 127)

Violence and, in particular, killing do not figure strongly in these accounts.
The language itself is significant. The term 'purveyor', a word normally
referring to the provision of fine food products, might suggest that becoming a 'specialist purveyor of the means of violence' is analytically equivalent
to becoming a specialist purveyor of fine pastries. This would imply that
engaging in violence and killing is no more difficult than other activities
requiring a degree of training.

Other accounts of military activity offer a very different emphasis. While
Giddens constructs an analysis of the deindividualization of violence, the
historian Joanna Bourke (2000) explores what she calls the 'intimate history
of killing' in warfare, her aim to 'put killing back into military history'. She
contends that killing is a very difficult thing to do, hence the importance of
military training, which she argues sets out to transform fear into anger, and
to channel this anger into a capacity to kill (Bourke 2000: 83). Rather than
deindividualizing violence, Bourke sets out to *personalize* it, her analysis of
embodied experiences of killing diverging radically from accounts of pro-
fessionals and purveyors.

The tensions in these approaches will be important to explore in the chapters that follow. One way to move beyond the 'state' versus 'non-state' debate
may be offered by the Dutch criminologist Willem Schinkel (2010). Noting
that the origins of the term 'terror' lie in the Greek and Sanskrit words for
fear, he suggests distinguishing between using the term 'terror' to identify
the action of states that govern through fear, a 'top down' process, while he
proposes using 'terrorism' to refer to non-state actors who seek to disrupt
forms of power, equally through fear. Terror, from this perspective, is the
action of states seeking compliance, while terrorism is a form of violence
prosecuted by non-state actors 'against random or symbolic targets to induce
fear among a wider audience, in order to influence some state' (2010: 143).

Violence, Embodiment and Agency

As we will see, much of the discussion of terrorism is framed in terms of
'strategic' or 'political' violence. This tends to emphasize the intentions or
the objectives of the actors who embrace violence, with the implication that
violence is chosen as a strategy or means to arrive at these goals. This draws
on a wider theory of rational action that seeks to explain behaviour by the
intentions of its authors, approaching violence as the outcome of a process

of decision or indeed 'calculation'. Implicit in this argument is a model of 'cost' and 'benefit', where violence is understood as a cost that actors are prepared to pay in order to obtain the benefit they seek.

How adequately does this rational actor model frame violence? The American sociologist Randall Collins (2008), echoing Joanna Bourke, argues that violence, and in particular, collective violence, is *difficult to achieve*. It is not enough to *decide* to be violent in order to become violent. Collins explores the violence that emerges in riots, and demonstrates that this is the product of a process of *interaction* between police and a crowd, where the embodied dimensions of this interaction are of critical importance for the successful construction of a riot. He highlights a number of phases involved in the construction of violence, each involving forms of embodied interaction (see also McDonald 2012). At the heart of this argument is the assertion that collective violence is something difficult to achieve, and its construction passes through embodied experiences of interaction more than the calculation of goals and means.

What is striking is the absence of violence as such an embodied, relational experience in very large sections of the literature on terrorism. Joanna Bourke's observation about the absence of killing in military history could equally apply to much of the discussion of terrorism. For reasons we explore below, an extraordinary amount of work on violence is focused on its *causes*, with these causes being located *outside the experience of violence* itself. Embedded in this we encounter a model of action or agency, one that we can describe as 'determinist' (Schinkel 2010), where some other event or reality is seen as the source of violence. Locating violence in such a determinist framework means that the subjective dimension of violence disappears, considered as being largely irrelevant to understanding violence as a social phenomenon (Wieviorka 2009).

Does this matter? In the chapters below we will see the extent to which this excludes dimensions of violence that may in fact be critical to understanding its development and transformation, such as fascination, fear, dread and exhilaration. Determinist analyses exclude from our consideration the possibility that actors embrace violence because they enjoy it as an experience, either as a form of release or as an imposition of suffering upon another, or the search for excess. The philosopher Arne Johan Vetlesen (2005) suggests that the popularity of rational accounts of violence may in part lie in the way they protect us from considering some of the most disturbing dimensions of violence, above all taking pleasure in the suffering of another. The French sociologist Michel Wieviorka (2009) argues that violence involves a dimension of mystery, something that is beyond our capacity to capture completely in conceptual terms. The awareness of the ways violence escapes models of rational action has been linked to the emergence of its mirror opposite as an analytical framework, the idea of the 'fanatic'. In this case the observer does not attempt to reconstruct the causes of violence; rather s/he seeks to identify the pathology at the root of fanaticism. As we will see, for many analyses adopting this framework, fanaticism is linked with religious experience, but in the process violence is removed from social relationships and reduced to an expression of pathology. Going beyond this polarization demands a more complex account of violence as experience.

The Experience of Violence

We are, as philosophers remind us, beings-in-the-world, and this being-in-the-world is fundamentally an embodied experience (Merleau-Ponty 1948/2004: 66). Where we seek to define violence uniquely as the product of calculation or costs and benefits, we remove the embodied, experiential dimension of violence from the way we understand it. Violence in many cases involves inflicting pain and suffering upon another person, and this opens out the question of affect and empathy – the capacity of an actor to feel the pain and suffering of another. This, more than calculations of cost and benefit, may be of critical importance in developing a social science of violence, highlighting the need to develop new ways of thinking about violence as *experience*. This may be of particular importance in understanding violence today, given the extent to which the experience of *the victim* has become so significant in contemporary social and cultural life (Wieviorka 2009). This highlights the need to develop forms of analysis that allow us to capture the cultural power of violence. The Yale sociologist Jeffrey Alexander writes 'we need to theorize terrorism differently, thinking of its violence less in physical and instrumental terms than as a particularly gruesome kind of symbolic action in a complex performative field' (2006: 91). This book sets out to contribute to this shift in perspective.

As we will see, the study of contemporary violence remains largely framed by a Janus-faced relationship between a 'rational actor' paradigm and a 'fanatical actor' paradigm, with violence considered to be the result of a decision or the expression of pathology. This polarization eclipses what Hans Joas calls the 'dynamics of violence' (2003: 192), a dynamic he suggests is close to, but ultimately very different from, experiences of creativity. Here Joas is highlighting experiences of transformation associated with violence, such as loss of self and its reconstruction, or the way violence can transform not only social worlds but also experiences of selfhood. This means part of the challenge confronting the social sciences is to understand the *experience* of violence. The German philosopher Axel Honneth helps to articulate what 'experience' means when he writes

> Experiencing something means much more than encountering persons, events, or things of which we merely take notice. In most encounters, we merely confirm a set of orientations we have already acquired ... But we 'experience' something when the situation is so unfamiliar to us, so novel, that we cannot apply our familiar knowledge and are surprised by the confused state of our intentions, knowledge and moods. In situations such as these, the significance of what we encounter is still unsettled, and we lack the interpretive tools to get control over this confusing and multilayered situation ... This is the case whenever the novelty of a situation captures us ... such that we cannot escape the confusion of our intentions, knowledge and emotions. In these situations, we speak – a bit helplessly – of being overwhelmed.
>
> (Honneth 2010: 778)

Honneth alerts us to violence transforming in ways that actors may not understand, to its ability to open up dimensions that appear beyond day-to-day reality. Such experiential dimensions may be at the centre of critical transformations in contemporary violence, evident in the increasing personalization of violence, in the search for the extreme, in the association of the religious with violence, or in the transformation we see in collective violent action, where violence seems to mutate from being an instrument to become a kind of totalizing environment that the actor cannot move beyond. This alerts us to dimensions of violence that appear *beyond experience*, associated in particular with horror, the extreme and atrocity (Cavarero 2008).

New Agendas

Violence has emerged as one of the most urgent social, cultural and political questions shaping the twenty-first century. The most obvious marker of this development is securitization, where potential and actual violence merge, the source of what we might call a politics or culture of fear. Violence also appears to be reconfiguring. Its association with images suggests that visual practices may increasingly be constitutive of violence, from the video recordings of suicide bombers to the photographs that emerged from the Abu Ghraib prison in Iraq in 2004. Violence appears to be changing in other ways as well, from the search for 'excess' to the relationship between death of the self and death of the other at the heart of contemporary suicide bombing (Khosrokhavar 2005). This development raises broader questions about violence against the self, from hunger strikes to self-immolation. At times, such violence can generate extraordinary resonance, evident in way the

self-immolation of a young man in Tunisia in December 2010 ignited democratic movements right across the Arab world (Khondker 2011). These are
urgent, but difficult, questions to explore. One way to approach them would
be to locate them within theories of society, reconstructing the ways violence
has been apprehended through the history of the social sciences. Another
would be to engage with the abundant literature on terrorism, seeking patterns and schools of analysis. This book will draw on these approaches, but
it will seek to link changing forms of terrorism with wider transformations
of violence, with a particular focus on the embodied relationships at stake
in violent action.

The first chapters of this book set out to identify core tools for the analysis of public violence. To do so, Chapter 2 highlights different periods of
terrorist violence, alerting us to the fact that such violence can take quite
different forms, while Chapter 3 introduces key debates and concepts.
Chapter 4 turns to explore the terrorism that emerged out of the student
movements in the United States and Italy in the 1970s, attempting to identify key processes at work as a social movement mutates into violence.
Chapter 5 continues this focus, this time engaging with transformations at
work in the Palestinian struggle, in particular the shifts evident between
the first and second Intifadas – the first Intifada being a struggle shaped by
optimism and collectively organized violence, and the second highlighting
the emergence of more personalized forms of violence, suicide bombing
in particular. Chapter 6 engages with violence that played a key role in
shaping theories of terrorism in the 1990s, the destruction of the Federal
Building in Oklahoma in the United States, and the Sarin gas attack on the
Tokyo subway system, both occurring in 1995. What was striking about
these attacks was their break with the revolutionary rhetoric of earlier terrorist groups, and the scale of death they attempted to bring about. These
attacks framed new debates around religious violence, introducing what
would become the influential theme of 'apocalypse' or violence seeking the
end of the world.

The book then turns to explore contemporary, globalizing violence,
above all its cultural and embodied dimensions. Chapter 7 engages with
imaginative and experiential dimensions of violence, focusing on dimensions of violence that appear increasingly present, such as masking and
the search for the extreme, and the increasing place of horror in contemporary violence. Chapter 8 engages with a critical dimension of the personalization of violence, namely the increasing importance of violence against
the self, above all associated with the development of the martyr, while
Chapter 9 continues the focus on the imaginaries of violence through a
focus on its increasing mediatization, from the circulation of photographs
from the Abu Ghraib prison in Iraq to the place of hidden worlds in the

London bombings of 2005. The final chapter, Chapter 10, draws these themes together, pointing towards what might be key dimensions of a new social science of violence.

A critical dimension of such a social science is its ability to develop conceptual tools that allow us to explore violence as an experience, one that is at the same time both embodied and relational. This demands a capacity to analyse the place of violence in constructing relationships between self and other, whether in militias, groups of friends or anonymous online chat groups. It demands a capacity to conceptualize and explore the relationship between the body and the self, from the experience of honour associated with community violence to the experience of self-destruction associated with the suicide bomber. It highlights the relationship between the author of violence and the victim, often excluded in accounts of purveying the means of violence. This points to the importance of attempting to understand dimensions of violence that extend *beyond experience*, evident in the search for limit experiences that may be becoming increasingly important in contemporary violence, from the horror of massacres to the fascination and culture of repetition suggested by the role of video images in contemporary violence. Violence, from this perspective, needs to be explored as a form of human agency shaped by culture and meaning, but where we also encounter limit experiences and dimensions that extend beyond language. Engaging with both these dimensions may be a critical task in constructing a new social science of violence. The hope of this book is that such a social science may contribute not only to understanding and responding to violence, but may also contribute to constructing social worlds less dominated by fear of the other.

2
Terrorism

A starting point for a social science of violence is the recognition that violence takes very different forms. This is particularly the case with terrorist violence: the actors are different, the victims are different, the violence itself differs in terms of its scale, its temporality and its meaning. To be able to move from discussing violence as an object to exploring it as embodied agency demands that we begin to explore actors, meanings and relationships. Doing so alerts us to one of the critical problems with the term 'terrorism', namely to the extent that it equates actors and forms of agency that are very different. In this chapter we begin to introduce some of the main forms of such violence, and in the process set the scene for the frameworks and debates to be introduced in the chapter that follows.

Propaganda by the Deed: Insurrectionary Violence

It is difficult for us today to imagine the panic generated by what was seen as a wave of terror spreading across Europe and the United States between 1880 and 1910 (Jensen 2008a). The period saw a series of dramatic political assassinations, including the assassination of the Russian Emperor Alexander II in March 1881 by a group calling itself 'People's Will', the assassination of President Sadi Carnot of France in 1894, the Prime Minister of Spain in 1897, the Empress of Austria in 1898 and the King of Italy in 1900 (Laqueur 1996). Almost exactly a century before the attacks of 11 September 2001, William McKinley, the 25th president of the United States, was shot while attending an exhibition in New York on 6 September 1901, subsequently dying of his wounds (Fine 1955). This assassination led McKinley's successor, President Theodore Roosevelt, to call for a war to rid the world of terrorism, an appeal that would have echoes a century later (Rapoport 2002). This violence involved both shootings and stabbings of national leaders as well as a wave of bombings, from the bombing of the Barcelona Opera House in 1893 (killing over 30 people) (Jensen 2004) to the Haymarket bombing in May 1886 in Chicago, where a bomb thrown at police breaking up a demonstration of workers led to shootings that killed and wounded over 100 people (de Grazia 2006).

Even though these events took place over a century ago, there are lessons for us when thinking about violence today. This violence was associated with the ideas of early anarchist thinkers such as the Frenchman Pierre-Joseph Proudhon (1809–65) (Jensen 2008a) and the Russian Mikhail Bakunin (1814–76) (Law 2009: 77), leading to a widely held belief, both then and now, that these philosophers and thinkers 'caused' this wave of violence. Of course, as we might expect, the story is more complex. Historians point out that this violence emerged out of conflict and social revolt in Europe in the second half of the nineteenth century. This ranged from the development of new types of worker organizations to attempts at insurrection, such as the short-lived success of the Paris Commune in 1871 (Gould 1993), when insurrectionists took over the capital for three months, before being crushed by government troops. For many people hoping for change across Europe, the Paris Commune had been a sign that insurrection might be a possible path to such change (Gould 1993), and over the decade that followed it a series of attempts at insurrection directly inspired by the Paris events followed, with uprisings in Spain and Italy between 1873 and 1877. All of these failed, and all were ruthlessly crushed (Jensen 2004: 123).

The emergence of anarchism as a philosophy was part of this wider context. While Karl Marx and others had founded an International Workingman's Association in London in 1864, looking to organize workers to bring about change (Marx and Engels 2007), the insurrections had promised another model of change, a more dramatic sweeping aside of the old order. The failure of these insurrections led on the one hand to ideas of small groups heading off to the mountains, effectively guerrilla expeditions (carried out in Italy in the late 1870s) (Jensen 2004), while others increasingly came to look to the individual act of revolt (Fleming 1980). This was articulated most famously by Peter Kropotkin, a young Russian nobleman in exile, who in 1881 called for 'acts of illegal protest, of revolt, of vengeance' to be undertaken by 'lonely sentinels'. Such acts that would 'compel attention' and bring about change in ways that were otherwise impossible. Each of such 'madmen' could, argued Kropotkin, 'in a few days, make more propaganda than thousands of pamphlets' (in Capouya and Tompkins 1975: 7).

What is at stake here? Historians point out that these models of insurrectionary violence draw on earlier traditions of social conflict and protest, particularly evident in the south of Spain, which involved kidnappings, the burning down of buildings or crops, and at times shootings (Jensen 2004). The experience of the emerging working class tended to generate solidarity, as disparate workers found themselves working in the new factories where they were increasingly subject to the unifying demands of machines and employers, and the emerging working class developing new types of collective action and organization (Gould 1993). This was a very different model of change from that of the 'lonely sentinel' and his/her desperate act. Increasingly those advocating this model of change opposed building organizations and political parties, emphasizing instead the importance of direct action (Linse 1982). This focus on individual revolt captured the utopia of a 'society without government'. While they looked to the emerging working class to bring about this new world, in most countries where anarchism developed its social base was not primarily among workers, but among literate artisans – mechanics, bricklayers, butchers, caterers, watchmakers, shoemakers and barbers (Jensen 2004). It seems clear that in part the anarchists were looking to fight the encroachment of large merchants and industrial systems that threatened their extinction, the ideology of anarchism speaking to the independent ethos of small business.

The wave of killings that developed from the 1880s was widely presented as being the co-ordinated action of an invisible international organization. But historians emphasize instead the diversity of people involved. While some were committed to the model of change articulated by thinkers like Kropotkin, many had little or no connection with anarchist groups or ideologies (Jensen 2004). They were none the less often presented as expressions of a sinister international conspiracy, setting in motion the repression of organized labour movements, and police brutality across a range of countries that 'ignited chain reactions of violence' where 'massive government crackdowns ... provoked even more spectacular assassinations and terrorist bombings' (Jensen 2004: 128).

There are several dimensions to this violence. Its origins lay in localized traditions of violent 'micro-insurrection', and the subsequent failure of mass insurrections. The references to an almost mythical proletariat underline that it was shaped by a desire for a revolutionary movement that was yet to be born. The extent to which this violence developed as a response to brutal police repression highlights the extent that violence and counter-violence can become a self-sustaining relationship, disconnecting itself from other social processes.

It is important to recognize that the violence of this period innovated in important ways. It moved away from cutting down vines, kidnapping or stabbing, coming to embrace the dynamite and gelignite that had been invented by Alfred Nobel in 1866, with some observers suggesting that this new technology of destruction had 'transformed the world' (Jensen 2004: 116). This may be an exaggeration, but it is clear that dynamite played a spectacular role in terrorist events in this period, such as the bombing of the

Barcelona Opera House in 1893 (Jensen 2008b). Despite advances, dynamite remained unstable and difficult to use, and it failed more often than it succeeded. None the less, its public impact was enormous, to such an extent that during his lifetime Nobel came to be associated with the wave of killings that relied on it. In 1888 a French newspaper wrongly believed Nobel had died, and ran an obituary calling him a 'merchant of death' (Stone 2001). Nobel's decision to leave his fortune to a series of prizes for the betterment of humanity can be seen in part as an attempt to dissociate himself from the violence sweeping Europe and the United States using the product he was responsible for creating.

While bullets were more effective than dynamite (and in fact killed more people during this period) (Jenson 2004), it was explosions that were spectacular. The spectacular nature of this violence underlines the important link between what came to be called anarchist terror and the development of modern mass newspapers. Newspapers played a key role in sensationalizing this violence, clearly contributing to and profiting from the sense of panic that developed. The threat of anarchist conspiracies was a constant feature of the new mass-market newspapers (while little evidence of actual conspiracies in fact emerged), and this wave of terror is closely associated with what came to be called the 'new journalism', which relied on shocking headlines and news that would both excite and entertain (Hobsbawm 1989). The bombing of the Barcelona Opera House in 1893 prompted a special edition of New York's *World*, leading to the highest sales (over 600,000) ever achieved by an American newspaper up to then (Jensen 2004).

A number of important questions emerge here. What sociologists recognize as 'social structure' clearly played a role in the development of the violence that came to be called anarchist terror. The period was one of major social dislocation and brutal responses to dissent. But equally, it is clear that it was not the dispossessed and workers who made up the majority of those involved in this violence. If any social group is represented here, it is neither working class nor industrialist – artisans and aristocrats were much more represented among these bomb throwers (Jensen 2008a), and this may have something to tell us about the social structure and terror. It may be that their distance from actual organizations of workers meant that the working class could take on an almost mythical nature, and this may offer insight into the forms of violence that mutate into terror. At the same time, the role of the media in this period is critical. This alerts us to the importance of violence as a form of communication, and the place of violence in emerging forms of mass media characterized by the search for sensation and entertainment. Dynamite was critical, not for its efficiency in killing, but for its capacity to create a spectacular event.

What is striking about anarchist terror is its sudden and almost complete disappearance after 1910. What was an object of almost mass hysteria in the mid-1890s had almost completely disappeared in Europe a decade later, with the exception of Spain. In the United States an explosion took place outside the Wall Street stock exchange as late as September 1920, a horse drawn cart carrying a bomb that killed some 40 people (Gage 2009). Those responsible were never found, but this also represented the end of this type of violence in the United States. Some sort of social, economic and political transition had been achieved, and what had come to be known as anarchist terror became irrelevant and archaic. Examining the European context, the historian Martin Miller argues that anarchist terror is best understood as a transitional phase between pre-modern and modern political violence (Miller 1995). New types of political and social organization had emerged, from mass-based social democratic parties and trade unions in Western Europe, to the parties of revolutionary elites that had emerged in Russia, with both these forms of political and social mobilization promising revolutionary change. The desperate act of the lone sentinel no longer seemed to look forward to a future world; instead it seemed part of a world being replaced by the industrial order, with its new conflicts and social imaginary.

National Liberation: Freedom Fighters or Terrorists?

While the national liberation struggles shaping the long period of decolonization involved what we might consider classical battles, in many cases they involved violence that did not aim at military victory over occupying forces, but at weakening the resolve of the occupying power. Such cases illustrate the extent that the term 'terrorism' is used to label the violence of one's opponents (Turk 2004) or reserved for violence that fails to achieve its goals (Hoffman 2011). The 'ideological warfare' Turk refers to is particularly evident to the extent that people once reviled as terrorists later come to be regarded as national heroes and statesmen. One of the clearest such cases is that of Menachem Begin (1913–92) and the fight for the creation of the state of Israel in what had previously been British administered Palestine. This conflict lasted some 15 years, leading eventually to the British withdrawal and establishment of the State of Israel in 1948. This was a conflict with significant echoes today, involving the right of Jews to immigrate to Palestine, whether Jews would be allowed to purchase land, and the future of Palestine itself after the eventual British withdrawal (Hoffman 2011: 260).

Born in Brest Litovsk, Begin had been involved in European Zionist networks, and immigrated to Palestine in 1942 (Hoffman 2011). A year later he was appointed commander of the main underground organization opposing British rule, the Irgun Zvai Le'umi (National Military Organization, often referred to by its Hebrew acronym Etzel) (Hoffman 2011; Begin 1951). Begin's role as a commander-in-chief of Irgun is detailed in his official Knesset biography. Irgun had first emerged in attacks against Arab fighters during the 1936 Arab revolt against British rule, from 1944 turning to focus directly on the British. Martha Crenshaw describes the violence undertaken by Irgun from 1936 as 'a form of collective retribution for Arab attacks on Jews... intended to intimidate the Arab population as a whole'. This developed, she argues, into 'a large-scale campaign of anti-Arab terror, including machine-gun attacks on Arab trains, grenades thrown at buses, and milk-can bombs placed in Arab markets' (Crenshaw 1995: 525; see also Bowyer Bell 1972). This campaign has been described as 'ethnic terrorism' (Byman 1998) to the extent that it aimed at inducing populations to flee areas through fear of violence.

As Hoffman notes, Irgun did not seek military victories against British forces, it avoided direct military confrontation. Instead it targeted institutions of government (Hoffman 2011: 263). Part of this campaign involved blowing up the King David Hotel, which then housed the British headquarters (Kushner 2003: 205; Hoffman 2006: 49), a bombing described by the British prime minister of the time as 'an insane act of terrorism' (http://hansard.millbanksystems.com/commons/1946/jul/23/terrorist-outrage-jerusalem; accessed 30 March 2010). Over 90 people were killed, mostly civilians (Hoffman 2006: 49). According to Begin, Irgun made warning phone calls about the impending attack, while the British deny any such calls were made (Kushner 2003: 181). What is clear is that techniques forged in the campaign against Arabs were evident in the bombing, with explosives being taken into the hotel hidden in milk cans. Whatever the circumstances, as Hoffman observes, the numbers killed means that 'the bombing remains one of the world's single most lethal terrorist incidents of the twentieth century' (2006: 49). Following this attack, Irgun's action against the British continued, in 1947 capturing and executing by hanging two British sergeants as retaliation for the arrest and execution of Irgun fighters. The bodies were left hanging in a public place, and this execution led the British to offer a £10,000 reward for Begin's capture (Kushner 2003: 181). In this period Begin was condemned by mainstream Jewish organizations as well as by the British.

By 1948, however, Britain's rule over Palestine had come to an end. The evidence suggests that the British public, weary of war, had no desire to continue its presence in Palestine when confronted with such violence (Dixon 2000: 99). Hoffman argues that Irgun's violence was the first of its kind to focus on creating spectacular events and at times horrific images, such as the British sergeants whose bloodied bodies were photographed while still hanging. He writes:

> The Irgun's terrorism campaign is critical to understanding the evolution and development of modern, contemporary terrorism. They were the first to recognize the publicity value inherent in terrorism and to choreograph their violence for an audience far beyond the immediate geographical locus of their struggle.
>
> (Hoffman 2011: 267)

According to this analysis, Irgun's violence did not aim at achieving military victory over British forces, its aim was instead to sap the British public's support for its presence in Palestine.

Begin highlights this dimension in his autobiographical account of the conflict, *The Revolt: Story of the Irgun* (1951). He insists that he and his collaborators were convinced 'if we could succeed in destroying the government's prestige... the removal of its rule would follow automatically. Thenceforward we gave no peace to this weak spot. Throughout all the years of our uprising we hit at the British government's prestige, deliberately, tirelessly, unceasingly' (1951: 52). While Begin does not use these terms, he understands violence as a means to smash the symbolic order and aura of invincibility surrounding the power of the occupier, while also being capable of bringing to life a new symbolic order, the nation. Violence, he argues, not only weakens the occupier, it can also destroy its credibility. Violence from this perspective can shatter a symbolic system.

While reviled as a terrorist during what can be considered a war of national liberation, Begin would eventually become Israel's sixth prime minister (1977–83), and in 1978 was awarded the Nobel Peace Prize. The model of violence Begin articulates in *The Revolt* is shaped by theories of regicide, killing the king. In regicide the king is not simply removed from power, the king is executed, and in the process a system of power is smashed (Hunt 1998). This played a key role in the public executions that took place during the French Revolution, where executing the king was experienced as smashing the symbolic system of power and meaning that the king holds together. This tradition had been important in Italy, where the Italian nationalist Garibaldi had been a believer in regicide, and where other nationalists had played a role in attempting to assassinate Napoleon III because of his failure to support the cause of the Italian nation (Jensen 2004: 127). It is significant that when accepting his Nobel Prize, Begin refers to Garibaldi as a figure who influenced him (Begin 1978: 196). This underlines the critical symbolic dimension of violence, its place in *systems of meaning* that will emerge as a central dimension in the chapters below.

Begin alerts us to a further dimension of violence:

> When Descartes said: 'I think, therefore I am', he uttered a very profound thought. But there are times in the history of peoples when thought alone does not prove their existence. A people may 'think' yet its sons, with their thoughts and in spite of them, may be turned into a herd of slaves – or into soap. There are times when everything in you cries out: your very self-respect as a human being lies in your resistance to evil: *we fight, therefore we are!*
>
>   (Begin 1951: 46, emphasis in original)

The legal theorist Shai Lavi notes that what is of primary importance in this account is not the outcome of the violence, *but the act itself*, understood as a form of resistance to oppression that constitutes a people. The use of violence, Lavi argues, 'was important for political existence itself, beyond any specific political aim ... For the Irgun, the use of force was not measured by its effective end, but rather by its inherent symbolic power' (2005: 209).

Such violence is best understood as 'performative'. The concept 'performative' emerged out of Austin's work in linguistic theory (Austin 1976), referring to forms of speech or 'speech acts' that do not describe an event or state of affairs, but rather *bring a reality into existence*. The classical example is the marriage vow: when a person says 'With this ring I thee wed', they are not describing something, instead they are making what Austin calls a 'performative utterance' that brings into existence a new reality, in this case the state of being married. Another example Austin uses is 'I name this ship ... '. In such performative utterances, speaking brings about a new state of affairs.

This is central to the account of violence articulated by Begin, gruesomely illustrated by Irgun's 1947 execution of two British soldiers by hanging as a response to the British execution of two of its fighters. The method of killing explicitly mirrored the earlier British execution. But in this case the bodies were left hanging in a public place, and pinned on them was a notice stating that they had been tried and found guilty by a 'tribunal' for spying and illegal entry. The note specifically rejects any suggestion that the killings were a reprisal, describing them instead as a 'routine judicial fact' (*Manchester Guardian* 1 August 1947: 5, cited in Bagon 2003: 124). Not only was Irgun mirroring British violence, through these killings it was claiming the sovereignty at the base of 'judicial' decisions. In this killing, Irgun is acting out the sovereign power that a people through a state may claim over life and death. These killings, to draw on Lavi's phrase, 'were important for political existence itself'.

The dimensions of 'freedom fighter versus terrorist' as well as this performative dimension of violence equally emerge in the case of another leader of the struggle against the British in Palestine, Yitzhak Shamir. Shamir was one of the leaders of Lehi, *Lohamei Herut Israel*, 'Fighters for the Freedom of Israel', a group referred to by its opponents as the 'Stern gang', naming it after its founder Avraham Stern (Heller 1995). This group is widely believed to have been responsible for a series of assassinations, including the assassination of the Swedish Count Folke Bernadotte, a distinguished diplomat serving as the United Nations mediator in the Middle East, who was judged as being too sympathetic to the Arab cause (Kushner 2003; Heller 1995; Stanger 1988; Bowyer Bell 1972). While Lehi denied any involvement, immediately after this killing the newly formed Israeli Provisional Government declared Lehi an illegal organization and disbanded it under newly promulgated 'Emergency Regulations for the Prevention of Terrorism' (Stanger 1988: 266). During the conflict with Britain, Shamir did not rule out terrorism as a form of action, declaring in 1943 'neither Jewish ethics nor Jewish tradition can disqualify terrorism as a means of combat' (cited in Crenshaw 1995: 527). While the newly created government of Israel declared Lehi an illegal terrorist organization following Bernadotte's killing, three decades later this was reversed, with the Israeli government honouring the organization in 1980 with the creation of a Lehi ribbon as a military decoration for its former members (see Israel Ministry of Defence, http://www.mod.gov.il/pages/heritage/Order.asp). In 1983 Shamir himself was elected prime minister of the country, and in 1992, speaking at a memorial to Lehi, he affirmed Lehi's heritage as central to the nation of Israel: 'we still need this truth today, the truth of the power of war...because without this the life of the individual has no purpose and the nation has no chance of survival' (cited in Crenshaw 1995: 527). This account of war echoes a model we have already encountered, one where violence is a medium through which the person can commune with a principle greater than themselves, in this case the nation.

The passage from terrorist to freedom fighter occurs in other well-known cases. In 2008 it emerged that Nelson Mandela, the former president of South Africa and winner of the Nobel Peace Prize in 1993, was still on a US 'terrorist watch list' (Hall 2008). While never having planted a bomb, Mandela had played a key role in the creation of the African National Congress's armed wing, Umkhonto we Sizwe (Spear of the Nation) (Mandela 1990: 122), an armed group that had been involved in a limited campaign of sabotage and bombings in public places in the 1980s, killing both black and white civilians. The most significant of these attacks, a 1983 car-bombing of the offices of the South African Airforce Headquarters in Pretoria, killed 19 people and injured over 200 (http://www.justice.gov.za/trc/decisions/2001/ac21003.htm; accessed 30 March 2010). During his time in prison Mandela refused to renounce armed struggle, and during the 1980s Amnesty International did not recognize him as a 'prisoner of conscience' (Kaufman 1991: 354), instead eventually 'adopting' imprisoned members of the ANC for violations of pass laws (Seidman 2001). Despite this history, two decades later Amnesty awarded Mandela the title of '2006 Ambassador of Conscience' (Amnesty International 2006).

The Student Movement and Terror, 1970–1980

In the chapters below we explore the ways violence transforms in contemporary national liberation conflicts. But what seems more complex to understand is how violence, and ultimately terror, emerged from within student movements in North America, Europe and Japan during the 1970s. In Europe the most important of these was the Italian Red Brigades, formed initially by Sociology students at the University of Milan. Over the period 1969–82 the Red Brigades killed or wounded over 160 people through assassinations, kidnappings, bank robberies and other actions (Varon 2004). While other groups emerged in Italy over this same period, the Red Brigades was the most bloody in terms of numbers of people killed, and the most spectacular, in 1978 kidnapping, trying and executing the Christian Democrat politician and former prime minister Aldo Moro (Drake 1995).

Dimensions of the Italian pattern are evident elsewhere. In the United States, a group from the Revolutionary Youth Movement succeeded in being elected to the leadership of Students for a Democratic Society at its 1968 Congress (Gentry 2004). This group would go on to form the Weathermen and, later, failing to develop mass action, the group renamed itself the Weather Underground Organization and decided upon a strategy of armed struggle against the US state. This led at first to a series of bombings against property, later escalating to the decision to bomb a dance at a military base – an action that failed, with the bomb exploding while it was being constructed and fatally injuring two members of the group (Varon 2004). Other groups to emerge during this period include the Red Army Faction in the then Federal Republic of Germany (Varon 2004), Action Directe in France (Sommier 2008a), the Cellules Communistes Combattantes in Belgium (Franq 1986), and the United Red Army in Japan (Farrell 1990).

These groups alert us to the complexity of violence. Some sort of transformation occurred when a section of a social movement, in this case the student movement, embraced violence as a strategy. In interviews given years after these events, prominent members of groups such as the Weather Underground argue that they took up violence because they had no choice, because at the time other paths to social and political change were blocked. In these accounts violence is often presented as little more than an instrument. But when we look back at the period, we see a more complex picture.

In 1969 when the Weather Underground adopted its strategy of violence, it is clear that key members of the group were increasingly fascinated by violence. A number make references to the ritualistic killing of Sharon Tate by Charles Manson that took place at the time, and it seems clear that violence is experienced in more complex ways than simply being a strategy reluctantly embraced (Miller 1999). In the German Red Army Faction we capture glimpses of a similar process summed up by a member of the group: 'When we employ violence, we change not only our objective world, but our subjective world...we break the stranglehold of the norms we have internalised' (cited in Varon 2004: 44). The violence that emerged out of European and North American student movements makes clear that we cannot simply regard violence as an instrument. We need to explore it as a more complex experience.

Violence and the Religious

The question of whether violence and terrorism have a religious dimension has emerged as crucial following the attacks of 11 September 2001. The attacks were undertaken by a group known as *al-Qaeda*, Arabic for 'the base' and the name of one of the camps set up in Afghanistan in the 1980s by the Saudi millionaire Osama bin Laden (Abou Zahab and Roy 2004). In 1998 bin Laden had called for a jihad or Islamic 'holy war' against Westerners, calling on all Muslims to kill Westerners until all Western troops had withdrawn from Saudi Arabia, the country of Mecca, Islam's holiest place (translation available at http://www.fas.org/irp/world/para/docs/980223-fatwa.htm). While he at first had denied any involvement in the attacks (CNN 2001), later bin Laden called the hijackers who had flown the planes into the towers 'Shaheed', or martyrs who died for their faith (Lawrence 2005: 112). Bin Laden at times directly drew on metaphors (Lawrence 2005: 214) that seemed to echo Samuel Huntington's argument that a world previously structured around political oppositions was giving way to a world increasingly shaped by civilizations that had their origins in religions (Huntington 1996). Many academic observers accepted this thesis, suggesting that the origins for the attack lay in a literalist understanding of the Qu'ran, Islam's Holy Book (for an example, see Venkatraman 2007). This seemed a widespread popular perception as well, some observers estimating that sales of the Qur'an increased five-fold in the United States in the period after the attacks – so much so that copies had to be airfreighted to the country from the United Kingdom (Gibbs 2001). The key to understanding this violence seemed to lie in a Holy Book written 14 centuries ago.

The suggestion that such violence could best be approached as a religious phenomenon seemed to converge with earlier events. Only a few months before the 11 September attacks, Timothy McVeigh, a former military serviceman, was executed following his conviction for a 1995 car-bomb attack which destroyed the Federal Building in the United States city of Oklahoma, killing over 160 people (Durham 1996). Many observers believed that McVeigh had been influenced by, if not connected to or supported by, the Christian Identity movement, a loose collection of groups proclaiming white supremacy and anti-governmentalism, some of which had been involved in violent attacks against African Americans and bank robberies (Hamm 1997). The idea of religious violence had also emerged in Japan, when members of what appeared to be a religious group called the Aum Shinrikyo, or Supreme Truth, were convicted for an attack in 1995 (the same year as McVeigh's attack) on commuters on Tokyo's subway system using Sarin gas (Lifton 1999). While only 11 people had been killed, the death toll could potentially have reached hundreds (Tu 1999). The founder of the Aum group did not appeal to political ideologies but to a cluster of beliefs drawn from Buddhism, Christianity and popular culture (Lifton 1999). Other examples of violence becoming increasingly important also seemed framed in religious rhetoric, from the suicide attacks of the emerging Palestinian group Hamas to plane hijackings undertaken by Sikh groups calling for a homeland they referred to as Khalistan, or the Land of the Pure (van der Veer 2000: 327). Influential observers of these different groups saw a pattern at work, one that had been signalled by the Islamic Revolution of 1978 in Iran. For Mark Juergensmeyer (1997), what was involved here was a rising religious opposition to the secular state, where 'traditional religion' (Juergensmeyer 1997: 17) attacked an increasingly weakened secular nationalism. This view was echoed in the influential account of the British sociologist Anthony Giddens, for whom al-Qaeda was a 'fundamentalist movement' (2003: xi), arguing that such

> groups and struggles can come into being in any sphere where traditional beliefs and practices are becoming corroded... To the fundamentalist, there is only one right and proper way of life, and everyone else had better get out of the way.
>
> (Giddens 2003: xii)

Such groups, according to Giddens, emerge when tradition is under threat, their aim being to 'roll back modernity'. Juergensmeyer takes this analysis further. He proposes that religious uprisings of Hindu, Buddhist, Sikh and Muslim groups in the 1970s were initially protests against the failure of modernizing states. But in the 1980s these began to internationalize, as did other messianic movements such as radical Jewish groups (who first emerged in the United States rather than Israel) and who believed that Israel's victory in the 1967 war over its Arab neighbours presaged the re-establishment of the ancient temple and the coming of the Messiah, or among Sikh groups fighting for Khalistan, who were also a product of the diaspora more than movements and conflicts within India. For Juergensmayer, a third stage became evident in the 1990s, signalled by the global jihad network that increasingly came to focus on United States' power. The emergence of this network was highlighted by the first attack on the World Trade Towers in 1993 by a group of activists, the core of whom had been involved in the 1981 assassination of Egypt's President Sadat. For Juergensmeyer, religion was not only the source such violence, it also played a key role in shaping one of its defining characteristics, its *excess*. What he called 'terror mandated by God' (Juergensmeyer 1997) stood outside normal logics of negotiation and compromise, and was considered an expression of betrayal of the holy mandate, driving a struggle where religion claims power of life over death.

This 'religious' interpretation of contemporary violent movements is, as we will see, countered by a more 'political' account, one which argues that these movements are better understood in terms of 'anti-imperialism' and a more political language rather than in terms of a crisis of secularist states and religious revolt. Embedded within this more political account of these violent movements is a model of action or agency. Often implicitly, and at times explicitly, as in Laqueur's (1999) thesis concerning 'new terrorism', religious violence is framed in terms of 'fanaticism', where the actor is considered to be outside any of the boundaries of rational action. The anti-imperialist and more generally political action models argue the opposite, proposing that such violence is the result of calculations of cost and benefit, even in the case of suicide bombings that emerged in the 1990s. Suicide action is paradigmatic of these different approaches: for some, it is the exemplar of the fanatic, while for others it is a strategy groups engage in to increase their prestige and 'market share' in an environment where radical groups are competing for support and resources. These competing analyses imply very different responses to such violence: a rational actor model implies a response in terms of negotiation and addressing what are perceived as the causes of grievance, while there would appear to be little to be gained by negotiation with religious fanatics determined upon destruction. As such, these competing analyses are not simply examples of academic debate. As we will see in the chapter that follows, they imply radically different responses to terrorism.

3

Competing Perspectives

To begin to engage with contemporary violence and terror we need some sense of the extensive literature and debates around terrorism. Within this literature a number of intellectual orientations recur. One cluster considers terror and violence as expressions of 'failure', whether social, cultural or at the level of the personality. From this perspective, violence is approached as a *symptom*. Another tradition considers violence as integral to and indeed an ordinary dimension of social life, conceiving it as an *instrument*. Other more recent analyses highlight the dynamics of violence, ranging from attempts to locate its emergence within social movements to interactionist approaches developing a micro-sociology of violence. For some of these analyses, violence is a relatively transparent instrument. Others highlight the complexity and indeed mystery around violence as an experience. At times questions about violence seem focused on deviant minorities, while at other times patterns of violence seem to open out questions at the heart of contemporary social life, as evident in the wide-ranging debate we introduced in Chapter 1 concerning the relationship between violence, obedience and conformity, one possibly mirrored today in the debate around the relationship between religion and violence. This means that the theoretical models we use to identify what is at stake in violence matter. This is the aim of this chapter: to start to understand what different intellectual traditions recognize as being at stake in violence, and why.

The Classical Model: Violence and Frustration

Drawing upon psychological studies of the time, the 1950s saw a more or less sociological consensus about organized violence. Violence was understood as a product of 'frustration', framed within a theory of 'frustration and aggression'. Psychologists such as John Dollard (1939) had proposed that this was a mechanism at work at the level of the individual personality, the concept being taken up in social analyses of what came to be called 'relative deprivation' (Gurr and Rutenberg 1967). This frustration thesis is central to the widely held argument that terrorism and violence are the products of poverty, inequality or the lack of education flowing from these conditions, a view restated in Britain immediately after the attacks of 11 September 2001 by Gordon Brown, the then chancellor: 'Poverty is a breeding ground for discontent. There is a sense of injustice. We have got to act if we are going to avoid the development of terrorist cells' (Landberg 2004). This argument seems almost self-evident because it offers a contemporary expression of the 'frustration–aggression' thesis: poverty, either absolute or relative, produces a sense of frustration that in turn is 'released' through violence. It is important to note that from this perspective there is little or no distinction between terrorism and violence, the two blurring into one category, understood as the product of frustration. While this frustration–aggression thesis often recurs in studies of terrorism (for an overview of just how widely, see Horgan 2005: 57), many psychologists dispute such a 'cause and effect' account of individual violence, and many equally question whether such a mechanism conjectured to exist at the level of the individual personality can translate to collective social processes (see Horgan 2005: 57).

Once we start to look, however, the available evidence fails to establish a causal relationship between economic inequality and terrorism, or indeed between economic inequality and violence in general (Krueger and Maleckova 2003). Studies of the social origins of those involved in the wave of terrorist violence in the 1980s suggest that, if there is a connection, those involved in terror have a level of resources and education higher than the population of which they are a part (Russell and Miller 1983), a pattern reaffirmed in contemporary studies. Marc Sageman's (2004: 78) analysis of occupational data of 134 persons involved in al-Qaeda related violence concludes that over 75 per cent come from upper- or middle-class backgrounds; at the time of becoming involved, a majority followed professional occupations (doctors, teachers), or were engaged in skilled employment (civil servants, students, small businesses). Less than a quarter were unemployed or in low-skilled jobs. Gambetta and Hertog's (2009) research into the backgrounds of those involved in jihadi terrorism underlines not only the extent to which education levels of terrorists are higher than average in the societies they come from, but that those involved in terror are more likely to be involved in professional employment, with the technical professions over-represented, in particular the profession of engineers (Gambetta and Hertog 2009).

When we consider the terrorism that developed in the 1970s in Germany, Italy, the United States and Japan, the world's richest countries, in each case, leaders of terrorist groups were more likely to come from elite universities rather than less privileged campuses, while the internal organization of these groups appears to mirror the social structure. In the Japanese United Red Army, for example, there was a clear hierarchy mirroring the prestige of the university that members attended – leaders of the Red Army, just as leaders of major Japanese corporations, came from the most prestigious universities such as Tokyo or Waseda, while lower- ranked members tended to come from less well regarded universities (Sommier 2008b). Such social hierarchies also appear in networks such as al-Qaeda (see Devji 2005). In a sense, if we can say anything about participation in terrorism, we can say that it tends to mirror more general patterns of participation in activism. This means that we need a quite different approach from one that locates the origins of terrorism in economic disadvantage.

Culture, Conflict and Violence: Clashes of Civilization

The thesis that frustration generates violence has made a comeback in recent years, shifting from older arguments about *economic* frustration to a new emphasis on *cultural* frustration. This is central to the influential 'clash of civilization' arguments associated with the work of Samuel Huntington (1993, 1996) and Bernard Lewis (1990). Huntington argues that an older world order structured by an opposition between two models of modernization, capitalism and communism, is giving way to a new order structured around an opposition between civilizations, which he defines largely in cultural terms. In this new world the principal opposition is between 'the West and the rest', and is most acute in the opposition between Western and Islamic civilizations, a result of what Huntington considers to be the failure of Islam to occupy the importance its adherents believe it deserves: 'The underlying problem for the West is not Islamic fundamentalism. It is Islam, a different civilization whose people are convinced of the superiority of their culture, and are obsessed with the inferiority of their power' (Huntington 1996: 217). What Huntington is doing here is re-articulating the model of 'frustration' proposed by social scientists in the 1950s, where frustration is the product of a gap between expectations and reality. Huntington draws heavily on the earlier formulation of the 'clash of civilizations' proposed by Bernard Lewis, who restates the classical theory of frustration in what he calls a theory of 'Muslim rage':

> The Muslim has suffered successive stages of defeat. The first was his loss of domination in the world, to the advancing power of Russia and the West.

The second was the undermining of his authority in his own country, through an invasion of foreign ideas and ways of life and sometimes even foreign rulers or settlers, and the enfranchisement of native non-Muslim elements. The third – the last straw – was the challenge to his mastery in his own house, from emancipated women and rebellious children. It was too much to endure, and the outbreak of rage against these alien, infidel, and incomprehensible forces that had subverted his dominance, disrupted his society, and finally violate the sanctuary of his home was inevitable.

(Lewis 1990: 47)

Lewis (1986) argues that what he sees as an anti-democratic impulse at the centre of Islam has prevented the modernization of Muslim majority societies, and their consequent relative decline generates increasingly bitter frustration. This analysis echoes the American sociologist Robert Merton's (1968) theory of anomie, understood as the product of the gap between aspiration and opportunity, expectations and reality. But rather than explain this gap and consequent frustration in terms of social structure, as did social scientists in the 1950s, Lewis argues that the source of this frustration lies today in culture.

There are important counter-analyses to this argument. The French political scientist Olivier Roy (2004) notes that Lewis develops his 'failed modernization' thesis uniquely in the context of a discussion of the Middle East. However, the majority of Muslims, notes Roy, do not live in the Middle East, and he argues that the supposed 'backwardness' of Muslim societies (at the centre of Lewis's thesis) disappears if we compare examples of Muslim majority countries with their non-Muslim neighbours: Indonesia with the Philippines, Kosovo with Macedonia, Senegal with Ivory Coast, and so on. When we do, the case for a distinct type of 'Muslim society' experiencing failed modernization is much less credible: in these cases per capita income is similar, or slightly higher, for the Muslim majority country; and fertility indexes are lower, and have dropped dramatically over the past two decades. Roy notes that even in those countries with Islamic governments, such as Iran, social practices and mores are moving in the direction of Western societies. In the case of the Islamic Republic of Iran, the legal age of marriage for women was lowered to nine years of age, while the actual age of women marrying has increased (Roy 2004: 14). In 2006 the median age of marriage for women in Iran was 23.5, and in neighbouring Israel it was 25.8. In the case of Iran this has risen from 18.5 in 1966, a change linked to economic development (United Nations 2008).

The Terrorist Personality

We can add a third type of analysis seeking to explain terrorism as a symptom of failure, adding to those focusing on social structure or culture. This focuses on problems of personality, with terrorism considered to be a manifestation of psychological abnormality. This is evident in the psychological literature, from claims that a 'terrorist personality' is the product of inadequate mothering that leads to dysphoria (depression and sadness) to claims that the path into terrorist violence has a physical origin, perhaps one of the most memorable being the suggestion that involvement in terrorism is associated with 'faulty vestibular functions in the middle ear' (Crenshaw 1981: 398 fn 29). Psychologists Andrew Silke (1998, 2004) and John Horgan (2005) carefully assess this abundant literature. Silke evaluates studies from the 1980s onwards, noting that they tend towards three principal constructions of the terrorist: terrorist as psychopath (antisocial personality), as narcissist (lacking empathy for others and centred on their own needs and ideas), and as paranoid (suffering from a pervasive mistrust of others). He observes that there is an almost 'Cheshire cat' capacity for such analyses to keep appearing where they are least expected. He then examines those studies and sources of clinical data that are available, and concludes that the evidence is clear: those involved in terrorism and extreme violence offer no particular psychological profile that is different from the rest of the population.

The idea that the terrorist must suffer forms of pathology and abnormality is often associated with the idea that they are unable to form normal meaningful relationships with others. The terrorist, from this perspective, is likely to be unattached, most likely will be outside any couple relationship or marriage, is unlikely to have children, and is generally either a loner or a hater – someone disconnected from normal human relationships and intimacy. But here again, the available data underlines that this perception is simply wrong. Marc Sageman's data include marriage data for 114 persons involved in al-Qaeda networks, and indicates that some 73 per cent of those involved are married, closely mirroring their age cohorts (Sageman 2004: 73). Edwin Bakker's study of persons imprisoned on jihadi-related terrorist charges in Europe finds a similar pattern of marriage rates (2006). The idea of the terrorist as socially isolated and maladjusted does not correspond to reality.

John Horgan's analysis of psychological studies concludes that there is a 'persistence of evidence to suggest terrorist normality' (2005: 65). Silke notes that it would be unlikely to find persons suffering from psychological disorders involved in terrorist groups. People with psychological disorders, he suggests 'do not make good terrorists. They lack the discipline, rationality, self-control and mental stamina needed if terrorists are to survive any length of time' (1998: 104). But given such data, why do assertions of psychological disorder and pathology continually recur in debates about terrorism, and why do we encounter an continous stream of calls for studies to capture the elusive psychological factor hidden behind terrorism? Having surveyed this literature across several decades, Silke offers a compelling explanation: 'We cannot believe normal people could produce terrorist acts, so we look for abnormality. As efforts to find gross abnormality fail again and again, attention has turned to more subtle shades of aberration' (1998: 67).

The question of the 'normality' of those involved in suicide actions emerged very powerfully in Britain in 2008, when a video filmed by one of the people involved in the July 2005 London bombings was tendered in evidence during a trial. Filmed on two separate occasions some time before the London attacks, in one part we see one of the bombers cuddling his two-year-old daughter, nestled in his arms in a sweet pink top. He kisses her, promises her he will miss her terribly, and tells her 'I have to do this thing for our future.' In another section tendered into evidence this same person introduces his daughter to his friends who are sitting, laughing and joking, and asks them 'What's your words of wisdom?', to which one replies: 'A few words of wisdom? Kill everyone there is' (transcript available at http://www.telegraph.co.uk/news/5236086/The-farewell-video.html). This video provoked enormous discussion in the United Kingdom and beyond. The recurring theme was the shock involved when we encounter a loving father cuddling his daughter, an obviously affectionate group of friends sitting around a living room, and a smiling young man saying 'kill everyone'. As the psychologist Andrew Silke argues, it seems beyond our comprehension that people who engage in mass murder can while away the afternoon with friends, love their partners, hug and kiss their children. One way to attempt to solve this tension, as Silke suggests, is to take the view that the terrorist is a pathological monster. Or we can struggle to identify and explore the social and cultural processes at work when ordinary people commit acts of extraordinary violence.

The Ordinariness of Violence: Violence as Instrument

Thus far we have introduced analyses that understand violence as the consequence of a failure of economic, cultural or psychological patterns. But there is a second, very important, framing orientation premised upon the normality of violence, locating this within theories of rational action or calculated action determined by goals (for a review, see Goodwin 2006). In the 1960s, when violent conflicts erupted in American universities, it was on the elite rather than the poorest campuses, making it difficult to argue that such violence was the product of frustration and disadvantage. In this context social scientists increasingly began to think about action and mobilizations in terms of resources and opportunities. And this, it was argued, applied not only to collective action in general but also to violence. Violence was not irrational, as the collective behaviour and frustration theorists had maintained, rather it was a form of rational action like any other. Anthony Oberschall (2004) argues that the decision to engage in violence is based on the calculation of costs and benefits. Charles Tilly asserts that the mechanisms at work in violent action are identical to those at work in collective action in general. Violence, he argues, is part of a wider 'repertoire' available to actors, and hence needs to be understood as part of 'politics as usual' (2002). For Tilly, the factors that determine which elements of this repertoire will be chosen are best understood in terms of opportunities, resources and strategic calculation.

From this point of view there is little value in debating whether certain strategies or actors are 'terrorist'. Tilly understands action as 'claim making', by which he means the steps actors undertake to gain rights, respect or some other goods within the political system, and he locates violence within this broader instrumental model. Tilly understands violence as inflicting 'physical damage' (2003: 3) on persons or objects, its goal being to induce change in the behaviour of others. Actors, from this perspective, *employ* violence, with collective violence defined as 'employ(ing) violent means of claim making' (2003: 13), a phrase echoing Giddens' 'purveyors of the means of violence' (Giddens 1987: 230). Tilly insists that people who use violence also use other tactics to achieve their goals, arguing against the idea that there is a specific category of people who employ violence. As a social historian he underlines the extent to which a wide range of actors use violence, from trade unionists, the urban poor, employers, ecology groups, to anti-abortion campaigners (2003: 237). The goals of those who employ terror as a tactic are, he argues, fundamentally no different from other social and political actors, arguing that 'participants in collective violence, including terrorist violence' struggle 'for power and profit in ways that overlap with the politics of their less violent counterparts ... Like conventional war, [violence and terror] represent the conduct of politics by other means' (2002). Terrorism is best understood as a 'political strategy'.

For Tilly, the key to understanding the emergence of violence and terror lies in the type of political regime most likely to reward it. While there is no direct correspondence between regime type and forms of violence, Tilly proposes that what he calls 'contentious politics' will most likely involve violence in 'low-capacity undemocratic' regimes (2003: 50), where a weak organizational capacity and a weak ability to modernize combine with an inefficient system of repression to create the regime type most likely to reward violence and terror. For Tilly, terror amounts to a particular kind of violence – 'sudden attacks on civilian targets' (2002). The 'mechanisms' involved in violent and non-violent action are the same, to the point, as Michel Wieviorka (2009) argues, this analysis is premised on the proposition that there is *no discontinuity between violent and non-violent acts, and between violence and terrorism*. As a result, an important shift occurs: rather than explore violence, the focus of analysis shifts to a general theory of action, with violence being regarded as one among a range of options that actors can pursue in order to achieve their goals.

This leads to a type of analysis pointed to by the Dutch criminologist Willem Schinkel (2004) – an approach he describes as determinist and formalist. By determinist he means that violence is ultimately approached as being determined by some other cause external to it. The meanings of violence are located *outside* violence itself. Violence then becomes discussed as an abstract event, where all forms of violence become equivalent, as for Tilly, when violence becomes a 'means of claim making'. There is a formalism involved in this approach, to the extent that it considers all kinds of violence, from throwing rocks to killing, as to 'inflict physical damage on persons and/or objects' (Tilly 2003: 3) or to 'deploy damage' (2003: 134). Is it adequate to define violence as the act of inflicting or deploying damage on persons or objects? Once defined in this way, it seems straightforward and indeed transparent, defined by the means–end relationship that gives it meaning. It is perhaps significant that the word 'pain' does not appear in Tilly's *The Politics of Collective Violence* (2003), nor do the words 'horror' or 'guilt', while the word 'suffering' appears just once. 'Damage' might be considered so generic that it removes us from the experience of violence, where to kill other people or to inflict immense suffering upon them become equivalent acts to throwing stones at them.

If we consider that meanings are only 'located outside violence itself' (Schinkel 2004: 16), we are no longer obliged to consider the violence at stake in violence, in particular dimensions that Schinkel suggests as the most disturbing – violence for its own sake, without morality or extrinsic meaning, something he suggests best approached as 'evil' (2004: 16). He perceptively proposes 'perhaps this is why this aspect of violence has been avoided in the social sciences. We are afraid of it' (2004: 16). Schinkel suggests that it might be time to 'end the exclusivity of the "why question"' when it comes to thinking about violence, and instead begin to think about the 'intrinsic attractiveness' of violence. The focus on an assumed causality, with its search for goals and causes, is 'far from convincing'. And it has a critical consequence: 'it omits a close analysis of actual violence from its research' (2004: 15).

Between Instrument and Imaginary

The Oxford Dictionary defines 'means' as 'an action or system by which a result is achieved' (http://oxforddictionaries.com/definition/means?q=means) and this captures the sense that Tilly gives to violence. Violence, understood as 'damaging acts' (2003: 15), is externalized as a 'means' (2003: 15). But in externalizing violence in this way, the instrumental approach excludes what arguably are critical dimensions of contemporary violence, and which may lie at the heart of terror: the *imaginary of violence* and dimensions of embodied experience which appear as increasingly central to extreme violence. The rational model understands violence as not only external to the actor, but as transparent and something that can be taken up or put down as circumstances require. But important dimensions of violence appear at odds with this 'violence as means' approach. One of the most important is when actors turn their violence upon themselves, as in the case of 'martyrdom operations' such as the attack on London's transport system, or when violence is turned inwards upon group members. Another important example, which we explore in the next chapter, is the case of the Japanese United Red Army, a student group involved in armed struggle in the early 1970s, where in its final days it killed 12 of its own members in an effort to purify itself (Igarashi 2007; Sommier 2008b). This did not only lead literally to the self-destruction of that particular organization, but also to the destruction of the post-1968 political left in Japan. Such violence directed inwards may have parallels in the more recent actions of the Aum sect in Japan in the 1990s that we explore in Chapter 6, where its first killings were also of its own members. Instrumental or strategic theories of violence offer us little insight into such processes where violence turns inwards. To grapple with this we need to engage with the place of imagination in violence, with dimensions of embodied experience such as longing, dread, pain, pleasure, belonging, exhilaration, tension, relief, imagination and rebirth.

Such experiential and imaginary dimensions of violence cannot merely be reduced to the pathologies of small groups. In Europe during the first decade of the twentieth century there was a widespread longing for war, a longing for a violent event that would purge and renew European societies and cultures (Joas 2003). The theme of transgressive, creative violence is not only part of terrorism, it occupied a central place in cultural movements such as Surrealism, where violence became increasingly aestheticized and associated with themes of self-realization, self-discovery and the breaking free of boundaries. The German historian Bernd Weisbrod points to the importance of violence as 'epiphany', an event through which a person discovers or comprehends something that previously was hidden. This is illustrated in the French artist André Breton's second *Surrealist Manifesto*, where he affirms

> The simplest surrealist act consists of dashing down into the street, pistol in hand, and firing blindly, as fast as you can, into the crowd. Anyone who has not dreamed of thus putting an end to the petty system of debasement and cretinization in effect has a well defined place in the crowd with his belly at barrel level.
>
> (Quoted in Wolin 2004: 181)

Such violence, argues Weisbrod, characterized by a vitalist cult of lived experience and a search for discovery of self, is the 'ultimate epiphany of modernity'. We capture something of such violence in the words of a West German student involved in the Red Army Faction in 1968: 'When we employ violence, we change not only our objective world, but also our subjective world ... we break the stranglehold of the norms we have internalized' (quoted in Varon 2004: 44).

In that sense, violence can establish itself as central to the way a group understands itself and its relationships with the world. This is highlighted by Richard Slotkin (1973) who explores the centrality of violence to ideas of regeneration that played a key role in the expansion of the American frontier in the seventeenth and eighteenth centuries. Slotkin argues that violence became the only way that Puritans could imagine relationships with the indigenous population, despite the fact that much wider relationships actually existed. While significant numbers of marriages existed between Puritans and native Americans, Slotkin argues that Puritan writers of the time ignored these, conceiving of the relationship between settlers and the indigenous population almost exclusively in terms of incidents of cannibalism and rape. Slotkin traces the development of 'a growing Puritan belief that the only acceptable communion between Christian and Indian, civilization and wilderness, was the communion of murder, hunger and bloodlust' (1973: 125). Violence can establish itself as a grammar of imagination, outside of which other things cannot be thought or comprehended.

The Obedience Paradigm

A subtle but pessimistic analysis of violence is proposed by social critics such as the sociologist Zigmunt Bauman, whose work we introduced in Chapter 1. He argues that involvement in extreme violence is not only not abnormal or pathological, it is in fact an expression of hyper-normality, the product of a culture of obedience he considers central to modern rationalized societies (Bauman 1989: 152ff). Most of us will be familiar with arguments introduced above about the 'terrorist personality' as someone who is frighteningly abnormal. Reflecting on the horrific violence unleashed against civilian minority populations such as Jews, gypsies and homosexuals by the Nazis during the Second World War, Bauman turns this literature on its head, arguing that those involved in extreme violence are best understood as being frighteningly normal. Extreme violence is not an aberration, he argues; rather it offers us an insight into the heart of modern society. Bauman is engaging with the cultural concern focusing on conformism and obedience that emerged in the 1960s, and which we saw highlighted by the debate around Adolf Eichmann's claim that his involvement in the Holocaust was simply a matter of following orders. Influential sociologists such as David Riesman (Riesman *et al.* 1961) were attempting to understand whether modern bureaucratic societies were generating a new type of 'outer-directed' person lacking an inner moral core and capacity for moral judgement.

Eichmann's defence formed the basis for the well-known experiment undertaken in 1961 by the Yale University psychologist Stanley Milgram (1965, 1974), who wanted to explore 'how far ordinary individuals will go' (1974: 5) to comply with instructions issued by an authority figure. Milgram's experiment asked volunteers to play the role of 'teachers', who were told that the study they were volunteering to join was to test how people learn. Their role as 'teachers', they were told, would involve administering electric shocks to students who failed to remember word pairs (1974: 20), in order to assess how such shocks helped people to learn. At the start of the test they were given a slight shock, to demonstrate that the test was 'real' (1974: 20). In fact, no shocks were administered to the 'students' taking the test. Instead, the aim was to test how far the volunteers would be willing to inflict shocks on others simply on the basis that they had been told to do so by someone in authority. While the 'students' in the experiment did not receive shocks, they pretended to move from gradual discomfort to extreme agony (screaming, crying, banging on the wall, crying out for the experiment to stop) as the volunteer 'teacher' gradually increased the electric charge at the direction of a researcher. Before the experiment, Milgram had asked his senior psychology students at Yale what proportion of people they thought would be prepared to go as far as to administer the 'maximum' 450 volts to a screaming 'student' simply on the basis that they were directed to do so by an authority figure wearing a white coat. The students expected this to be in the order of 1 per cent of those being tested. In fact 65 per cent of people went to the ultimate point of inflicting what they believed to be agony on another person, simply because they had been told to do so by a person in authority (Milgram 1974: 69).

Milgram's experiment was designed in 1961, a few months after the beginnings of Adolf Eichmann's war trial in Israel, and he wanted to test whether it was possible to accept that extreme Nazi violence was possible through 'following orders', as Eichmann's defence team was claiming. Milgram noted that the participants in his research project were normal people who in principle objected to inflicting pain on others (Milgram 1965), but when told to do so by a person in authority, 65 per cent would inflict agony on another person. He concluded that 'Ordinary people, simply doing their jobs, and without any particular hostility on their part, can become agents in a terrible destructive process' (Milgram 1974: 6). The problem that required explanation on the basis of his research, argued Milgram, was not the abnormality of those who inflict violence, but the potentially horrific power of ordinary people's obedience to authority.

A decade later an equally famous, and equally controversial, experiment was conducted at Stanford University by Philip Zimbardo (Zimbardo 1972). In this case 24 undergraduates were given the roles of guards and inmates in a mock 'prison' in a basement at Stanford University. Potential research subjects answered an advertisement placed in a student newspaper, to be paid a daily rate for their role as research participants. The participants selected to play the role of prison guards were given batons, uniforms and sunglasses to avoid eye contact with prisoners. Those designated as prisoners were dressed in ill-fitting clothes and humiliating stocking caps, they had to wear a chain around their legs and did not have a name but a number. Within just a few days the volunteers became totally absorbed into the roles they were being asked to play: those playing the role of guards, finding themselves in a situation of absolute power, became increasingly violent and sadistic, designing increasingly humiliating forms of punishment for prisoners, ranging from push-ups, confinement in cupboards to other forms of brutality. Some prisoners were told as a punishment they were to be denied their payment for participating in the project. A number accepted this, remaining in the prison rather than simply walking out since they were no longer being paid. Zimbardo argued this demonstrated that these students had internalized the role of prisoners, no longer realizing that they were in fact free people being paid for their involvement in a research project. While being free to leave at any point, they had come to accept that they were imprisoned. Originally planned to last three weeks, the situation in the 'prison' deteriorated so rapidly that Zimbardo was forced to terminate the experiment after six days. This model of socialization as a generator of extreme violence was later used by Zimbardo and co-researchers to explore the violence of police torturers and murders in Brazil (Huggins *et al.* 2002).

These 'learning' and 'prison' experiments have provoked ongoing discussion of issues ranging from the ethics of deception in the first case to causing actual suffering in the second, as well as the extent to which situations produced in an experimental context can be used to understand the actual social world (Orne and Holland 1968). Some psychologists have asked to what extent the sadism that emerged in Zimbardo's experiment may have resulted from the way he prepared participants for their roles as prisoners and guards (Haslam and Reicher 2007). Capturing much deeper cultural anxieties about the dangers of a conformist society that were emerging in the 1960s, Milgram's proposition that violence is the product of obedience had a major impact in wider theories of society, taken up by Zigmunt Bauman and his analysis of the Holocaust. But what if it was not obedience that had led so many of the volunteers to administer what they believed were horrendous levels of pain to others? The experiments were filmed, and the Norwegian philosopher Arne Johan Vetlesen observes that many of the people administering the shocks were giggling at the time they did so – what if, asks Vetlesen, those administering the shocks were not doing so out of respect for authority, but because they found themselves in a situation where they could indulge in a desire that most of the time they repressed – the desire to inflict pain upon another (2005: 107).

Michel Wieviorka argues that Milgram's thesis that extreme violence is ultimately caused by 'obedience' does not tell us enough about the specific cultural, historical, social and political conditions involved where atrocities take place (2009: 117). And, in fact, actual studies of extreme violence deployed in massacres and atrocities suggest a more complex process than simple obedience. The historian Christopher Browning (1992) explores the violence undertaken by the German Police Battalion 101 in Poland during the Second World War. This Battalion was made up of middle-aged German family-men, husbands and fathers, many in middle-class occupations, who were too old to be drafted into the regular army. They were drafted instead into the reserve police, responsible for dealing with order and control of civilian populations in occupied territories. Their first tour of duty saw them sent to Poland in July 1942. On their first day of active service, three weeks after arriving, they were driven in trucks to the village of Józefów, home to some 1,800 Jews (1992: 2). Their task was to round up the Jewish inhabitants, separate the men to be sent to labour camps, and then to execute all the women, children and old people. The members of the Battalion did as they were ordered, killing over 1,500 people on that day, many being bayoneted to death. The Battalion remained in Poland for the next two years, its missions focusing on killing civilians. It is estimated that during its period of duty in Poland, the Battalion was responsible for killing over 38,000 Jews (Browning 1992: 142). Here too, observers have attempted to find some kind of abnormality that might offer an explanation for the way ordinary men became involved in such atrocity. But Browining comes to the same conclusion as that arrived at in studies of those involved in terrorism – the people involved in such violence were normal middle-class husbands and fathers.

The violence of Battalion 101 cannot be regarded as the product of a 'detached' obedience as the Milgram thesis suggests. Instead the involvement of these middle-aged men in violence appears unstable, fluctuating between different meanings. At one time they celebrate killing (Browning 1992: 20), at another they proceed far beyond any demands for cold obedience, clearly taking pleasure in humiliating those whom they were to kill. At other times they need to get drunk to be able to perform the tasks asked of them (Browning 1992: 69). As Wieviorka argues, the story appears more complex than the suggestion that involvement in atrocities can be explained in terms of a unique principle of obedience.

Dissatisfied Elites, Passive Masses, Dynamic Processes

Martha Crenshaw (1981) argues that terrorist violence needs to be understood as a means of achieving a political goal. However, she insists, it is not the poor and dispossessed who are likely to engage in terrorism. The recruiting ground for terrorists, she argues, is the elite, while terrorism is best understood in terms of calculations of cost and benefit, rather than the irrational action of 'fanatics'. Crenshaw argues such rationality is manifest in two dimensions: first, the relationship that a terrorist group establishes with its environment; and, second, in organizational logics that occur within the terrorist group itself. The distinctive dimension of terrorism, she argues, lies in the fact that it is a form of violent coercion that aims to hurt and intimidate, rather than to achieve a military victory. Certain things thus take on significance. Surprise attacks compensate for weakness in numbers and military capacity, and such attacks are most likely to develop in a context that is perceived in terms of opportunity, in particular when a government is perceived as experiencing weakness.

Crenshaw argues violence is likely to emerge in particular political contexts, suggesting that we need to distinguish between the causes that *permit* terrorism (1981: 384) and those likely to be involved in violence actually *developing*. Terrorism, she argues, is the product of elites who are disaffected, who want to bring about change, but who lack the popular support necessary to engage in more mass-based strategies. Two factors thus play a key role, she suggests: elite disaffection on the one hand, and mass passivity on the other (1981: 384). Implied here is the idea that if the masses were mobilizing for change, more mass-based strategies would replace the development of terrorism. However, she suggests, a third factor also needs to be present: a repressive regime, but one where repression is weak or inefficient. In such a context terrorism becomes an option to bring about change: it is easier and cheaper than strategies aiming at mass mobilization, above all where repression makes mass mobilization difficult, if not impossible. It is in such situations where legal expressions of opposition are blocked, but where a regime's repression is inefficient, that revolutionary terrorism is 'doubly likely', as what Crenshaw calls 'direct' and 'permissive' causes coincide (1981: 384). For Crenshaw, the blockage of legal possibilities for change is a 'direct' cause of terrorism, while the extent that inefficient regimes are associated with the availability of targets and weapons, combined with poorly organized repression, serves as a 'permissive' factor: 'When the group perceives its options as limited, terrorism is attractive because it is a relatively inexpensive and simple alternative, and because its potential reward is high' (Crenshaw 1981: 387). This analysis underlines the extent to which the political system and the relationship between political actors shape the emergence of terrorism.

For most authors writing in a rational actor perspective, violence and revolutionary organizations are understood in instrumental terms: they are instruments to achieve goals. While working within this tradition, Crenshaw is alert to experiential dimensions such as the pleasures of risk, excitement, intensity, belonging, status and loyalty associated with involvement in violent groups. This alerts us to important dimensions of such groups: in Germany, for example, Andreas Baader, the leader of the Red Army Faction, called for international proletarian revolution as liberation from what he called 'consumer terrorism', yet cultivated a Marlon Brando figure of cool wrap-around sunglasses, open shirt and tight jeans, and took great pleasure in driving a Porsche Targa convertible sports car while on the run from police (Aust 2008: 165).

Crenshaw underlines the extent that the emergence and development of terrorism involves collective or group processes. There is little use in looking to grievances or discontent to explain the development of terrorism, she argues: oppression and injustice are widespread, a sense of grievance is universal. The development of terrorism is, however, a much more limited phenomenon. As such, 'structural explanations' such as inequality or domination are of limited use: 'the formation of organizations, not environmental conditions, is the critical variable. Entrepreneurship is an essential ingredient: the leaders who establish an organization must skilfully create and manipulate incentives to attract members' (1987: 21). Organization theory, Crenshaw argues, helps us understand certain critical dimensions of the trajectory of terrorist organizations. While they may emerge as a means to an objective, after a period of time many organizations come to have 'organization maintenance' as their principle objective. They develop structures, resources, income streams and prestige that become ends in themselves. Simply referring to ideology or stated goals fails to take into account this critical dimension of group trajectory. Developed within economics as the 'theory of the firm', these insights into organization behaviour may help us understand why groups continue in existence long after they cease to believe that their original objectives can be achieved. This observation is important in understanding the dynamics at work in terrorist groups that have amassed important resources, as in Northern Ireland (Silke 2000). It also alerts us to important dynamics within such groups – many terrorist groups engage in illegal activities, from robbing banks or drug sales. Initially, these are understood as serving the goals of the group. But as these goals become less likely to be achieved, the illegal activities become more and more the primary reason for the continued existence of the group. This highlights critical issues involved when groups attempt to disengage from violence.

Crenshaw's work is one of the earliest to underline the centrality of what Hans Joas (2003: 187) would later call the 'dynamics of violence'. Across this literature we can see different attempts at conceptualizing such dynamics. Sidney Tarrow (1989) higlights a 'cyclical' model of social movement activism. Michel Wieviorka proposes a theory of what he calls 'antimovements' and their 'inversion'. Finally, Randall Collins (2008) sets out to construct a 'micro-sociology' of violence. Each of these offers important insights into violence and its transformation.

Demobilization and Radicalization: Political Cycles

For the American political scientist and sociologist Sydney Tarrow, the emergence of terrorism as a form of violence needs to be understood within a dynamic of radicalization associated with the demobilization of social movements. Such movements, he argues (1989: 95ff), proceed through three 'stages': an initial stage of mobilization, when what he calls 'political opportunities' become available for 'early risers'. A second period follows as the movement strengthens and its demands become more widely taken up. In this period the movement's demands no longer appear so radical, it begins to become routinized and institutionalized, moving from the role of 'challenger' to that of 'insider'. The third and final period of the cycle, demobilization, is characterized by two directions: exhaustion and polarization. Many people previously involved in the movement are now likely to be in government institutions, while the less committed will have dropped out, leaving the movement in the hands of its most radical and committed elements. A dynamic of polarization becomes evident, as moderate movement participants become involved in institutions of government, leaving movement organizations and associations in the hands of the most radical, who remain committed to the future of the movement and who are increasingly likely to use confrontation as a tactic to prevent the movement's institutionalization, which they consider would lead inevitably to its neutralization.

For Tarrow this cyclical dynamic is the source of a logic of violence, a process pointed to by Isabelle Sommier (2008b: 26). When a social movement is mobilizing it is characterized by moderation, it is reaching outwards and including wider numbers of people. The dynamic of demobilization, however, is one of radicalization, as borders and non-negotiable principles are asserted as the movement shrinks back to its committed core who resist both institutionalization and disengagement. Institutionalization and radicalization are two sides of a social movement's demobilization. For Tarrow this is illustrated by the Italian student movement of the 1970s, where both institutionalization and violence emerged side-by-side in the latter stages of the 'protest cycle' (Tarrow 1989).

Donatella della Porta's (1995) study of political violence in Germany and Italy comes to the same conclusion. For della Porta the declining period of a protest cycle is characterized by two opposed but complementary developments: increasing institutionalization of the movement on the one hand, while on the other 'small groups resort to more organized forms of violence' (1995: 53) (as compared to the unorganized violence that characterized the earlier period of the movement). Drawing on Tarrow's cyclic model, she underlines a further critical dimension: the interaction between social movement activists and police. She argues that if the type of violence emerging out of the 1960s student movements radicalized into the most lethal forms of terror in Germany and Italy, this is because of the fascist legacy in both these countries, which meant that students interpreted police repression as a sign of the re-emergence of fascism (1995: 194).

While violence may be present at the beginning, peak and decline of a movement, Tarrow argues that *organized political violence* will be associated above all with the period of movement decline. There is no need, he argues, to link the development of such violence with the pathology of the actors involved. The key lies in political dynamics.

Antimovements and Inversions: Social Dynamics

French sociologist Michel Wieviorka (1993) also locates the emergence of violence within a theory of social movement transformations, drawing on the work of Alain Touraine (1988). Touraine argues that movements are not primarily organizations, nor directed primarily towards the political system, but are fields of tension, creativity and action. In particular, he suggests that movements are constituted around three poles, which he terms 'identity', 'opposition' and 'totality'. *Identity* is a field of tension where actors experience themselves as being capable of bringing about change and being creative, while also confronting experiences that limit and dispossess them. In the case of the labour movement, these two sides are evident in the creativity of skilled workers on the one hand and in the experience of being dispossessed of creativity and autonomy by the assembly line and deskilled work on the other. *Opposition* refers to the social actors that social movements consider as their opponent, such as industrialists in the case of labour movements. *Totality* refers to the issues at stake in these social conflicts, issues that call into question directions of social development. Social movements, argues Touraine, are not defined by political cycles but constitute themselves through action and conflict in a social field constituted by these three poles: identity, opposition and totality.

Wieviorka builds on this analysis, suggesting that terrorism emerges out of particular constellations of social movement that he refers to as 'antimovement' (1993: 13). While a social movement will be constituted by the three poles of identity, opposition and totality, in certain cases these dimensions 'invert', where rather than seeing them combined in the way that characterizes social movements (maintaining distinction and tension between them), they become fused (1993: 5). In the case of an 'antimovement', the pole of *identity* ceases to refer to any social entity (workers, women, students, youth) but becomes defined uniquely in terms of abstract principles (such as justice, history, purity). The pole of *opposition* equally ceases to refer to an actual social opponent (such as employers, men, the older generation), and becomes defined in martial or military terms, within an imaginary of war rather than conflict: the social opponent becomes increasingly abstracted, an increasingly powerful and threatening enemy, such as law, the state or the system, fused into a single menacing being. The pole of *totality* becomes redefined as well, less and less connected with actual social utopias, and ceases to have any connection to actual social worlds and practice, where it can only be achieved by a radical break with the present world, as opposed to its transformation. Images of a future social world become replaced by myth.

All social movements have within them the potential to generate such antimovement dynamics, as all have the ideal of a world where their opponent will have ceased to exist. Often this gives rise to the development of sects, organized in terms of strict boundaries of purity and impurity. Such groups, argues Wieviorka, are best understood as 'antimovements', where in certain cases such antimovements can radicalize to the point of embracing violence.

He describes this process as 'inversion'. In such cases, reference to any social identity not only disappears, it becomes replaced by what Wieviorka calls *subjectivism*, where an absent or dormant social identity is replaced by the violent actor's commitment. While the labour movement may be sleeping, the violence of the terrorist will wake it from its slumber. Reference to any other social actor disappears into a world constituted uniquely through desire and will: 'substituting himself in a unilateral if not fanatic manner for a social entity whose existence has become an impossibility, or promoting himself as the necessary catalyst for the awakening of a dormant class, the terrorist makes himself out to be the consciousness of all who have been alienated, deprived of the ability to act, or who remain unconscious of the historical role they have to play' (1993: 8). In a similar fashion, the social opponent becomes 'objectified', no longer recognized as being made up of human beings, transformed instead 'into a concrete target to attack, properties to destroy, a person to physically eliminate, or a system to annihilate' (1993: 8). The principle of totality becomes equally transformed, there is no longer any reference to a future utopia or description of the society one is fighting for, or even a mythic description of a new order. Instead

> the ends of one's acts become confused with their means, with all sense of vision being reduced to plans for the destruction of all that stands in that way of the actor's subjectivity. It is no longer the creation of a new society that is most important, but rather the destruction of the existing order.
>
> (Wieviorka 1993: 8)

This type of violence leads to the use of the term 'fanatic'. But Wieviorka insists that what is at stake here is not a psychological aberration but a fusion of actor and cause (1993: 9). Terrorism is not simply about choosing violence as an instrument, or its location within a political cycle, but involves the construction of secret, total worlds of fusion where nothing is out of place. In this dynamic, argues Wieviorka, the goal becomes fundamentally one of destruction, expressed in terms of a hyper-subjectivism (where the actor understands himthemself to be the agent of history), while the opponent becomes objectified and depersonalized. This leads to a form of hyperactivity, where the subjectivity of the actor becomes threatened if no longer active, and where the world becomes reduced to a power struggle between opposing forces. This creates forms of megalomania, a belief that action can 'dictate history' (Wieviorka 1993: 12), leading to a world of desire and menace, love and hate, a very different world from the model of terrorist violence proposed by Charles Tilly, one of 'politics as usual'. While the fusion of subjectivity and cause may give the appearance of the fanatic, for Wieviorka the origins of this fusion lie in social processes, not individual pathologies.

A Micro-sociology: Situational Dynamics

Work by the American sociologist Randall Collins (2008) points to a renewal of interactionist approaches to the study of violence. He argues that violence is not a pervasive potential that needs to be controlled by culture and civilization, nor a simple choice among a range of options that actors have available to them. Rather than view violence as being easy, he argues that it is a difficult achievement for embodied actors, and that the task of sociological analysis is to understand the ways actors overcome what amount to significant obstacles to violence. He argues that wider social and cultural contexts are not the key to understand violence; what is important instead is the interaction that takes place in 'situations' where violence develops: 'features of situations ... determine what kinds of violence will or will not happen, and when and how' (2008: 20). This focuses analysis on the embodied co-presence and physical encounters of people in locations where violence may develop, such situations being shaped by 'confrontation, tension and emotional flow' (2008: 2). For Collins it is this 'confrontational tension' that makes up the 'central reality' of violence, meaning that to understand violence we need to shift the focus from macrosocial questions such as civilizations or crisis, to focus instead on the embodied co-presence and interaction of the protagonists of violence. In particular, analysis needs to identify and understand what Collins calls 'emotional energy' or the ways actors 'become entrained in each other's emotions and bodily rhythms', the dynamic that he argues is at the centre of the 'situational process' (2008: 19).

This micro-sociology offers important insight, for example, into the ways police and protesters interact, from jeering and threatening to mocking or simulated violence, involving a dynamic of interaction that Collins studies, in particular through the analysis of images. In the process, he captures what we might call the 'dance' of violence, the attempt by actors to intimidate, infuriate or ignore their opponents, and through which we can see the way actors become caught up in emotion and body rhythm. This emphasis on inter-subjective embodied experience points to the limits of analyses that consider violence uniquely as choice, as if violence flows uniquely from the calculation of actors. For Collins, what is critical is confrontation that occurs in situations, understood as a social space where bodily rhythms interact. This is central to understanding violence.

From Ideas to Experience: Actual Violence

What is striking so far is the divergence of approaches we have encountered, opposing macro and micro, cause and effect, agency and symptom. Embedded in these models are diverging approaches not only to thinking about societies, but also to what constitutes human action, and to the place of meaning in that action. Rather than move to some higher level of abstraction in an attempt to resolve these tensions, which, as we have seen, would turn violence into a formalistic category, over the chapters that follow we turn to explore more closely actual experiences of violence, in an attempt to identify what we can use from these different intellectual models, but also what seems to stand beyond them. The next three chapters will focus on attempting to identify key points, transitions and questions in the dynamics of violence, from where we will shift to explore the ways that violence is globalizing today.

4

Terror, Violence and the Student Movement

The student movements of the 1960s set in motion social and cultural transformations that we are still experiencing today, above all in the search for personal experience and autonomy (Melucci 1996). But these movements also gave rise to groups committed to armed struggle to achieve revolution (Zwerman *et al.* 2000). In some countries, such as France, groups such as the Maoist *Gauche Proletarienne* (Proletarian Left) went to the edge, kidnapping a business leader (Wolin 2010: 27), yet after holding him captive, decided to release him, in the process pulling back from placing violence at the centre of their action (Sommier 2008a). In Britain, a group calling itself the *Angry Brigade* emerged between 1970 and 1972, its actions being limited to a short period of attacks on property, in a kind of theatrical violence influenced by the 'situationism' that had emerged in the French student movement of 1968 (Plant 1992: 126; McDonald 2010). But in other cases student action mutated into more sustained violence. In the United States, students who had been elected to lead the once powerful SDS (Students for a Democratic Society) dissolved that organization in 1968 and created another that eventually became committed to armed war with the American state, the *Weather Underground* (Miller 1999). The most sustained and deadly violence emerged in Italy, where between 1969 and 1982 over 2,700 attacks took place, leading to the deaths of some 351 people (della Porta 1992: 151). A number of violent groups emerged in this period, the most deadly being the *Red Brigades*, a group that would go on to kill scores of people, including the kidnapping and execution of one of Italy's most important political leaders, Aldo Moro, in 1978 (Drake 1995). In Japan in the late 1960s increasingly violent confrontations between student demonstrators and police saw student groups arming themselves with staves, helmets and rocks, with several groups later developing 'military wings' that understood themselves to be revolutionary elites. Two of these groups merged in their final days to form the Japanese United Red Army, a group that in late 1971 took refuge in Japan's mountains, where in its dying days it killed 12 of its own members (Igarashi 2007). While these groups were very different, at certain points their paths converge in ways that help us to understand important dimensions of the transition to violence and the increasing centrality of violence in the imaginary of these actors.

Freeing Oneself through Confrontation

The young people who would later create the Red Brigades were originally student activists in Italy's wealthiest northern industrialized cities. Most had become involved in student activism in university occupations at the centre of the wave of activism that took place in 1968 (Statera 1979). These occupations were powerful periods of personal and collective transformation. The Italian historian Luisa Passerini's (2004) interviews with participants highlight the theme of self-discovery and transformation, of freeing oneself from fear and internalized forms of control. Action, such as occupying lecture theatres, is experienced as freeing oneself from internalized domination, a transformation not limited to the world of ideas, but extending to embodied experience, to new ways of being together (Passerini 2004: 71). These accounts underline how much action is not simply an instrument to achieve a goal, but involves experiences of discovery, of finding oneself part of a world that one did not imagine even existed, of discovering oneself to be a different person, with potential and possibilities one could not imagine.

The students described the occupations as 'cultural guerrilla war'. Protestors with megaphones would storm lecture theatres, ridiculing lecturers and physically preventing classes from taking place. One student recalls the period with a sense of unease, stating 'really there was a lot of violence, we were out of control. Nobody could do anything at the university', while another suggests that the action created a momentum that could trap its protagonists: 'this cultural guerrilla war was a game, but I don't know how much we all liked it...A mass movement doesn't much like to be contradicted' (Passerini 2004: 78–9). The action increasingly sought to shock, to blaspheme, to create a break with the past (older generation, parents), while also asserting that the students belonged to 'the people', evident in the increasing use of profanities. The search to shock, to smash and to embarrass was an attempt to achieve freedom and self-transformation through transgression.

By late 1968 the occupations were over (Statera 1979). Students were divided between action on campuses or supporting labour strikes, typically through demonstrations at factory gates. The period of optimism and hope in a new world was progressively weakening, with the student movement seeming trapped in actions that appeared to be repeating the past, offering no new meaning. Intensity, experience and the possibility of revolutionary change seemed to be elsewhere, in the centres of raw industrial power and energy, the huge factories, fortresses of the Italian Communist Party (PCI), where, it seemed, a mobilization was building that would sweep aside the old order (Drake 1999). This was not simply a view held by radical students, but also by professional sociologists who argued that 1968 marked the beginnings of a resurgence of class conflict in Western Europe (Crouch and Pizzorno 1978). Academic observers, distant from these events, tend to identify structural processes, political opportunities, decisions or strategies. What we need to grasp as well is embodied experience of which the actor struggles to make sense: the world is changing, they are changing, they can feel what is happening, a key dimension of action is the struggle to make sense and also to feel sense. Passerini describes her own involvement in producing daily action leaflets that she distributed at the factory gates:

> Serve an idea, a movement. Gather news of the struggle, write it up in the leaflet, give it back by circulating it. Link, transmit, act as a passageway, be the vehicle. The PCI workers at the gates of the engine works watched us sceptically. The looks we exchanged with other workers were heavy with reciprocal expectations, with an understanding not fully articulated, with trepidation for what might happen. An intense flow of nonverbal communication continued, over and above the information dispersed about what had happened in one day in one department. I experienced a sense of the end of the world, a mental state of emergency, like an inner perception of an imminent end, with the urgency to act before it was too late. The rhythm of daily life accelerated in order to live up to the circumstances, absorbed in the approach of the eschaton, which might be a triumphant outcome or a catastrophic result. Time curled like a wave repelled by a dyke. Life was marked by continual deadlines, but what was supposed to fall due? The final hour, the encounter between our time and the time of the definitive uprising of the downtrodden masses. I wasn't in possession of myself, I was advancing in enemy territory, forced on the attack in the absence of a fixed place in which to come face to face with myself.
>
> (Passerini 2004: 103)

This account captures an experience that marked a generation (see Glynn 2009). Passerini describes her experience of trying to invent a new form of open couple relationship, inspired by the French philosophers Jean-Paul Sartre and Simone de Beauvoir, in a deliberate attempt to limit attachment.

She concludes with an exploration of love, hatred and the search for the extreme:

> Out of all this was born a violent notion of liberty, an extremism that concealed a certain self-hatred. Be done with the image of the woman-mother, warm and affectionate refuge; assert toughness, coldness, detachment, distance. But the 'open' relationship with a man became very closed, the site of fusion between ideas and ideals, of reaction to experiences with other people, of unrecognized sufferings, establishing a hierarchy dominated by the couple. I don't remember the feeling of jealously from that period. Something inside me suffered, but it didn't find ways to experience the feeling, it expressed itself silently.
>
> (Passerini 2004: 45)

Passerini is describing a radical and profound personal disruption, from the relationship with her boyfriend to the magnetic attraction of the factory. What is at stake here is not simply a struggle about ideas, but also to *feel* part of her body and her world. She describes an experience where the boundaries of self become uncertain, and reminds us that action within social movements is not simply about decisions to employ instruments, but is a powerful embodied experience at first beyond the capacity of the actor to make sense of, made up of tensions and 'trepidations'. Her account is like an encounter with a powerful work of art, one that stops us in our tracks and throws us off balance. At first we don't know why, and making sense of what is happening to us is an experience that demands not simply the mind but also the senses.

This path to the workers' struggle was shared by the small group of students at the University of Trento who created the Red Brigades (Griset and Mahan 2003: 174). At first they set up study circles and journals aiming at transforming the university, but in 1969 they abandoned this and moved to the industrial heartland of Milan, to create what they called the 'Metropolitan Political Collective', based in a run-down building, where they organized political seminars, discussions and workshops as well as experimental theatre and art exhibitions (Drake 1999). The period came to be called the 'hot autumn', as a wave of strikes accelerated in the second half of 1969 (Wieviorka 1993). The newly created collective aimed at joining and politicizing worker conflicts, with members taking jobs in key factories, in particular Milan's large Siemens and Pirelli plants (Pisano 1979).

The Workers' Struggle

The experience of these activists was similar to that described by Passerini in her account of accelerating time, of increasing tension, of an approaching 'eschaton' or turning point that would open out to either radical transformation or catastrophe. For these students, Italy was entering a revolutionary period, one where violence would be central to bringing about change. Confrontations were taking place against factory closures in rural towns. Milan's giant Fiat factory was occupied by workers (Cuninghame 2011: 325). The time was ripe for a 'qualitative leap' in the struggle. As the 'hot autumn' progressed, the sense of living in a time of increasing tension intensified, associated with a widespread fear of a looming coup d'état, where the history of 1922 would repeat itself and the army would take power. This sense of looming disaster increased with a series of attacks alleged to have links to the security services, beginning with a massive explosion in the Piazza Fontana in Milan, killing 17 people and injuring over 80 (Foot 2009). A wave of arrests of left-wing activists followed, one prominent anarchist dying after falling from the fourth floor of a police building, widely seen as an extra-judicial killing (Foot 2007). This period was fundamental to the imaginary associated with creating 'brigades'. The decades of fascist rule from 1922 had been opposed by partisan brigades, and the students' decision to create a new 'brigade' emphasized the fascist threat while claiming the heritage of Resistance. The term Brigades emphasized the continuity with the Resistance, while taking up proudly the term 'reds', up to that point a derogatory term used by conservative newspapers and politicians (Sommier 2008b).

The workplace conflicts that exploded in the 'hot autumn' were often 'wildcat' actions, largely undertaken by unskilled workers who had immigrated to the cities from the country in the post-1945 economic expansion. These actions were often directed against remote trade union leaders just as much as at employers, manifesting important dimensions of the 'proletarian' identity pointed to by Alain Touraine (1988): sabotage and other forms of disruption aiming at breaking free from work experienced as alienating and meaningless. Skilled workers will never destroy their tools, they are instruments of their creativity. For unskilled workers, tools and machines are often instruments of their domination, becoming a target for sabotage. This new workforce was celebrated by the philosopher Toni Negri, a key figure in the development of philosophies of *Potere Operario* (Worker Power), as the *worker-mass*, workers who had no knowledge of the traditions and culture of trade unions, and who had not been socialized into the demands of industrial production. For Negri (1979) such workers were the new 'revolutionary subject', and violence was central to their action. (This 'mass worker' is reworked as the *Multitude* in Negri's recent work [Hardt and Negri 2004]). One such form of action that emerged in the 'hot autumn' involved 'internal marches', where workers would stop work, march through the factory disrupting production, destroying the authority of foremen, humiliating them and at times forcing them to lead the march (Giachetti and Scavino 1999). This echoed actions of the Italian Resistance, where collaborators were humiliated by being placed on donkeys and marched through villages.

The Red Brigades began its action by creating cells at major production plants such as Siemens and Pirelli (Jamieson 1990). In August 1970 they distributed leaflets during a strike at Siemens, denouncing workers who were not involved, referring to the management as an 'army to be used against us' and '*torturers*' (Red Brigades, *Communiqué One*, November 1970, author's translation, emphasis in original). As workplace conflicts intensified and workers were sacked, Brigade members moved to a new type of action, setting alight cars belonging to managers and union leaders, describing this as fulfilling 'rulings of the People's Court' (*Communiqué Two*) blurring class conflict at the workplace with an imaginary of armed resistance to the occupation.

War

The language of war marked a shift in forms of action (Sommier 2008a: 41). This was evident in March 1972 when a Siemens manager was kidnapped, photographed with a gun jammed into his jaw, and subjected to 'Proletarian Trial in the People's Prison', the verdict being to release him 'on parole' (Wagner-Pacifici 1986: 52). This kidnapping set in motion a concerted police campaign to arrest members of the group. A narrow escape of its key leaders led to a decision to go underground and become a clandestine organization. In 1973, kidnappings extended, not only to industrialists, but also trade union leaders considered by the group to be 'collaborators'. Those kidnapped were judged and accorded 'provisional release' on the grounds that they had acknowledged the wrongs of their actions. But by 1974 there was an increasing sense among the members of the Brigades that this strategy was not working. Their action was either rejected, or worse, ignored by most trade union members (Wieviorka 1993). The labour mobilizations that had peaked in 1969 were declining, and the labour movement itself appeared to be fragmenting (Drake 1999). Key figures in the Brigades argued that the limits of the factory-based strategy lay in the ability of multinational corporations to relocate their production, neutralizing direct action in the factory. The challenge was to move beyond managers and collaborating unionists, and attack directly the cause of the Brigades' limited impact: the state (Moretti 1994: 20, cited in Ruggiero 2005).

A new vision of the SIM (Multinationals' Imperialist State), articulated in 1975, allowed the Brigades to 'tie together everything' (Wieviorka 1993). The Brigades would no longer seek to be an armed presence in labour conflicts, but would engage directly in guerrilla war with the Italian state. The Brigades expanded into two columns, 'regular' members who lived in clandestinity, and 'irregular' supporters, with cells developing across several northern cities (Zwerman *et al.* 2000). The strategy of action shifted to political murder, beginning in June 1976 with the assassination of judges whom the Brigades considered to be opponents, followed by a wave of killings. By now the Brigades had become completely disconnected from the social objectives supposedly inspiring them (Ruggiero 2005). Their primary purpose became the accumulation of clandestine military strength: 'military episodes in most cases were no longer decidable as moments of wider social conflicts, but as products of a military group seeking self-promotion (2005: 301). Targets were chosen not because of their links to particular political issues, but to demonstrate military prowess. The most spectacular such action was undertaken by the Brigades on 16 March 1978, in the kidnapping and subsequent execution of Aldo Moro. At the time, Moro was president of the Christian Democrat party, and the day of his kidnapping was scheduled for the signature of a 'historic compromise' between the Italian Communist Party (PCI) and the Christian Democrats. Moro was ambushed in the middle of Rome, his five bodyguards killed in a firefight (for a detailed account see Moss 1981; Wagner-Pacifici 1986; Drake 1995: 2). The political class refused to negotiate, and Moro, following a series of communiqués, was 'tried' by the Brigades and assassinated on 9 May. The period following was one of escalating violence.

Observers such as Michel Wieviorka (1993) argue that this increase in violence paradoxically points to the group's decline. In the Brigades' strategy of war, the state became a force of evil to be destroyed, but at the same time also became increasingly abstract to the point where any opponent was considered part of the state: police, political leaders, journalists, newspaper editors, academics were all considered part of 'the state', and all were considered targets. At the same time increasing forms of 'autonomous' violence were emerging in Italian cities in the context of social and political crisis. In Milan, for example, groups of young people would loot luxury shops while shouting revolutionary slogans – the difference between political violence and delinquency was blurring (Wieviorka 1993). The Brigades were becoming defined by a logic of a private war against the state, their violence increasingly disconnected from wider movements and political actors, their actions increasingly focused on reproducing themselves rather than establishing relationships with social actors (Ruggiero 2005), suggesting the pattern of 'organization maintenance' pointed to by Martha Crenshaw (1981). The Italian state's response was to declare war on the Brigades, setting in motion a new type of state violence, where members of the Brigades were killed rather than detained (Wieviorka 1993). The Italian sociologist

Donatella della Porta (1996) underlines important transformations within the Brigades during this period, linked to the shift to clandestinity. Previously the Brigades had a relatively decentralized organizational model. Members would maintain other activities, either as students or workers, with an open structure allowing recruitment into the Brigades primarily through friendship and family networks. This open structure also meant people could leave the Brigades relatively easily (della Porta 2009). Della Porta notes the importance of broader cultures of violence within which the Brigades emerged: a majority of those who joined the Brigades had prior experience of physical confrontation with the police, with many having experience of acting as marshals during demonstrations where physical confrontations were common with the police or right-wing opponents.

The arrest of the first generation of leaders in 1974 converged with an increasing sense both of the limits of the open structure and the first form of violence, typically associated with burning opponents' cars. The shift to war against the state was in part a response to the limits of this strategy, and in part a response to the infiltration and arrest of the Brigades' founding generation (della Porta 1996). The shift from attacks on property to political murder took place over 1972 and 1974, passing through the intermediary stage of kidnapping. This shift was associated with a militarization of the Brigades, which became reorganized into 'columns' in the principal cities where they were implanted (della Porta 1996). The demands of clandestinity meant that the forms of financial support previously readily available from networks of friends became much more limited, and so a new type of violence emerged, which would be the task of the 'logistics' wing of each column. These were to be responsible for violence to raise funds. Industrialists would be kidnapped, no longer for political reasons, as in the earlier period, but for ransom. The group began to engage in bank robberies as well, again not as a political action, but to raise funds. The Brigades were becoming increasingly closer to traditional forms of crime and banditry: bank robberies and kidnapping for ransom (Catanzaro 1991).

The Inertia of Violence

The Italian sociologist Raimondo Catanzaro (1991) insists that it is not sufficient to understand groups such as the Red Brigades from 'the outside', as a response to competition with other groups and political opportunities. He underlines the importance of internal dynamics, and argues that the relationship to violence is central to the transformations the Brigades experienced. In the early days, he argues, violence was understood as defensive, justified as a response to the violence of 'the system'. As the Brigades developed, violence became less and less a means to an end, instead increasingly coming to define the group and becoming an end in itself. Catanzaro's (1991) interviews with former members point to an increasing fascination with violence, an almost erotic relationship with guns and the potency that they offered – members would spend their afternoons cleaning their guns, holding them and at times almost caressing them. In this process, he argues, the search for action was less and less framed in terms of wider social conflicts, and increasingly experienced as a search for personal identity.

In the period following the assassination of Aldo Moro, the political space open to the Brigades became more and more constrained (Wieviorka 1993). The comminqués published by Moro's captors make it clear that, after two months' detention and subjection to 'trial', killing him served no political purpose', his 'trial' failing to produce the puppet of the Imperialist State that the Brigades had expected their captive to be. Moro's killing further isolated the group, but the path to killing Moro was experienced as an inevitability (Catanzaro 1991). Once captured, Moro could not be released or the whole strategy of war would appear meaningless – five guards had been killed in his capture (Drake 1995: 2). The Brigades war against the state had spawned a form of violence that was generating its own momentum. In the context of shrinking political space, violence increasingly appeared as the only path offering 'a break with the castrated and obsolete world of politics' (Catanzaro 1991). Violence was less a means to a goal, *it had become the only way that the Brigades could demonstrate their existence to themselves and others.* As the strategy of war with the state developed, violence came to be experienced as a path from which the actor was unable to disengage. Increasingly cut off from wider networks, the clandestine members of the Brigades found more and more aspects of their lives micromanaged by the leadership, even to the point of rules specifying how clean apartments should be or rules for hairstyles and grooming (Red Brigades nd). This social world was claustrophobic, involving long periods of boredom matched by extraordinary demands to detail activities (mirroring the bureaucratic Italian state) (Sommier 2008a).

Catanzaro argues the increasing centrality of violence in this final period was associated with what he terms a 'double depersonalization' (1991: 191). Former Brigades members describe the person they are about to maim or kill in a language of a category or symbols, victims are no longer experienced as human beings. One former Brigade leader, in an interview with the Italian magazine *L'Espresso*, defended Aldo Moro's execution, affirming 'You know we did not kidnap and kill Moro the man, but [rather] his function. We reject the accusation of political homicide' (cited in Drake 1995: 118–19). But not only is the victim reduced to a category – the Brigade members experience a similar depersonalization of their own role. Killing is not experienced in terms of personal responsibility, but involves realizing a larger historical process, with many Brigades members from this period describing their role as being the simple 'instruments of revolutionary justice' (Catanzaro 1991). Within this logic, as actions become depersonalized, the actors increasingly experience themselves as trapped. In the beginning, instrumental violence served political violence – robberies and kidnapping were to obtain funds to meet the infrastructure needs of the organization. But as political violence was less and less experienced as serving a purpose, particularly after the killing of Aldo Moro, members appear resigned to a future where violence becomes not only inevitable but also meaningless (Catanzaro 1991). As the political momentum declines, instrumental violence becomes more and more central to the life of the group, experienced as a trap. Another former member describes himself as having joined the Brigades as an idealist, only to find himself involved in robberies to finance going on holiday (Catanzaro 1991: 195).

Death to Traitors

As the Brigades became more isolated from social actors and conflicts, their political discourse became more and more abstract, with final communiqués written in impenetrable jargon. An important shift occurs, one to which Wieviorka's theory of movement inversion (1993) alerts us: the enemy as described in the later communiqués shifts from the capitalist class or the state to an increasingly totalizing image of a corrupt society. At this point the Brigades' opponent becomes not only increasingly abstract (evident in the increasing place for jargon in communiqués) but also increasingly powerful. Not only does the state control social life, but its power threatens the Brigades itself. Now, if any member of the group raises the possibility of leaving, this is no longer regarded as a matter of personal preference; it represents a threat to the group, an act of disloyalty (della Porta 2009). The person thinking of leaving is now a traitor, as is anyone who shows signs of wavering commitment. This new dynamic was amplified by changing responses of the Italian state, which introduced new laws facilitating 'repentance', whereby Brigade members could hope for eventual freedom if they renounced violence and became informers. As opportunities for meaningful political violence 'outside' effectively disappeared, political violence now turned increasingly inwards, targeting members or former members who had repented. In 1981 Patrizio Peci, a senior Brigade member, had become a prominent informer, giving police information that led to the arrest of those involved in killing Aldo Moro (Galfré 2010; Drake 1995). He was untouchable in prison, but his brother, Roberto, believed to have been an active member of the Brigades during 1976–7 before being arrested and later released on minor charges, was not so protected (Crook 2001: 661). He was kidnapped and held captive for 54 days, during which time he was tried by a 'People's Court' and executed, his body left in the street in Rome, with a sign attached to it reading 'death to traitors' (Guidelli 2005).

Roberto Peci's 'proletarian trial' was filmed on Super 8 film and sent to a national television station after his execution (this film is available in the public domain). In it we encounter echoes of the videos produced by al-Qaeda 25 years later. The film consists of an extreme close up of Peci's face, against a background of revolutionary slogans pasted on the wall behind him. The film opens with the camera panning over these slogans, with Italian partisan music playing in the background. It then locks on to Peci's face, and for the rest of the film we hear the calm voice of his accuser asking him questions about his role as a traitor, while Peci replies as he is required to do, his face framed by the slogans behind him. The camera remains focused on him as the sentence of death is communicated to him by the voice that remains faceless. As the distraught Peci drops his head into his hands, the revolutionary music comes back in. The condemned Peci, the revolutionary slogans, the revolutionary music all become part of the one communication: forced to confess his guilt, Peci's death becomes part of the struggle for the revolution. His death signals the increasing power of the revolution, communicated by the increasing volume of the revolutionary songs that accompany the sentence. Political violence has found a new target, traitors. It also addresses a powerful message to members who are tempted to repent – if they cannot be killed, members of their family will be. There is a long tradition of such 'transversal' vendettas among criminal organizations in Italy, and it was now embraced by the Brigades as revolutionary violence. As the political project became increasingly replaced by a language of pure and corrupt, good and evil, the Brigades increasingly came to function as a sect, and their violence turning inwards.

Killing the Body

One of the most disturbing examples of violence turning inwards took place in Japan in the Japanese United Red Army, made up of the remnants of other groups in the dying period of revolutionary violence in Japan (Steinhoff 1989). Its strategy had focused on attacking police boxes, capturing weapons, and from there proceeding to attack and kill bureaucrats in government offices, including a failed attack on the prime minister's office in late 1969 (Igarashi 2007). Following a series of failures, the group was on the defensive, by late 1971 it was isolated and hiding out in the Japanese mountains

(Igarashi 2007). In December of that year group members began a series of group criticism sessions to test the extent that each member was faithful to the cause of 'kill or be killed'. These sessions involved 'self-critique', where group members who had demonstrated some form of failure or lack of commitment would allow themselves to be beaten by others, this being a demonstration of their willingness to reform themselves (Box and McCormack 2004). Group members would be beaten unconscious, but when they regained consciousness they would have achieved 'genuine communist subjectivity' (Igarashi 2007). This was all part of members transforming themselves into 'killing machines', with an increasingly urgent attempt to deny any experience of emotional or physical need (Igarashi 2007: 129). From this perspective, any desire for bodily comfort or pleasure was interpreted as 'enemy territory', having to be overcome for the revolution to succeed.

Between December 1971 and January 1972 this group tortured and killed 12 of its own members. Catanzaro refers to the 'depersonalisation' of both actor and victim in relation to the Red Brigades, and significantly, Igarashi also uses this term to explore transformations at work in the Japanese Red Army. The aim was to purge desire for comfort or pleasure, with violence being the means through which members could cleanse themselves of their attachments to capitalist society. Through being subjected to beatings members could achieve revolutionary subjectivity, in particular through being beaten unconscious. To hesitate to accept a beating or to be reluctant to beat a comrade were both interpreted as signs of inadequate commitment. The beatings became increasingly brutal, and after the first case where a member died, this failure to recover was interpreted as a sign of their lack of revolutionary commitment. This violence was changing, ceasing to be a means of assisting comrades with their self-criticism, becoming instead 'evidence of the victim's own guilt' (Igarashi 2007: 132).

A key area in which group members set out to purge themselves of such attachments was sexuality. Looking to demonstrate their transformation, members would confess in group sessions to having minor sexual thoughts about each other. These sessions were followed by acts of self-improvement, at first extra rifle training outside in the cold, then kneeling for hours in preparation for writing sessions where they would detail their failures as the first step in their rectification (Steinhoff 1992: 204). A critical point in the escalation of this process occurred when a female member undergoing this process accused a male member of molesting her while she was asleep. Both parties were to be beaten as punishment, the male for entertaining sexual thoughts, the female for portraying herself as a 'martyred heroine' (Steinhoff 1992: 204). The aim of the transformation was to overcome private emotions, so that love for others would become love for the group (a desire that we also encounter in the Weather Underground).

These first beatings elicited further confessions from the couple, seemingly justifying beatings and punishment as a means where group members could honestly look at themselves and engage in self-transformation. Both were beaten further, tied to posts and left without food or water. Both eventually died (Steinhoff 1992: 205).

Another member suffered the same fate after being accused of paying attention to his clothes and hairstyle. In January 1972 this logic reached its gruesome endpoint when a female member was ordered to *beat herself* on the grounds that she wore her hair long, she wore make-up, and she continued to wear a ring that she had prior to joining the group. She did so for some 30 minutes, doing so in a circle of group members, till her face became a bloody mess. She failed to beat herself unconscious, at which point the group joined in. She was left tied up after the beating, a state she remained in until she died four days later (Igarashi 2007: 132). Another female member, also beaten to death, was accused of developing opportunistic associations with men, while her husband accused her of being active during sexual intercourse (Igarashi 2007: 133). These and other killings of members highlight the extent that repressing femininity was integral to the group's attack on embodied subjectivity. It was part of the danger to be tracked and destroyed.

From Student Movement to People's War

The dynamics of violence that emerged in the United States in this period, when part of the student movement mutated into 'war against the state', manifests important similarities with both the Italian and Japanese experience. In 1967 students at New York's Columbia University believed that the university was affiliated to US military programmes, a discovery that set in motion a campaign against the university's involvement in the war in Vietnam (Varon 2004). At the time the university, located near the African-American area of Harlem, was also in the process of building a new gymnasium, and had chosen to build this on land originally designated for low-cost housing in the Harlem district. The students believed that not only had the university decided to take this land, it had also decided that the building should be designed with its rear facing Harlem, and the edifice's front pointing towards the white and affluent sections of New York (Bradley 2009: 39ff). For these idealistic students, this decision symbolized the university's indifference to the local black population. Initial student action involved occupying the construction site, the action receiving widespread support across the campus, as well as from black organizations within Harlem. The campaign widened, with students demanding that the university admit black students and withdraw from involvement in the war in Vietnam. This was not the first student occupation of a university, but this was a prestigious Ivy League campus, and its location in New York meant proximity to national media (Varon 2004). In its attempts to extend this movement, the rallying call of Students for a Democratic Society (SDS) became 'Many Columbias!' (Hayden 1968).

For the university dean, the student action involved no more than 'inchoate nihilism whose sole objectives are destruction' (Lusky and Lusky 1969). Mark Rudd, one of the leaders of SDS at Columbia, and a future founder of the Weather Underground (Rudd 2010), responded to the accusation through an open letter in April 1968:

> You are quite right in feeling that the situation is 'potentially dangerous'. For if we win, we will take control of your world, corporation, your University and attempt to mould a world in which we and other people can live as human beings. Your power is directly threatened, since we will have to destroy that power before we take over...We will have to destroy at times, even violently, in order to end your power and your system – but that is a far cry from nihilism.
>
> (Rudd, open letter to Grayson Kirk, 22 April 1968,
> in Caldwell 2008: 60)

Rudd ended his letter with a phrase that would become the slogan of the action at Columbia and beyond:

> There is only one thing left to say. It may sound nihilistic to you, since it is the opening shot in a war of liberation. I'll use the words of LeRoi Jones, whom I'm sure you don't like a whole lot: 'Up against the wall, motherfucker, this is a stick-up.'
>
> (Caldwell 2008: 60)

The student occupation was peaceful. It was the response that was violent. Occupying students sat on the ground singing peace and protest songs, chanting 'no violence', while New York tactical police took control of the campus and arrested some 700 students, with dozens of students being injured (Varon 2004: 26). Students were dragged out through a police line, and beaten as they went (film of these events is available in the public domain). Rudd was later expelled for his role in the occupation. But the university did not return to normal: sit-ins and class boycotts continued, many courses were cancelled, and grades not issued (Varon 2004: 28). A week after the events at Columbia, Martin Luther King was assassinated. The time was less and less one of hope.

By the end of the 1960s, the hopes of the counter-culture had largely collapsed, symbolized by the killing that took place at the free concert at

Altamont, California, in December 1969 (Wood 2003: 336). For student leaders, society was increasingly understood as a system of domination, while the principal means of bringing about social change was to oppose the forces of US imperialism, in the country itself and internationally. This took on increasing importance within SDS (Miller 1999), above all in the Revolutionary Youth Movement. Student culture and action increasingly came to be regarded as 'bourgeois'. What was critical was to build an alliance of young people who would support the struggle of black people in the United States and oppressed peoples in the Third World. To be successful the movement had to 'destudentize' itself and build a new anti-imperialist youth movement. In June 1969 a group circulated a manifesto entitled *You don't need a weatherman to know which way the wind blows* (*New Left Notes* 1969), drawing on Bob Dylan's *Subterranean Homesick Blues*. In it they map out a vision for a mass movement, not built around reforming the university, but through struggles against police power, 'the pigs', understood as the embodiment of the imperialist state:

> The pigs are the capitalist state, and as such define the limits of all political struggles; to the extent that a revolutionary struggle shows signs of success, they come in and mark the point it can't go beyond. In the early stages of struggle, the ruling class lets parents come down on high school kids, or jocks attack college chapters. When the struggle escalates the pigs come in; at Columbia, the left was afraid its struggle would be co-opted to anti-police brutality, cops off campus, and said pigs weren't the issue. But pigs really are the issue and people will understand this, one way or another.
>
> (*New Left Notes* 1969: 24)

The new strategy aimed at building an 'active mass base, tying the citywide fights to community and citywide anti-pig movement, and for building a party eventually out of this motion', one which would serve as the basis of 'the world strategy for winning the revolution'. This had to build a movement 'oriented toward power'. This movement would 'become one division of the International Liberation Army', its battlefields added to the many Vietnams to defeat US imperialism. The authors conclude their document with the objective, 'Long Live the Victory of People's War!', constructing a parallel between the Vietnamese confrontation with the US armed forces and the confrontation they envisaged with the police.

For these students, a 'people's war' promised a new unity between different struggles. It was to be built through opposition to 'the pigs', and would begin with *Days of Rage*, a protest action corresponding with the trial of the 'Chicago Seven' scheduled to take place in Chicago in October 1969. The aim was to take control of the streets and 'Bring the war home'. Ten thousand young people were to converge on Lincoln Park, and from there take control of a large part of the city, in the process bringing into being the people's war, one where the struggle against police in the United States would be seen to parallel the struggle against the United States army in Vietnam (Varon 2004). The slogan 'Bring the war home!' was not a metaphor. These students understood themselves to be fighting a system of power that manifested itself through force: through the army internationally, and through the police domestically. A movement previously struggling for *Many Columbias!* was now mutating into one committed to *Many Vietnams!*

Smashing Monogamy

By this stage the members of the Weathermen were living in some 15 collective houses across several cities. Life in these houses suggests a changing relationship between individual and collective experience. These communal groups set about 'smashing monogamy', with couple relationships frowned on as exclusive, and increasingly opposed. Group sex was not uncommon, as were cases where members would have sex with whomever the leadership decided. Acid trips were part of the experience. Money earned was handed to the group, personal possessions were seen as bourgeois, and long sessions known as 'Criticism-Self-Criticism' were undertaken, where the group would break down and then rebuild its members (Gentry 2004; Thoburn 2008: 104). While not as violent, this deconstruction and reconstruction of members by the group mirrors the dynamic we saw in the United Japanese Red Army. One former Weather Underground member describes this criticism process as a 'purifying ceremony involving confession, sacrifice, rebirth, and gratitude' (Ayers 2001: 154). There was little personal time, with activities spent alone such as reading or listening to music frowned upon or forbidden. These were not democratic communities: in each, all power was held in the hands of the leaders, the Weatherbureau (Varon 2004). These were not ascetic communities that set out to deny the body any pleasure, as in the Japanese case, but the accounts of those who lived in these houses underline exhaustion and constant pressure, above all through the criticism sessions and the lack of personal space and autonomy.

Looking back on this period, Mark Rudd describes what he calls the 'gut check': 'We developed all kinds of our own repertoire of psychological tricks, like something called the gut check where we'd challenge each other to be more violent and to be therefore more revolutionary, or to be more disciplined, to give up our bourgeois luxuries' (Rudd in Siegel and Green 2003). Another early member who left the group before it went underground describes a loss and discovery of self linked to the revolution. She had left her husband, was a postgraduate social work student, paying her way through college through topless dancing, emphasizing her 'style' as one of mini skirts, high heels and boots. She describes the group's documents as 'too theoretical', but affirms that she was attracted by the romance of the call to leave everything for the revolution. It was a break with the dull suburban life: 'My white knight materialized into a vision of world-wide liberation...' (Stern 2007: 72). She would later describe herself as being attacked because she wanted to maintain a monogamous relationship (2007: 174).

The Weatherbureau's directive for group sex can be seen in two ways. The directive to 'smash monogamy' was to use the body and bodily experience to destroy a dimension of the established order. In that sense, the directive for group sex can be understood in a similar way to other demands that the body be 'put on the line'. On another level, we can see that the campaign to 'smash monogamy' emphasizes the primacy of the group and the distrust of private, intimate relationships that the group, or more specifically its leaders, cannot control.

When the People Fail to Appear

The People's War involved local actions, such as occupying school classrooms, and members running into schools in poor neighbourhoods shouting 'Jailbreak!' (Varon 2004). But the most organized effort to 'bring the war home' centred on the Days of Rage, the planned convergence on Lincoln Park in Chicago (Sommier 2010; Gentry 2004). Varon (2004) reconstructs the events that took place on the day: rather than 10,000 young people answering the call, fewer than 300 people were present, essentially members from the shared houses. They were outnumbered by the police surrounding them. Speeches were made, helmets put on, members practising using sticks and baseball bats. The group started marching towards the Gold Coast neighbourhood, an affluent area where the 'Chicago Seven' trial judge resided. To get there they had to pass through poorer neighbourhoods. The first brick was thrown through a bank window, shouting erupted, they moved ahead, smashing windows and cars, mostly not affluent cars but those of workers. The expected police reaction was violent: six people were shot, 70 arrested and a city official was paralysed. The next day a 'women's milita' set out to repeat the actions of the day before, but was easily controlled by the waiting police (Varon 2004).

The Days of Rage were experienced as a disorienting failure – the people had failed to turn up to the people's war, and the movement that the Weathermen had been certain that they represented did not appear. In the period that followed, violence within US society became even more endemic, with police in Chicago killing charismatic leaders of the Black Panther party while they were asleep in bed (Escobar 1993). The original optimism of SDS, with its Enlightenment confidence of the perfectibility of man (Hayden 2005), was displaced by anger, disorientation and rage.

Everybody Has to Die

In December 1969 in Flint, Chicago, the Weathermen held a last public event before going underground. It was named a 'War Council' (Miller 1999). Varon (2004) describes the room as being covered with portraits of slain heroes such as Che Guevara or Malcolm X, the space festooned with images of guns (including a large papier mâché pistol hanging from the ceiling). Activities included karate and singing songs glorifying violent rupture. A Chicago city official, Richard Elrod, had been paralysed as a result of injuries sustained during the Days of Rage, and the group sang about him to the tune of Bob Dylan's *Lay Lady Lay*:

> Stay Elrod stay
> Stay in your Iron Lung
> Play Elrod
> Play with your toes a while.
>
> (Varon 2004: 159)

The speeches capture an increasing fascination with violence. Mark Rudd declared 'It's a wonderful feeling to hit a pig. It must be a really wonderful feeling to kill a pig or blow up a building!' (Rudd 2010: 189). Violence promised a way to achieve rupture and disrupt an increasingly powerful system. The speeches reflect a powerful desire to shock and transgress, another leader affirming 'We're against everything that's good and decent in honky America. We will burn and loot and destroy. We are the incubation of your parents' nightmare' (Varon 2004: 160). The association with America's nightmares was most clearly expressed in relation to the recent murder of the actress Sharon Tate (eight months' pregnant at the time) and five other people, killed in her home by members of The Family, a group led by Charles Manson. Tate and her companions had been tortured, rooms had pools of blood on the floor, and slogans daubed on the walls in the blood of the victims. The word 'war' had been carved on to one of the victims' bodies, while Tate's body was left with a fork sticking into her abdomen (for an analysis of these murders, see Atchison 2010). Nothing of value was taken; these seemed to be killings for the sake of killing. Mark Rudd quotes another leader of the Weather Underground celebrating this killing, calling for those present to 'Dig it! First they killed those pigs, then they ate dinner in the room with them, then they even shoved a fork into pig Tate's stomach. Wild!' (Rudd 2010: 189; see also Miller 1999). For the rest of the meeting, participants would greet each other holding up three fingers in what became known as the 'fork salute' (Varon 2004: 160). What is striking about the violence at this 'War Council' is the way it appears so pervasive. Violence seems to offer a solution when no other appeared to exist, as we see in one exchange:

> Are you going to fight everyone who doesn't agree with you?...Do you really think every white person in this country should die...do you really?
>
>   If they're not going to do shit, well...yes, I do. If people won't join us, then they are against us. It's as simple as that. That includes the working class, and kids, if necessary.
>
>   Everybody has to die?
>
>   Everybody has to die.
>
> (Varon 2004: 166)

During a debate, one member asks what happens if the revolution occurs before 'the masses' are fully organized into revolutionary consciousness, suggesting that fascism will be required to keep order. Another replies 'If it will take fascism, we'll have to have fascism' (Varon 2004: 166). These discussions foreshadowing the death of everyone who does not support the revolution are not a call for a final solution involving the killing of millions, nor are these appeals to embrace fascism. Violence here is less of a programme, it allows these revolutionaries to imagine a word where what appears currently impossible – the revolution – can exist.

The War Council marked a shift from attempting to build a mass movement to a strategy of clandestine violence, its principal form of action centred on bombing. The strategy had been foreshadowed by a bombing of the monument to the police in Haymarket Square in Chicago immediately before the Days of Rage. The following years witnessed bombings focusing on police, prisons and government buildings. The original bombing campaign intended waging war on the US military by attacking military personnel at a dance, and a bomb for this purpose was being constructed in New York City in 1970 when it accidentally exploded, killing three members of the group (Varon 2004). This, it appears, led to a rethink, and to a strategy focusing on bombing buildings and symbols as opposed to killings. On 21 May 1970 the group issued its first 'communiqué': 'Hello. This is Bernardine Dohrn. I'm going to read A DECLARATION OF A STATE OF WAR...Within the next fourteen days we will attack a symbol or institution of Amerikan injustice' (in Green and Siegel 2003; see also Varon 2004:

180). Two weeks later the NYC police headquarters was bombed, with the Weather Underground issuing a statement claiming responsibility (Varon 2004: 181).

Violence, Desire and Rupture

The events we have explored in this chapter offer both insights and questions about the transition to violence. Crenshaw argues that terrorism reflects the distance between radical elites and passive masses, where the absence of a revolutionary movement leads an elite to adopt terror as a strategy. This dynamic is present in both the Red Brigades and the Weather Underground. It is particularly evident in the American case, when the failure of the Days of Rage set in motion the transformation evident in the War Council. But while Crenshaw focuses her analysis on violence as a strategy, what we encounter at the War Council is above all violence as an imaginary. Many of the published memoirs of former members of the Weather Underground focus on the War Council as a pivotal event. The historian Jeremy Varon notes that these authors attempt to distance themselves from the event: one describes it as a 'group psychosis', another as 'total insanity', while an anti-war activist who was at the meeting but not a member of the Underground described it as 'grotesque'. Varon underlines that the violence as constructed at the War Council at Flint has a significance beyond political protest.

Members present at the time argued that the Weather Underground's violence was a response to the violence of the state, above all to the killing of Black Panther activists. Todd Gitlin, a fierce critic of the Weather Underground, argues that these young people were experiencing a kind of 'violence shock' (1993: 313), with the Vietnam War and police violence directed at demonstrators disrupting previously safe worlds. Varon notes that the War Council's ritualized violence aimed at helping these young people to 'develop their own capacities for aggression'. The Manson murders, argues Varon, exercised their attraction because they appeared to lack purpose (nothing was stolen; the main aim appeared to be an orgy of violence), reflecting Dostoevsky's definition of modern crime: 'nothing is forbidden, everything is permitted'. Varon argues 'to elevate Manson was to take on the mask of radical otherness, to announce oneself ... as at least "capable of doing anything" ... praising Manson, the Weathermen rhetorically blurred the revolutionary imperative to "use any means necessary" for political ends with a fascination with normlessness and total license' (2004: 163). The Weathermen's opposition of chaos to order, destruction to the status quo, essentially involved 'inverting the hierarchies within a binary structure, leaving the structure intact' (2004: 163).

The horror, violence and excess evident at the Flint War Council, the Red Brigade's descent into the hunt for traitors, the United Red Army's torture and execution of its own members, all correspond closely to the model of inversion proposed by Wieviorka: the absent actor is replaced by the terrorist, the opponent becomes a totalizing system, the capacity to imagine a different world collapses. For Varon, the horror and mock cruelty at Flint underlines the extent to which these radicals were repeating or mirroring the very violence that their resistance sought to oppose. For Kenneth Kenniston, a psychologist and sympathetic observer of the movement, this period of crisis of the American New Left was one of 'the discovery that violence lies not only within the rest of American society, but in the student movement itself' (Varon 2004: 168). From this perspective, the violence of the movement was not simply a product of or reaction to dominant forms of violence in American society; instead it was part of that violence. A similar analysis can be made of the violence of the Red Brigades. The more its violence sought to target the state, the more it increasingly *mirrors* that of the state – in its 'people's tribunals', its sentences, its punishments and in its petty control of the day-to-day lives of its members that we also witness in the Weather Underground and United Red Army. In the process we see a radical transformation of these groups as violence comes to focus inwards and they become less and less connected with other social actors; as the attempt to produce a movement mutates into violence that eventually becomes so central that they can no longer imagine action outside a paradigm of war, not only against an increasingly mythical and all-powerful opponent, but against their own bodies.

5

Violence and Nation: The Palestinian Experience

Violence plays a central role in the constitution of nations (Giddens 1987). But when we start to explore actual violence, we find it takes very different forms. These forms and the transitions between them are powerfully illustrated by the place of violence in the struggle of the Palestinian people. The complex history of this struggle is beyond the scope of this chapter, but it highlights three quite different forms of violence: the Fedayeen violence of state-supported militias located outside Palestine; the violence of the first Intifada or uprising (1987–93); and the violence of the second Intifada (2000–04). In the first period of 'international terrorism', Palestinian violence was largely a proxy for states; in the first Intifada, violence was closely linked to building social and political organizations; while in the second Intifada it took a radically different form: political committees were replaced by militias, while a radically new type of violence emerged, that of the suicide bomber. These transformations have had major implications for the Palestinian struggle, and beyond this, they highlight critical dimensions of what is at stake as violence mutates.

The Fedayeen and International Terrorism

Before the Intifadas, violence associated with the Palestinian struggle was of a very different nature. During the declining days of the British Mandate in Palestine there was little sense of a Palestinian nation. The Palestinians were poorly organized and possessed little relationship with the British and had little support in the Arab world. During this period the Palestinians were not so much a nation but a community defined by traditional social relationships, a social world of clans dominated by large landholding families (Robinson

1993). The creation of the state of Israel was a cataclysmic event for this community-based society, above all to the extent that it was associated with expulsions and measures such as the Absentee Property Law which today would be considered ethnic cleansing (Forman and Kedar 2004). The expulsion of the Palestinians would bring about the collapse of traditional forms of social authority and a situation in the refugee camps in the 1950s described by Wieviorka (1993) as the 'death of society', involving the collapse of social structure, culture and norms also evident among other displaced populations. By the late 1950s, the words Palestine and Palestinian had almost ceased to be used (Wieviorka 1993). But this decade also witnessed the birth of organizations committed to Palestinian liberation, as power shifted from the older landed elite to a new university-educated generation in exile (Robinson 1993). This process was accelerated by the emergence of wider Arab nationalism. A League of Arab states had been formed in 1943 with the goal of supporting Arab independence and opposing the formation of a Jewish state in Palestine, and, as part of this rising nationalism, in 1964 the League founded the Palestine Liberation Organization (PLO) and the Palestine Liberation Army (PLA), placed under Egyptian control, with Palestinian identity subsumed under a wider Arab identity (Wieviorka 1993: 225).

Michel Wieviorka links the birth of Palestinian nationalism to the defeat of Arab armies by Israel in the Six-Day War of 1967, a movement centred on the Fatah faction within the PLO. Fatah believed that it was impossible to undertake an uprising within Israel and the occupied territories, a view reinforced by the dramatic military superiority demonstrated by Israel through its victory over Egypt and its allies. So the period from 1967 saw the birth of a strategy shaped by two converging processes: the rise of Palestinian nationalism in the refugee camps, and the determination of the defeated Arab states to continue their war with Israel through other means (Wieviorka 1993). After the defeat of 1967, the aim was to transfer the war to the domain where Israel was vulnerable. Training camps were established with funds from Syria, Iraq, Libya and Egypt (Sayigh 1992). This period illustrates what came to be known as 'international terrorism', with PLO actions during this period acting as a proxy for the states organizing and financing them. During this period the PLO was based outside the occupied territories, one of its strongest areas of implantation being Europe. It embraced a kind of action that it did not create: plane hijacking (Holden 1986), the aim being to create actions that were important in terms of spectacle, breaking with previous anti-colonial violence that had involved guerrilla fighters focusing on military targets. But while it was becoming increasingly prominent internationally, the PLO was to a significant extent directed by the states supporting it. Tensions between these states were increasingly played out within the PLO itself, which after 1973 splintered into groups and factions aligned with supporting states who conducted war between each other via Palestinian proxies (Quandt *et al.* 1973: 67ff).

Wieviorka (1993) notes that the actions undertaken in this period had little relationship to the Palestinian national struggle, driven instead by the interests of the states sponsoring and using factions within the PLO. This period was one of relatively open state-supported terrorist networks where the Palestinian struggle served as a convergence point for members of groups as diverse as Baader Meinhof from Germany (Varon 2004: 65), the Japanese Red Army (Sommier 2008b: 76) as well as individuals in search of adventure who converged on training camps in Jordan, from there undertaking actions in Europe. These actions ranged from letter bombings, attacks on aircraft and murders, to the kidnapping of OPEC oil ministers in Vienna in 1975 (Hamm 2007: 158) or the kidnapping and killing of Israeli athletes at the 1972 Munich Olympics (Magloff 2011). Contemporary evidence now highlights the extensive involvement of state secret services in this period, such as the role played by the East German Stasi (Schmeidel 2008).

Wieviorka argues that these actions had almost no relationship with the Palestinian experience in Israel or the occupied territories (Wieviorka 1993). Their disconnection from national struggles and their dependence upon security services highlight a paradigm of 'international terrorism', where terrorist actors serve as proxies for state action. Those involved in these actions typically were recruited from refugee camps that were geographically removed from the occupied territories, coming in particular from Lebanon (Farsoun and Zacharia 1997). Wieviorka argues that while this spectacular revolutionary violence lacked real connection to Palestinian struggles, it none the less played an important role. Through it, the idea of a Palestinian nation was reconstituted. If in the 1950s the term Palestine looked as though it would disappear, this period of revolutionary terror, corresponding in important ways to the model of elite violence proposed by Crenshaw, played a key role in creating a Palestinian national identity.

This national identity had a strong polarity between 'outside' and 'inside', and between male and female. On the outside were the *fida'i* (one who sacrifices his life in struggle) wearing the Palestinian scarf or *kufiyya*, making the Palestinian struggle visible on the world stage. On the inside new images of national struggle also began to emerge, either the revolutionary peasant rising from the ground with gun in hand, or the peasant woman dressed in an embroidered dress (*thawb*) holding her children as she remained defiantly 'rooted to the land' (Lybarger 2007: 24). Amal Amireh emphasizes how central this gender imaginary would become to the Palestinian national narrative, with the land constantly referred to as female, as raped and subjugated, while the loss of land would come to be equated with a loss of manhood and masculine potency (2003). This model of the external (masculine) fighter and the internal steadfast female increasingly drew upon patriarchal under-standings of honour and the need to respond to its violation, in a model where religiosity, culture and social life become fused:

> these ideas had been part of the ethos of village and small-town life and contin-ued as values within the refugee communities. Religious structures, Muslim and Christian, reinforced these orientations in various ways. The nationalist refor-mulation, however, produced a secularized patriarchalism, symbolically linking 'honour' to the 'people's revolution'.
>
> (Lybarger 2007: 24)

These identities would undergo a profound mutation as the Palestinian struggle transformed.

The First Intifada: Civil Violence

With the PLO based outside Israel and the occupied territories, political organizing within the territories began in the 1970s and accelerated in the 1980s, linked to the expansion of universities and a new generation who had grown up under occupation (Lybarger 2007). These networks and groups would play a key role in the events that would take shape as the first Intifada, the first sustained uprising against Israel in the occupied territories. The Intifada, or uprising, began in December 1987, only ending officially with the signing of the Oslo Accords in 1994 (Hammami and Tamari 2001). Its original dynamic was close to that of a riot, in that it was a response to a precipitating event – in this case, an Israel Defence Force (IDF) jeep that crashed into a vehicle, killing four Palestinians. This set in motion a wave of spontaneous anger, centred on the refugee camps and working-class areas in the occupied territories (Bucaille 2006).

French sociologist Laetitia Bucaille (2004) argues that the first Intifada was a powerful example of a civil uprising. Significant numbers of shop-keepers refused to pay taxes, while other groups mobilized as well. In response to the decision by the Israeli government to close schools and uni-versities, teachers offered free classes in homes, doctors offered free health-care, and fruit and vegetables were grown in domestic gardens to boycott Israeli produce. The Intifada aimed at building a mass movement and self-management through civil disobedience, with Chenoweth and Stephan arguing that over 95 per cent of the actions involved in the uprising were non-violent (Chenoweth and Stephan 2011: 119). The mobilization also pos-sessed an important cultural dimension, where forms of cultural resistance to occupation were developed, such as the *dabka*, a traditional dance of the region, seen as incarnating Palestinian identity and struggle (Swedenburg 1990). At a time when political meetings were illegal, the *dabka* became both a popular celebration and one of the principal ways young people could meet, so much so that it was banned by the Israeli military during the Intifada (Bucaille 2004).

It is important to recognize just how much the Intifada disrupted what had become the established model where the fighter is male, with the nation as female and in need of protection. The Intifada involved a radical transformation, with women's committees taking on a key role in organization and action, and a new linking of revolutionary and feminist themes (Jean-Klein 2003). Women were at the centre of organizing neighbourhoods, in particular when areas were sealed off by the IDF – they were the ones instituting sharing and cooking collective meals, caring for the injured, and confronting IDF soldiers (Bucaille 2004). This role was particularly associated with middle-aged women, a role that came early in the Intifada to be associated with the 'heroic mother': the middle-aged woman, usually in her national embroidered dress, in the middle of the demonstrations, developing tactics to save children being arrested or beaten by Israeli soldiers. The actions of such women gave rise to the national heroine known in popular literature as 'Um al-Shaheed' or the 'Mother of the martyr'. Through popular songs and poems such as *'Mother of the martyr rejoice. All the youth are your children'*, the image of this woman became central to Palestinian popular culture (Abdo 1991: 25). The significance of this transformation cannot be overemphasized: the shift from a military to civil uprising meant, for Rita Giacaman and Penny Johnson (1994), that women were moving from a role of followers to leaders; for Sharif Kanaana (1994), the transformations brought about through the Intifada were so significant that they 'feminized Palestinian society' (see also Darweish 1989).

Isquat, Purity and Social Vengeance

By 1992, after four years of uprising, a profound transformation was becoming evident in the culture and organization of the Intifada. Laetitia Bucaille (2004) captures this when she describes events that took place at a funeral of a young man killed by the IDF in April 1991. Word of his death spread quickly; friends, family and acquaintances hurried to attend the funeral, to take place at a Christian church. His body was placed on a wooden bench, held up for all to see, almost falling into the crowd. Anger, grief and desolation cut through the crowd, shouting and screaming in distraught rage. In the presence of death, restraint is abandoned. One of the dead young man's friends called out: 'with our souls and our blood, we will sacrifice ourselves for you' (Bucaille 2004: 20). The themes of hope, civil organization and celebration of Palestinian culture that were so important early in the Intifada had become eclipsed after years of uprising and increasingly brutal repression. In their place, Bucaille underlines the increasing significance of what we can consider 'Puritan' dimensions of the struggle. Nationalists and the newly present Islamist groups were converging around the idea that before it could successfully confront the enemy, the Palestinian people would have to be reinvented, to be restructured around traditional and religious values (Bucaille 2004: 22). The ideology of resistance increasingly came to emphasize unity and the imperative of not questioning the social order. Bucaille points to a changing place of pleasure and joy within Palestinian society at this time, pleasure and celebration being seen increasingly as dissipating energy that should be directed to the struggle. But what is more, these were seen as being associated with weakness and with people vulnerable to exploitation by the increasingly potent enemy. In the latter stages of the Intifada, cafés were closed, shopping excursions to Israel and even visits to the beach forbidden by militants, while marriages, once a demonstration of joy and the social status of the family, were celebrated with discretion (2004: 22).

In this desperate context, the fear that any weakness could be exploited by the enemy became increasingly important. The enemy was no longer 'outside', but, as we saw in the previous chapter, the enemy was also 'inside'. In this case it was the drug addict needing a fix, the drunken person who might inadvertently give away information, the sexually available woman – all could become potential informers, letting the IDF know whom to target in killings and raids (Amireh 2003). This new fear extended to those involved in the struggle itself. Bucaille recounts the experience of 'Jihad', a long-time supporter of Fatah and an active *shebab* (young fighter) who had been imprisoned by the IDF, who was caught one evening by fellow militants kissing his girlfriend. They warned him: 'watch your step, you'll end up a collaborator' (2004: 22). The idea that kissing one's girlfriend could lead to becoming a collaborator was an expression of *Isquat*, or 'causing to fall'. *Isquat* referred to the widely held belief that Israeli agents were at work among Palestinians, seeking to trick young men into compromising sexual activity with women (Amireh 2003). The next day the young man would be taken for interrogation by the IDF, where he would be shown compromising photographs, and forced to collaborate in order to protect his honour.

A further transformation parallels the demand for purity and the fear of *Isquat*. From its beginning the Intifada had been a terrain where competing social groups vied for control of the Palestinian national agenda. The uprising had begun in refugee camps and the poorest areas, and from the beginning those mobilizing had attempted to force prominent families and

traditional social elites to become involved in the struggle – this was one
of the key aims of insisting on a boycott of Israeli products or refusing to
pay taxes. As the Intifada was collapsing, this demand increasingly took
on dimensions of what Bucaille calls 'social vengeance' (2004: 28), where
demanding co-operation from shops increasingly gave way to looting those
regarded as insufficiently committed to the struggle, blurring social mobilization and criminality. As Puritan themes become increasingly important,
the place of women in the struggle also began to take on new meaning.
Women were not simply a symbol of community, but increasingly of its
purity (Haj 1992). Women whose husbands, sons, brothers or fathers had
died or been killed in the struggle, or who were in prison, would stop wearing make-up and attractive clothes as an expression of mourning and grief.
In working-class areas, those most mobilized in the Intifada, women began
to cover themselves with the veil, not the traditional Palestinian *hattah* or
headscarf (Hammami 1990). Wearing the veil increasingly became a symbol
of supporting the Intifada and protesting the occupation, a 'patriotic obligation'. This practice overlapped with the theme of social revenge, closely
associated with anger directed at those believed not to have fully supported
the Intifada, who had left others to assume the burden and suffering, and
who were increasingly seen as responsible for its failure. The veil was first
embraced in less Westernized poorer zones, and it is from here that young
men or *shebab* moved out to enforce new rules of modesty in the streets of
more cosmopolitan neighbourhoods. At first the *shebab* would insult women
walking bareheaded in the streets. Later, gunmen used the threat of force to
oblige women to comply, in particular wealthier women seen as not being
committed to the liberation struggle (Bucaille 2004).

The first Intifada collapsed in 1993, the year before the Oslo Accords created the Palestinian Authority and accorded limited autonomy for Palestinian
territories. Bucaille argues that by then the earlier class alliance at the origins
of the Intifada had come apart. The leaders who had steered the Intifada
at its beginning had been killed or were in detention, leaving responsibility to a newer generation who resorted much more easily to violence, and
in particular to violence directed against other Palestinians. Increasingly
vicious conflicts erupted between Fatah and the newly formed Hamas as
they competed for control of turf (Bucaille 2004: 25). The later stages of the
Intifada witnessed its increasing weaponization, as young stone throwers
were replaced by gangs of gunmen who moved easily between taking shots
at Jewish settlements and extorting protection money from Palestinian nota-
bles. The killing of traitors through summary execution became increasingly common (Stockton 1990). Bucaille's fieldwork in the Gaza town of
Nablus points to the extent that young *shebab*, who had originally taken
direction from Fatah, refused to stop their summary executions of people

they considered traitors: 'the Fatah activists in the medina were more eager to punish members of their own society than to work for the liberation of all' (Bucaille 2004: 28). In the final months before the withdrawal of Israeli forces, these young militants accelerated their attacks on collaborators and members of the social elite, taking control of the dying days of the Intifada, imposing increasingly cruel and violent methods, and wrecking the logic of civil disobedience (Bucaille 2004: 28; Dudai and Cohen 2007). This logic of social revenge was mirrored by increased intensity of attacks on unveiled women. Early in the Intifada, the Unified Command had issued an edict that women were not to be harassed, no matter what their dress but the end of the Intifada was a different reality: by 1989, 12-year-old boys were pelting unveiled women with stones in the working-class areas of Gaza (Bucaille 2004: 130; Hammami 1990).

It was towards the end of the Intifada that fear of *Isquat* also reached hysterical proportions. As Palestinian violence increasingly turned inwards, one of its principal targets consisted of detecting and rooting out those who had fallen in this way. Activists from all groups, Nationalists, Islamists and Marxists, extracted confessions from those whom they believed had fallen – often through the use of torture. Amal Amireh notes that as the Intifada was collapsing and fear of widespread collaboration with Israel escalated, this fear became increasingly associated with fear of other forms of perversion, such as men being seduced by their sisters or their mothers, or mothers seducing their children, producing an atmosphere where 'everyone was a suspect, especially women' (Amireh 2003: 759). This fear has remained part of the Palestinian experience. In 2009 a young Palestinian woman pleaded guilty to spying after having been seduced and filmed making love with an undercover Israeli security agent, after which she was blackmailed into passing on information about militants. No significant information was actually passed on, but she was sentenced to 20 years' hard labour (McCarthy 2009).

The Birth of Hamas

The collapse not only of the Intifada but of Palestinian society itself is central to the emergence of a new type of actor that would reshape the Palestinian struggle: Hamas (Hroub 2000). The origins of this group date from 1973 when a small group, all of whom had trained in Egypt, energized the old Muslim Brotherhood groupings in Gaza, creating the Islamic Centre (*al-mujamma' al-islami*) as the Palestinian Muslim Brotherhood (Knudsen 2005: 1376). They had all been born shortly before the war of 1948, and had settled in the Gaza Strip, where they were excluded from political office because of their refugee status – Gaza at that time was part of Egypt (Knudsen 2005:

1377). All had trained as doctors, engineers or teachers. None possessed religious qualifications. Israel's annexation of Gaza in 1967 encouraged the initial development of this group, the Israeli authorities supporting the growth of the Brotherhood as an alternative to the secular nationalism of the PLO (Milton-Edwards 1992: 49). It in turn focused on charitable activities and, with the support of funds from Saudi Arabia and Kuwait, on gaining control of existing mosques and building new ones – the number increasing from some 200 to 600 in the 20 years from 1967 to 1987 (Knudsen 2005: 176). Milton-Edwards notes that the *Mujamma* 'was not noted for its activities against the occupation authorities', and the incidents where it did use force 'were infamous in that they were directed against fellow Palestinians' (1992: 49): in 1980 supporters attacked and burned down the offices of the Palestinian Red Crescent society, Palestinian nationalist leaders were beaten in Gaza, and wedding parties were disrupted for being 'un-Islamic' (1992: 49n). But while facilitated by a benign attitude from the Israeli authorities, Israeli support alone cannot explain the growth of *al-mujamma'*. Rema Hammami (1990) argues that its social activism engaged with key issues in Palestinian culture, suggesting that it offered 'a model of society and social behaviour relevant to the problems of the majority of poorer residents in Gaza', in particular addressing problems of drug and alcohol abuse. While left-wing political organizations were attempting to prevent Palestinians working in Israel (when over 50 per cent of Gaza's workers were employed in Israel (Roy 1995), *al-mujamma'* proposed a more practical and achievable solution, 'a return to a moral social code as embodied in their interpretation of Islam' (Hammami 1990: 25).

In spring of 1988 younger members of *al-mujamma'*, with the support of some of the older generation worried by the loss of support they were experiencing in the context of the Intifada, created Hamas, an acronym for the Movement of Islamic Resistance (*harakat al-muqawama al-Islamiyya*). Initial support for Hamas was relatively limited, reflecting the fact that the Islamists had been absent from the fight against occupation, which had been essentially a secular nationalist struggle. From the beginning Hamas undertook its own actions, rejecting any involvement in the Unified Command structure co-ordinating the Intifada. It organized its own strike days, published its own manifesto, and launched a campaign across Gaza for women to wear the *hijab*, with slogans such as 'Daughter of Islam, abide by *shari'a* dress!' (Hammami 1990: 25). In May of the same year, religious youth associated with Hamas broke into school classrooms and demanded that schoolgirls wear *hijab*, and in September of the same year another group attacked schoolgirls in the street. These first campaigns drew on the pervasive anxiety around *Isquat*, with Hamas leaflets arguing that Israeli intelligence services were undermining the morality of Palestinians in order to recruit them as collaborators (Hammami 1990). The attempt to reconstruct Palestinian society was not only undertaken by the emerging Islamist groups. Problems of violence, drug use and theft were endemic to life in the refugee camps. Loren Lybarger's (2007) interviews with people living in the camps underline an increasing sense of the need to reconstruct the moral order in the context of the conflict with Israel. University students were increasingly repelled by the factional logics mobilized by Fatah and leftist groups, suggesting that the Islamists were offering more than exhausted political ideology. For many, secularism meant a lack of moral purpose, individualism, self-interest and, ultimately, chaos and the destruction of collectivity.

Corruption, Violence and Despair

In August 1993 the Oslo Accords were agreed between the PLO and Israel, creating a new Palestinian Authority that would be charged with rebuilding a fractured society. The Authority was made up of Palestinians who had been in exile, cosmopolitans perceived as remote and foreign, particularly in Gaza, an area largely cut off from movements of people. These newcomers increasingly came to be called 'Tunisians', a reference to the PLO headquarters in exile. This view is captured by one of the founders of Hamas, shortly before his arrest by the Palestinian Authority in 1995, who describes the PLO as 'corrupt...debauching themselves, drinking, singing and dancing, carrying on like they did in Jordan, Lebanon and Tunis. But what they forget is this is Gaza' (cited in Milton-Edwards and Crooke 2004: 301).

With the creation of the Authority, the old elite set about re-establishing its power though links to the new incoming governors, in particular through corruption (Milton-Edwards 1996). The period witnessed increasing violence, with Authority security forces increasingly directed to controlling Islamist attacks on Israelis (Usher 1996). Not having negotiated the Accords, the Islamist groups rejected the Authority and its compromise with Israel (Kristiansen 1999). Torture became increasingly common (Roy 2001). The extent of this increasing repression is indicated by the creation of the Palestinian Authority's State Security Court in February 1995, following suicide attacks on Israeli troops in Gaza. The Court's sessions could take place at midnight, the judges appointed to the Court were serving members of the security forces, while those to be tried were given no advance notice and denied independent legal representation. Trials lasting only minutes leading to sentences of imprisonment of up to seven years were not uncommon (Amnesty International 1997; see also Kassim 1997). These trials and summary imprisonments illustrated just how little of the hope of a unified

Palestinian nation remained, the hope that had been at the centre of the Intifada.

A New Violence: The Second Intifada

Implicit in many discussions when we refer to 'more' or 'less' violence is the idea of violence as an object, something that can be 'purveyed'. But the Palestinian experience highlights violence as an embodied relationship, both to the other but also to the self. This is highlighted by the profound transformation in the type of violence that would become central to the second Intifada. This second uprising, known as the al-Aqsa Intifada, began in September 2000 following a visit by then Israeli opposition leader Ariel Sharon to the al-Aqsa mosque. The visit took place just two weeks after commemorations of the 1982 massacre of Palestinians at the Sabra and Shatila refugee camps in Lebanon (MacBride *et al.* 1983). A demonstration followed Sharon's visit, where Israeli security forces opened fire killing some 20 Palestinians. This killing, condemned by the United Nations Security Council (Resolution 672, 1990) was central to the beginnings of the second Intifada (Pressman 2003).

The difference in forms of action between the first and second Intifadas is striking. While the first Intifada had involved self-organization, in the second Intifada there were no neighbourhood committees, no experiments in popular education, no free medical clinics. The act widely regarded as turning protest into a new Intifada was undertaken by a 19-year-old Palestinian who in the days following the massacre, went into a quiet Jewish section of Jerusalem, and wielding a 15-inch knife stabbed to death an unarmed woman, a gardener and a policeman, and wounding a schoolboy before being shot himself (Chartrand 1990). Avishai Margalit (2003) suggests that it was these killings by a lone actor that would be used by Hamas to build the momentum that would become the second Intifada, manifesting a radically different kind of action. In the first Intifada, groups set out to build local organizations and committees; but in the second, an individual set out in search of Israelis to kill. There had been precursors to this kind of action in earlier 'one-way' attacks. In 1990 members of the Palestine Liberation Front attacked beachgoers at Tel Aviv's Nizanim beach, followed in 1991 by a series of stabbings on buses in Israel, actions described as 'one-way missions involving extraordinary risk' (Yom and Saleh 2004: 1). Bucaille (2004) notes a similar pattern among Fatah militants she interviewed who were involved in an attack on the IDF in April 2001. These fighters rejected wearing bullet-proof vests, despite the fact that they were readily available.

These emerging forms of violence highlight a changing relationship with risk and death, a transformation that we need to locate within the wider imaginary of struggle associated with the Intifada. The first Intifada, argues Farhad Khosrokhavar, 'gave everyone the feeling that they had recovered their honour' (2005: 110), it was a break with defeat and humiliation, and from a Palestinian history defined by loss of land and by the crushing superiority of Israeli military might. Khosrokhavar underlines that not only was this history defined by defeat, but also by a sense of *inferiority*. He notes that Palestinians widely watch Israeli television, and when they do so they see an Israeli society that is not simply based on hatred of Palestinians, but one that is culturally dynamic, internationally open and innovative – in stark contrast to the Palestinian experience. He argues that what was so important about the first Intifada was that it allowed Palestinians to overcome this crushing inferiority and shame. This situation, however, had radically changed at the time of the beginning of the second Intifada. The Palestinian government was widely regarded as corrupt, lacking any vision, and increasingly implicated in torture and killings of its own people as its very survival came to rely upon repressing attacks on Israel (Roy 2001). At the same time the land set aside for Palestinians was being fragmented increasingly by settlements in a pattern described as 'enclaving' and 'exclaving' (Falah 2003), creating a form of colonization very different from that experienced in countries such as India or Algeria, where colonized peoples might go years before ever encountering a British or a French person (see Razack 2010). In Palestine, daily life requires negotiating checkpoints involving humiliation and arbitrary treatment (Kotef and Amir 2007), while colonization involves not simply loss of land, with water also being diverted to Jewish settlements (Isaac and Selby 1996; Falah 2003; Khosrokhavar 2005). Broken into pieces and reduced to a 'multiplicity of localities' each with its own political status, Khosrokhavar argues that Palestine after the Accords found itself an aborted nation, mutilated by Israeli settlements and dominated by a shadow state whose leaders' main concern was to 'refuse to allow society to have a political role and to help its authorised representatives get rich' (2005: 111).

There is a sense that rather than coming to life, the Palestinian nation in the years following the Oslo Accords was dying (Khosrokhavar 2005). This helps us to understand the shifting forms of violence we see at work. The first Intifada was symbolized by the young stone-thrower, part of a wider civil movement not only contesting Israeli dominance but also patriarchal and class dominance within Palestinian society itself. The Intifada was framed by a future, by a temporality shaped by the belief that real and significant change was possible, and could occur within the lifetime of the actors involved. In the second Intifada, civil and organizational dimensions of mobilization were all but absent. Israeli response to its power being contested was also very different, increasingly involving collective sanctions, and live rounds being fired at demonstrators. The effect of this was dramatic, with a majority of those Palestinians killed in this period not being involved in armed actions or even demonstrating at the time of their deaths, but going about their normal routines (HDIPI 2001; Larzillière 2004). This repressive violence meant that it was no more dangerous to become involved in an armed action than to simply attend a demonstration. In a context where there was no longer any real hope of transformation, as Khosrokhavar (2005) argues, 'political time' had effectively collapsed.

This absence of perspectives of change is central to the types of militias that emerged after 2000 and to the types of violence in which they engaged. French sociologist Penelope Larzillière (2004) interviewed members of these militias, and was struck by the extent that they embrace a culture of risk. The lifestyle of the militia members, she notes, is essentially nocturnal, where the relationship to the body plays a central role. She argues that the violence engaged in is not particularly strategic, it is shaped by calculations of possible benefit and danger, but is disorganized, its objective being limited to killing Israelis with little regard to the risks involved. It is framed by a culture of the search for extremes, from lack of sleep to taking risks. The militia members' body style and body presence mirror that of the occupying forces, in particular the nonchalance of Israeli troops at checkpoints as they oblige people to wait, with militia members equally sporting wraparound sunglasses, the swagger and a style of dress made up of bits of uniform. She observes that joining a militia gives the young person the possibility of creating a self-image that is not one of 'victim'. But it also increasingly draws on the mode of self of the young Israeli troops managing the occupation: 'militarism and the capacity to inflict hurt and suffering' (Larzillière 2004).

The violence that came to characterize the second Intifada not only manifests a changing relationship with risk, but also in it we encounter a changing relationship with death, above all evident in 'martyrdom operations' or suicide bombings. The first of these occurred in April 1993, when a car bomb exploded next to a bus carrying Israelis near Mechola in the Jordan Valley (Kimhi and Even 2004). Yom and Saleh estimate that between then and September 2000, 27 suicide missions claimed 120 of the 290 Israeli deaths attributed to Palestinian attacks, while in the early years of the Al-Aqsa Intifada, 112 suicide bombings accounted for 474 of 918 Israeli deaths (Yom and Saleh 2004). This violence was accompanied by a changing organizational pattern involving the militarization of the second Infitada, where instead of civil committees the key actors were brigades associated with different organizations. In 1992 Hamas created the Izz ad Din al-Qassam brigades that in 1994 undertook a series of suicide actions against individual

Israelis following the massacre of worshippers at a mosque (Knudsen 2005: 1381).The Fatah organization had a military wing since its inception, but in late 2000 it created the Al-Aqsa Martyrs brigade (Brym and Araj 2006). Significantly, the creation of this brigade follows, rather than precedes, the type of violence evident in the individual attack discussed above, where a lone young man, not a member of any organization or group, went into Israel to kill. The first actions of the Al-Aqsa Martyrs brigade mirrored this, involving the shooting of settlers (three teenage religious school students in May 2002), the suicide bombing of a group of women and children waiting outside a synagogue (May 2002), and the suicide bombing of a grandmother and her granddaughter (May 2002) (Frisch 2003). All these targets lack any military significance.

Let the Whole World Be Erased

We see key dimensions of this new paradigm of violence in the killings undertaken on 4 October 2003 by a 29-year-old Palestinian woman, who blew up herself in a crowded restaurant in the Israeli city of Haifa, killing 21 people and wounding another 50 (Graham 2004: 192; Hafez 2006: 49). A graduate with law qualifications, she had recently taken up a new position in a legal firm in Jenin. In the period before the bombing, members of her family had been killed during a security forces raid that took place at the family home in the days leading up to a family wedding (see this account in Levy-Barzilai 2003). A Jordanian newspaper quoted a speech that she made at one of the funerals:

> Your blood will not have been shed in vain. The murderer will pay the price and we will not be the only ones who are crying. If our nation cannot realize its dream and the goals of the victims, and live in freedom and dignity, then let the whole world be erased.
>
> (Cited in Levy-Barzilai 2003)

Before setting off the explosives in the restaurant she filmed a 'final testament'. In it she says:

> I know that I shall not bring back Palestine. I fully know this. However, I know that this is my duty for Allah. Believing in the principles of my faith, I respond to the call. I now inform you that, Allah willing, I shall find what Allah has promised to me and to all those who take this path – gardens which Allah promised us, in which we will live forever, Allah willing. Having believed in this, how do you think I can accept all the passing worldly temptations? How can I go on

living on this earth when my spirit has become attached to an Omnipotent King? My entire aspiration has become to see the glorious light of Allah. It is His land and it is His religion, but they want to extinguish His light. We all know this. It is therefore my duty to the religion of Allah – and my obligation to Him – to defend it. I have nothing before me other than this body, which I am going to turn into slivers that will tear out the heart of everyone who has tried to uproot us from our country. Everyone who sows death for us will receive death, even though it be a small part [of what they deserve].

> (Translation MEMRI, Special Dispatch 776, 2004,
> originally posted to the Islamic Jihad website)

'Let the whole world be erased' captures the temporality of this action. This young woman describes turning her body into shrapnel and tearing through the bodies of the colonizers, just as the settlements have penetrated and torn through the hopes of the Palestinians. Her reference to the impossibility of the Palestinian nation realizing its dream points to a theme underlined by Khosrokhavar, namely the 'impossibility' of the Palestinian community that is at the centre of the action of the suicide bomber. The idea of *erasing* the whole world implies not only violence, but an action that takes place in an instant. Time collapses into the act of the explosion. What is at stake in this new violence, but almost completely absent in the first Intifada, is a critical question that we explore in the chapters which follow. Khosrokhavar underlines that these actors are convinced that the Palestinian nation has become impossible not only because of the Israeli occupation but also because of failure and division among Palestinians themselves. This type of bombing, he argues, highlights a form of action where it is no longer possible to change the world through living, but only through dying (2005: 109ff). The Palestinian nation is torn apart by Jewish settlements, its politics mired in corruption, its economy sinking into a morass of smuggling, illegal activities and crime. The attraction of Israel, with its wealth and cosmopolitan pleasures, is enormous, so much so that Khosrokhavar argues Palestinian culture is increasingly 'schizoid', torn between attraction and revulsion at the forces destroying it (2005: 124). This is evident in the mimetic attraction among militia members of the demeanour and style of the occupation forces pointed to by Pénélope Larzillière (2004). For Khosrokhavar (2005), this situation is increasingly lived as intolerable, as a form of destructive experience. This, he argues, is the key to the development of violence where change cannot be brought about through living, but only through dying.

The pattern we encounter in the Palestinian experience evokes certain dimensions of the violence we explored in relation to the student movement. As the Red Brigades became more and more isolated, violence increasingly turned inwards in the attempt to root out traitors, while in the Japanese United Red Army enduring violence came to be seen as purifying, as a way to free oneself from the attractions of the consumer society. While the Weather Underground did not set about executing its members, it also directed a form of violence inwards, evident in the control of its own members and the demand for constant self-criticism. This development, however, becomes radicalized in the Palestinian struggle, as violence becomes increasingly directed inwards in the attempt to root out traitors (in particular, through summary executions) and in the fear of *Isquat*. These developments underline the complexity of the experience of violence, and the difficulty of reducing violence to the status of a simple instrument to be taken up or put down as the context determines. What is most striking in the Palestinian case is the shift away from a form of controlled violence located within a civil struggle to a type of violence focusing on bringing about the death of the other, with less and less regard to risk, ultimately developing into a type of violence where death itself comes to be understood as the way to bring about change that cannot be achieved through life.

As this type of violence became more common towards the end of the twentieth century, sociologists began to interpret its development in religious terms. But while religious themes appear to be linked with this form of violence, the Palestinian experience of transformations in violence suggests a more complex process than one where 'religion causes violence'. If anything, what we encounter in the Palestinian experience may illustrate the opposite, a history where violence transforms what religion means.

6

Apocalypse Now?

During the 1990s a shift in paradigms for thinking about violence and terror became increasingly evident, as both academic researchers and policy-makers declared there had been a shift from an older form of 'political' terrorism to new forms of 'religious' terrorism. For Walter Lacquer (1999) religion was central to the fanaticism defining what he called 'new terrorism'; David Rapoport (2004) argued that religious terrorism constituted a 'fourth wave' following periods of anarchist, national liberation and revolutionary terrorism; Mark Juergensmeyer (2003) argued that the world was witnessing a new 'cosmic' violence as national identities gave way to religious identities. Most often these analyses drew on theories of frustration, tending to limit the social significance of the religious to a role of responding defensively to wider social change. Of course, historically religious imaginations have not simply been about maintaining the status quo; they have often been at the centre of revolutionary movements. The historical sociologist S. E. Eisenstadt (1999) underlines the role of religious utopias in the French, English and American revolutions, arguing that these revolutions to a significant extent secularize religious themes. Other movements of radical social transformation have also drawn upon religious imaginations and utopias, from the Rastafarians and indigenous movements (Hall 2003) to the redemptive imagination of the American civil rights movement (Asad 2003). But even if we accept the limited role offered to religion by strain theory as a defence against social change, we are left with a question: why should such a defence become violent?

Arguably the most influential response to this question has been proposed by Mark Juergensmeyer, who contends that to the extent contemporary conflicts are seen through religious lenses, the actors involved believe that no compromise can be entered into. He argues that these conflicts are increasingly experienced as 'cosmic' (2003: 148), where a final confrontation between good and evil is believed to be at stake (2003: 34). In such circumstances the normal rules of compromise and limitation of violence no longer apply: 'there is no need to contend with society's laws and limitations when one is obeying a higher authority. In spiritualizing violence, therefore, religion has given terrorism a remarkable power' (2004: 221). This understanding of violence extends well beyond academic debates: in 1999 the FBI published a strategic assessment of potential terrorist groups in the United States, ranging from neo-Nazis, skinheads, Christian Identity, the Ku Klux Klan, Black Hebrew Israelites and others, grouping them under the title *Project Megiddo*, named after the Hill of Megiddo (Armageddon) where the Christian Bible's Book of Revelation locates the final battle between good and evil. For the FBI, these groups share 'apocalyptic religious beliefs' (the report is available at http://purl.access.gpo.gov/GPO/LPS3578). This paradigm has also been used to explain the attacks of 11 September 2001, with al-Qaeda being regarded as a 'doomsday cult' controlling its members by using brainwashing (for a review, see Wright 2009).

Juergensmeyer argues that participating in a cosmic war allows the actor to escape from 'humiliating and impossible predicaments' and in the process 'provide themselves with a sense of power...and nobility'. He sees this type of action as being associated increasingly with martyrdom, which he argues, from the point of view of the actor, 'will lead the way to conquest and redemption' (2008: 432). The growth of the apocalyptic violence paradigm was not simply the product of academic debate. It seemed to make sense of two attacks that shaped thinking about violence and terror in the 1990s, both of which took place in 1995: Timothy McVeigh's attack on the Oklahoma Federal Building, and the Aum attack on the Tokyo subway. In this chapter we explore both of these and consider the apocalyptic violence thesis, in the process attempting to reconstruct the social worlds and imaginaries that made such violence possible.

The Destruction of the Federal Building

Early on the morning of 19 April 1995 a pick-up truck packed with 2,200 kilos of fertilizer explosives parked in front of the Federal Building in Oklahoma City. Less than half an hour later it exploded, killing 169 people, including 15 children, and injuring many more (Hamm 2007: 179). At this point had been was the most destructive terrorist attack to have been committed on American soil, and initial speculation focused on Middle Eastern origins (Barkun 1996: 256). Soon afterwards, however, a veteran of the first US Iraq War, Timothy McVeigh, was arrested, and two years later was found guilty of murder, and executed in 2001. Through this process it would emerge that McVeigh, while not a member of any organization, was associated with several groups involved in what had come to be known as the 'Christian Identity Movement' (Barkun 1996: 274; Hamm 1997: 7), a loose cluster of white-supremacist groups and individuals involved in actions ranging from taxation refusal and bank robberies, to violence targeting homosexuals and racial and ethic minorities, including the burning of black and mixed congregation churches (Sharpe 2000; Barkun 1997; Schlatter 2006).

McVeigh's attack had taken place on the second anniversary of the siege of the Mount Carmel Center at Waco, Texas, that led to the deaths of some 74 members of a group known as the Branch Davidians (Hamm 2007: 153; Barkun 1994; Wright 1995: x) during a siege being conducted by law enforcement agencies. These deaths emerge as a critical factor in Timothy McVeigh's actions (Dean 1998: 103). At his trial McVeigh's defence team showed a video, *Day 51: The true story of Waco* (available in the public domain) (Michel and Herbeck 2001: 118), and Waco was central to material McVeigh published in the days before his execution, when he sought to offer an account of his actions (McVeigh 2001). The Branch Davidians were a breakaway sect from the Seventh Day Adventist Church who believed in the imminent return of Jesus Christ, and who had sold all their possessions and moved to 'Mount Carmel', a site in Texas, to await his arrival, an event that they believed would set in motion the Apocalypse, or the end of the world (Lawson 1995). Kenneth Newport's close analysis of the transcripts of the negotiations during the Waco siege (Newport 2006: 271ff) suggests that the leader interpreted the siege of the Mount Carmel Center as an event that could trigger the Apocalypse (for an account of the siege, see Hall 2002; Newport 2006).

There is, however, little evidence that McVeigh understood his actions in terms of such 'endtimes'. He describes the bombing of the Federal Building as an attack on the US Federal Government, not an event to bring about the end of the world, evoking the language and imaginary of a pre-emptive strike:

> I chose to bomb a federal building because such an action served more purposes than other options. Foremost the bombing was a retaliatory strike; a counter attack for the cumulative raids (and subsequent violence and damage) that federal agents had participated in over the preceding years (including, but not limited to, Waco)... Therefore this bombing was meant as a pre-emptive (or pro-active) strike against these forces and their command and control centres within the federal building. When an aggressor force continually launches attacks from a particular base of operations, it is sound military strategy to take the fight to the enemy.
>
> (McVeigh 2001/2005)

Religious Terror, Pious People?

Juergensmeyer writes 'what puzzles me is not why bad things are done by bad people, but rather why bad things are done by people who otherwise appear to be good – in the case of religious terrorism, by pious people dedicated to a moral vision of the world' (2003: 7). This appears to imply that there is an association between religiosity and good, or at least that people who are, or who claim to be, religious are more likely to be predisposed towards good than the average of the population. An alternative is proposed by the criminologist Mark Hamm (2004), who rejects framing the question in terms of good people doing bad things. His study of the subcultural world out of which McVeigh emerged does not point to a world of 'pious people', but to a violent subculture shaped by white power music, by a paramilitary style (closely cropped hair, clothes similar to military fatigues, a fascination with weapons), and by a language of race and ethnic hatred where minorities and Jews are portrayed as agents of a vast conspiracy. One where ideology, weaponry and practices of male bonding (weekends away shooting etc.) allow for the creation of collective cultures where those involved can 'go berserk' (Hamm 2004: 327) on perceived enemies: homosexuals, Jews, blacks and foreigners. Significantly, within this world Hamm finds little evidence of apocalyptic thinking – instead he encounters a violent subculture that exercises a seductive power. Rather than apocalyptic beliefs, he argues the case of Christian Identity in the United States underlines the importance of music, literature, symbolism and style in the construction of terrorism (2004: 326), highlighting the extent to which this world is shaped by criminality, ranging from firearms offences, bank robbery and taxation refusal to credit card fraud. Hamm suggests that the reference to the Apocalypse is in fact a minor dimension of the culture and action of these men, proposing instead that what is more important is the search for fame, intensity and excitement – values at the centre of US culture. From this perspective, it is perhaps not without significance that McVeigh requested that his execution be transmitted live on television – a request that was refused (Sarat 2001).

Conspiracy, Violence and the Imaginary

What is striking about McVeigh is less a sense of an approaching end of the world, but his engagement with much more worldly dimensions of American popular culture, in particular 'anti-governmentalism' and conspiracy theory. From what we can reconstruct, it is clear that Timothy McVeigh lived in a world shaped by such theories. At its simplest level, this means that he believed the world to be shaped by hidden forces and sinister groups, and that he understood himself to be involved in a struggle against such hidden forces. As the American sociologist Michael Barkun argues, this 'culture of conspiracy' is widespread in contemporary societies, and McVeigh demonstrates important expressions of this culture (Barkun 1996). In the year before the Oklahoma bombing, McVeigh visited 'Area 51', a US government installation in the desert north of Las Vegas widely believed to hold captured UFOs (Barkun 2006: ix). His friends are reported to have affirmed that on several occasions McVeigh stated that he believed that he had received a microchip implant without his knowledge during the time he served in the US forces in the Gulf War, aiming to monitor his location and actions (Barkun 2006: 101; Russakoff and Kovaleski 1995).

Barkun (2006) points to the central dimensions of conspiracy belief. First is the idea that nothing happens by accident – every event has behind it some type of explanation, some form of intentional action. In that sense, there is no chance or random event, or processes that are out of control. The world can be understood in terms of intentionality. Second, nothing is as it seems, since the hidden actors shaping events deliberately set out to conceal themselves. Third, everything is connected. In a world without accident or chance, the actions of the powerful leave a trace in the pattern of events. Understanding such patterns is the key to understanding the action of the actors concealed behind them. As Barkun emphasizes, this understanding of the world is both frightening and reassuring: frightening because it underlines the potency of the power and presence of evil, in a way that can lead to dualistic world views opposing good with evil. But it is also reassuring, in that it promises intelligibility – if the patterns and hidden links can be identified, the world can be understood. This, perhaps, is the most potent dimension of conspiracy theory, its promise of a world that is meaningful rather than arbitrary: 'the clear identification of evil gives the conspiracist a definable enemy against which to struggle, endowing life with purpose' (Barkun 2006: 4).

The Banal and the Extraordinary

The period since McVeigh's attack has seen an extraordinary expansion of conspiracy theories seeking to explain events ranging from the death of public figures from US President Kennedy to Princess Diana, the rise of diseases such as AIDS or patterns of drug addiction, to the attacks of 11 September (Locke 2009).

The Hollywood blockbuster *Men in Black* was based on the widespread belief in the United States that 'men in black' are involved in operations to guard government secrets, such as the presence of aliens (Dean 1998: 155). Other widely embraced conspiracy beliefs are constructed around the role of secret organizations such as the Illuminati or groups whose origins supposedly go back to the twelfth century Crusades (Barkun 2006: 45ff), such as the Order of Knights Templars (Barkun 2006: 213) – themes of extraordinary success in popular film and airport fiction. Such hidden groups, it is believed, are behind the orchestration of events over the past millennium, and today are at the heart of attempts to create a 'New World Order' (West and Sanders 2003). These themes are not only important in Western popular culture, they also occupy a major place within Islamist organizations: the Hamas Charter, for example, quotes extensively from the *Protocols of the Elders of Zion*, a forgery purporting to uncover a secret Jewish plot to control the world (Hagemeister 2008). The Hamas Charter also condemns other groups as 'secret societies', ranging from the Freemasons to Lions and Rotary Clubs (a reliable translation of the *Charter* is Maqdsi 1993).

Part of the recurring structure of conspiracy theory is its contrast between the very small and the very large. Spark highlights the importance of a 'profligate mish-mash of detail' characterizing conspiracy theory, noting the importance of small traces charged with meaning, such as the secret codes some radical right groups believe are embedded in the rear of road signs in the United States to help invading forces find their way. The codes are hidden in the rear of the signs because it is presumed that the invaders will drive on the other side of the road (Spark 2001). This small detail makes intelligible the otherwise enormous claim of a vast conspiracy to introduce secret signage across the United States to assist the invading forces of the New World Order: the conspiracy is a bridge between the banal and the extraordinary.

Simon Locke (2009) underlines the extent to which conspiracy theory is part of a wider culture of blame. But rather than seek to identify a specific person as being responsible for events, conspiracy theory seeks out a general category of persons who are representative of something that exists above and beyond them. Locke argues this extends to a more general 'conspiracy culture' closely linked to modern experiences of suffering. To the extent that conspiracy theory attributes blame, it offers answers to questions such as 'why me?' or 'why us?' (2009: 578). Rather than an expression of the rise of the religious, Locke follows Sir Karl Popper, who considers conspiracy theory, or the idea that every event can be explained in terms of a group of people who wanted it to happen, as an expression of secularization and the decline of religion's public impact (see also Pigden 1995).

Fear, Desire, Fantasy

What clearly drives the emergence of the idea of 'apocalyptic' violence is its excess. While the Weather Underground robbed banks using weapons to threaten people or blew up monuments, and the Red Brigades killed up to five individuals in its most bloody action, McVeigh killed 168 people, including children. This excess seemed intelligible as 'cosmic' violence charged with carrying out the will of a vengeful God.

But rather than look to the injunctions of religious texts, it could be more useful to explore the relationship between fear, desire and fantasy at the heart of conspiracy culture. Mark Fenster (2008) draws on Slavoj Žižek's understanding of fantasy to argue that conspiracy theory is best understood as a particular form of desire or fantasy, one that 'takes its own failure into account in advance' (Žižek 1989: 126). From this perspective, embedded within conspiracy theory is an acceptance that the perfectly transparent world it longs for is impossible given the state of corruption and opaqueness of the world in which it finds itself. This sets in motion a dynamic of displacement at the heart of conspiracy theory:

> Displacing these fears of impossibility onto fears of conspiracy, condensing these fears into notions of murderous, licentious presidents and secretive cabals, the conspiracy theorist enjoys his symptoms, indulging in its practice, revelling in its excess, never fully reaching the fulfilment of desire lest he be confronted with the realization that the notion of a wilful, secretive conspiracy by an elite cabal is not quite right.
>
> (Fenster 2008: 109)

As we saw in the previous chapter, excess and impossibility came to occupy a central place in the second Intifada, with Khosrokhavar arguing that the *impossibility* of community was central to its violence, as the earlier civil violence of grassroots organization gave way to the personalized violence of the suicide bomber. I argued that the relationship between fear and fantasy also emerges as decisive. In that case, it was the fear of *Isquat* (falling down) and the fantasy it released (of daughters seducing fathers etc.). Such dimensions highlight the way that violence extends beyond the frameworks of everyday 'politics as usual'.

Fantasies of Destruction

On 20 March 1995, a month before McVeigh's attack, five men boarded five different subway trains in Tokyo's rush hour. The trains were scheduled to pass through the stations servicing the major government administration departments and the national parliament. Each of the men carried a plastic bag of the highly toxic nerve gas, Sarin, wrapped in newspaper. As the trains approached the government district, each punctured the Sarin bag, and leaving them on the floor of the train, stood up and alighted at the next stop (Juergensmeyer 2003: 104). The bags began to drain. Commuters began to fall ill, in most cases not knowing what was causing the nausea and collapsing around them. In one case a commuter kicked the Sarin bag off the train and on to a platform; in another passengers pushed an emergency stop button, but only after the train had travelled several stops (Transportation Research Board 2006: 35). In total 12 people died as a result of exposure to the deadly gas, while later estimates based on hospital attendance suggest that some 6,000 people suffered injuries as a result of the attack (Tu 1999).

The five men were all members of the Aum Shinrikyo, a 'new religion' that had developed in Japan since the mid-1980s. At first glance they don't appear to correspond to what we would expect of 'violent fanatics'. Each was highly educated, having graduated from prestigious universities with engineering or medical qualifications (Juergensmeyer 2003: 104). In previous years they had all left behind their earlier lives to go and live in a community formed by a visually impaired yoga teacher who had completed school for the blind and begun to practice as an acupuncturist and practitioner of Chinese medicine (Lifton 1999: 14). In his mid-twenties Aum's future founder joined a Buddhist religious group, later leaving to teach yoga from his one-room apartment in Tokyo. In his early thirties he travelled to India, on his return to Japan telling his students that he had found enlightenment (Lifton 1999: 21). In July 1987 he changed his name and created a new group, the Aum Shinrikyo (Supreme Truth), which two years later would be registered as a new religion with the Tokyo Prefecture, one of tens of thousands of 'new religions' created in Japan in the 1980s. Aum's teachings were drawn from Buddhism, Taoism and Christianity, as well as the prophecies of Nostradamus, these ideas combined with a regime of body practice involving exercises, yoga and meditation (Juergensmeyer 2003: 110). Followers could proceed through stages of learning to the goal of Enlightenment. Those who had reached a sufficient stage were able to become *shukke* (a 'renunciant' who has left home), moving into one of the group's communities and donating all their assets to the group (Lifton 2007: 66).

At its beginning the culture of this group was optimistic. The original yoga and meditation group formed in 1984 had sought to foster personal improvement through teaching, study and practice. But while aiming at spiritual awakening, this optimism was also accompanied by a negative view of the world as corrupt and materialistic, where to remain trapped in day-to-day life would condemn people to negative karma which, following death, would lead to hell and rebirth as a lower form of life. According to Aum's teachings, embracing the group and its ascetic practices would allow people to reject the world, and in the process purify themselves and attain salvation. The aim of the sect was to create 30,000 spiritually advanced beings (Lifton 1999). Only this could avert what the founder had begun to predict, namely a nuclear war in the fateful year 2000. Negative karma was growing, and the Kobe earthquake of 1995 that killed some 5,000 people was a sign (Iida 2000). Only the power of the elect 30,000 could dispel such negative karma that would otherwise lead to the destruction of the world. This group would be the monastic order of *shukke*, who would live in utopian communities known as Lotus Villages, creating a utopia on Earth named Shambala (Lifton 1999: 46).

What is striking is the extent to which these beliefs cobble together themes from popular culture of the time: fascination and apprehension regarding the year 2000 combine with the Hollywood theme of heroes saving the world from destruction. As the Aum sect develops, what we see is the gradual eclipse of the utopian dreams of Shambala and the increasing importance of nightmares of destruction. In early 1989 the founder wrote *Day of Perishing* (Lifton 1999: 47), where this change of tone became evident. Rather than averting the destruction of the world, this was now judged as inevitable, with Aum declaring that only its followers could hope to survive. The world was doomed, not because of the failure of the Aum sect to achieve its goals, but because humanity had failed to embrace the Aum path. Humanity was guilty: having heard Aum's message and rejected it, it deserved the fate awaiting it. All Aum could do was save the faithful (Reader 2000: 193–5).

Embodied Experience

This changing view of the future of the world was linked to a changing place of embodied experience within the sect. In the summer of 1988 Aum began to demand of its followers that that they undertake self-mortification such as fasting or undergoing extreme cold (Trinh 1998), a reflection of traditional practices of self-cultivation through renunciation of pleasure that we also encountered in the United Japanese Red Army (Steinhoff 1992). Reader (2000) describes this as a 'culture of coercive asceticism', noting that those who failed to comply with these demands increasingly came to be punished by beatings, imprisonment or denial of food. The meanings of such punishment changed, becoming explicitly justified as saving a member who otherwise was believed to be doomed. The internal life of the sect did not simply focus on the mortification of its members. Progression could also be advanced through the purchase of products, from the used bathwater of the guru (300,000 yen per glass) to a drop of his blood (1 million yen) which would allow the recipient to attain superhuman powers (Lifton 1999: 36).

This period would become a turning point for the sect. In late 1988 a disciple died during one of the ascetic practices (Eate 2008). He had been hung upside down, with a rope tied to one leg, for periods of up to 90 minutes, between which he had been submerged in freezing cold water. The death occurred at the time the sect was due to receive news of its application to the Prefecture for recognition as a religion (which would facilitate the purchase of property and brought a lenient taxation regime). It was decided that the death should be concealed, and the dead disciple's body was burnt and disposed of. Reader argues this death posed a problem of doctrine: if someone could die as a result of the sect's practices, how could Aum's teaching be said to save its followers who did what was demanded of them? This led to an inflection in teaching: not all could be saved, only the most deserving (2000: 23). It was from this period that violence became increasingly central to both the leader's writings and to sect practice. In 1992 Aum's leader declared himself to be Christ, who would be able to save his followers but would have to die himself (Lifton 1998).

While Aum's utopian dimension continued through attempts to create Lotus Villages in rural areas, these were increasingly being opposed by local communities. Aum's leaders came to interpret this rejection as similar to the rejection of Jesus Christ. This sense of an increasingly hostile environment was central to Aum's decision to launch its first gas attack in the city of Matsumoto in June 1994, where it was feared that legal proceedings would prevent the sect's attempt to purchase land. Aum's leaders decided that the best way to prevent a decision that could block their attempt at land purchase would be to kill the judge presiding over the case. A residential apartment block housing the Court examining the Aum land purchase was targeted, with Sarin gas being distributed late at night from a truck parked in a car park. Seven people, including two judges and one court official, were killed (Hardacre 1996), with over 200 people being injured (Tu 1999).

This external violence mirrors the violence that was becoming increasingly important within the sect itself. From October 1994, members who expressed doubt or concerns were likely to be subjected to electroshock, with the sect's hospital administering over 600 shocks within a period of three months to members manifesting 'inappropriate ideas' (Trinh 1998; the Japanese author Haruki Murakami [2001] interviewed several former sect members who describe their experience of electroshocks, one saying she received shocks after refusing sexual advances). During 1994, members who left were kidnapped and returned, imprisoned in small transport containers for months until seeing the error of their ways (Reader 2000: 11). Parcels containing poison gas were sent to journalists regarded as opponents (Trinh 1998). In May 1992 the sect gained approval to install an industrial incinerator at its compound at Kamikuishiki, and this began to be used for the disposal of bodies (Trinh 1998). In this latter phase Aum devoted increasing resources to producing weapons. Sarin and XV gas were produced successfully, experiments in weaponizing chemicals were undertaken at a property owned in rural Australia (Watanabe 1998), and trips were made to Russia with a view to purchasing nuclear weapons (Cameron 1999). Several members of the sect were prominent Japanese Yakuza (Mafia) (having joined early when Aum was focused on healing), and these links proved invaluable in obtaining the contacts necessary for weapons purchase and production (Trinh 1998; Introvigne 2002).

From this point there is an increasing sense that Aum had begun feeding upon itself. Some estimates suggest as many as 50 sect members were killed during 1994 and their bodies disposed of in the incinerator (Trinh 1998). In February 1995 a lawyer was kidnapped and died while being questioned about his sister, who had left the sect (Trinh 1998), his disappearance setting in motion a public outcry and police action, with an imminent raid on Aum headquarters being planned. This impending police action can be seen as a trigger for the Aum attack on the government quarter, mirroring the attack on the Court buildings in Matsumoto a year earlier. Aum leaders had been alerted to the raid, most probably by members who were part of the police or through contacts involved with organized crime (Olson [1999] explores the close links between Aum and organized crime or Yakuza groups). Trinh argues that the decision to undertake the subway attack was made only two days before it was to take place, suggesting the haste involved, and the Sarin had to be specially produced. This rush meant that this was not a fully successful batch, at only 30 per cent strength – and this meant that the massive number of potential deaths was reduced (Trinh 1998).

Subjectivities, Pain and the Search for Selfhood

What sense can we make of this extraordinary transformation? A group that began as a yoga and meditation class mutated over a period of years into something that attempted to bring about mass death on Tokyo's train system. While the sect emphasized creating a world of the saved who would in turn save the world, it was deeply embedded within contemporary culture. This is particularly evident in its beliefs, from its fascination with the portents of the year 2000 and the prophecies of Nostradamus to its self-understanding as a band of heroes saving the world (Lifton 2007). Yumiko Iida (2000, 2001) locates the development of groups such Aum within profound transformations occurring within Japanese society in the 1990s, attempting to understand Aum's emergence and development within the context of broader questions concerning embodiment, subjectivity and violence. She links Aum to the increasing 'virtual' nature of Japanese consumer society, pointing to the increasing place of the 'artificial' within this world, from pets to video games, suggesting that the consumption patterns characterizing Japanese capitalism were producing an 'infantalization' of Japanese society, where consumption was becoming an increasingly 'artificial pleasure loop'. Other critics of Japanese capitalism, both radical and conservative, equally expressed increasing concern about the emergence of a 'sign economy', one where selfhood is less and less a question of depth and character, and increasingly a question of surface (see Allison [2009] for an analysis of 'pokemon capitalism'). Iida argues that this world of surface and signs has particular implications for the relationship between body and self, and this relationship was clearly central to Aum's practices. She argues that within the model of Japanese consumerism that emerged over the 1980s and 1990s the body changes its status, moving from being the foundation of the self to increasingly becoming a controllable environment, where enhancing how one relates to oneself is determined by how others relate to one's body: 'the pleasure of consuming the self is mediated by others' consumption of it, which is in turn consumed by the self' (2000: 435). Rather than focus on the apocalyptic dimensions of Aum, she underlines the extent to which its development needs to be understood in terms of these dimensions of Japanese consumer culture.

This focus on the body also converges with other dimensions of the sect. Handing over all decisions to the group, Aum offered those who joined it a safe home, a protected space where they could grow up again. One young woman who joined Aum describes her experience as a search for meaning and connection, where 'in giving oneself to this inner world of love and purity, by submitting to the higher virtue of the cult, one would feel freed from the burden of dealing with the brutal world outside', describing the experience of joining Aum as a 'retreat back to the mother's womb' (Iida 2000: 442). This dynamic of retreat and re-creation of self arguably characterizes all sects. We saw how the Weather Underground set about remaking its members through the 'gut check' and group sex, while the Japanese United Red Army set out to reconstruct its members so that they could achieve 'communist subjectivity' (Igarashi 2007). These groups were embedded in the revolutionary student culture of the 1970s. Aum's transition to violence took place two decades later, and rather than a reference to world revolution and 'people's war', we encounter the relationship between a virtualized popular culture, the occult and science.

Iida highlights Aum's debt to *manga* and computer games. Its first text signalling a new imaginary of violence, *The Day of Perishing*, was not a theological treatise but a *manga* comic. Members could progress through offerings and tests in a system directly modelled on the fantasy game *Dungeons and Dragons* (Goto-Jones 2009: 122). Aum was significantly influenced by a Japanese television show 'Spaceship Yamato' (Lifton 1999: 46), which saw itself as rescuing humankind from the threat of aliens, producing a pseudo-experience of living in a fantasy world similar to the virtual world of a video game. Aum members could increase their power in ways similar to video games, through obtaining objects that had superhuman power, such as water that the guru had bathed in, a drop of his blood, or through purchasing headgear that would allow the wearer to synchronize their brainwaves to those being emitted by the sect's leader (Olson 1999: 516). The whole logic was centred on increasing one's powers through progressing through levels, in a process that depended on passing tests and accessing secret knowledge, where progression could be accelerated by special powerful objects or by the payment of money. This clearly parallels the structure of a computer game.

The importance of magical objects within the cult reflects a wider pattern within Japanese society, one that Ian Reader describes as the 'democratization of magic', a paradigm he sees at work right across the new religions that emerged in Japan over the 1990s, which were all characterized by a rejection of ordained ministers who monopolized magical power (Reader 1988, 2006). In the case of Aum, this magical access to power was associated with occult practices that allowed access to secret knowledge. As Iida suggests, such occultism can easily coexist with a scientific world view, to the extent that both seek to explain every detail of human existence in terms of cause and effect. In this case, hidden forces are believed to be at work, and these can be accessed and controlled by magical practice. The convergence between the occult and science, both of which are centred on exercising control, helps us to understand the otherwise difficult to comprehend fact that the Aum cult was largely made up of university graduates from the scientific disciplines. This link between the occult and science may also help explain the often observed over-representation of engineers and computer scientists in the jihadi groups that emerged in the late twentieth century (see Gambetta and Hertog 2009).

What makes Aum different from a computer game is the extent to which the tests that adherents had to pass came increasingly to involve subjection of the body to pain – at first one's own body, and as one progressed through the levels, the bodies of others. Observers who locate Aum within the broader transformations at work within Japanese culture link its resonance among many educated young people to its capacity to respond to the unease generated by what is often experienced as an absence of values within Japanese culture that 'make life worth living'. This absence may set off two types of response: either retreat (evident in Japan among young men who refuse to leave their bedrooms, the *otaku*) (see Ito 2004), or practices that may involve explosions of violence that seek to reveal the self (Iida points to the importance of the gruesome murders which took place in the Japanese city of Kobe in 1995, when a boy of 14 years of age beheaded school mates, leaving their heads in public places with poems he had written stuffed in their mouths). From this perspective, Aum can be understood as a social world 'that confirms the limits of the self, the boundary between the self and the outside', one where the subject knows that 'the body is alive because it is in pain'. Rather than regard Aum's violence in terms of apocalyptic themes, Iida suggests a different dynamic:

> The Aum incident mirrors immanent problems of contemporary Japan – a fragmented, disembodied and claustrophobic subjectivity, whose desperate attempts to recover a lost integrity had reached a point of violent explosion.
>
> (Iida 2001: 243)

Religion to Violence, Violence to Religion?

It is perhaps not surprising that the Tokyo and Oklahoma attacks were interpreted in terms of 'apocalypse' and 'end of days', in particular in the United States, given the importance of such themes within American popular culture (Wojick 1999). These attacks occurred in the period leading up to the year 2000, and to this extent appeared to be part of a bigger picture of events such as the murders/suicides of some 914 people in Jonestown (Guyana) in 1978, the destruction of the Branch Davidians (1993), the murders/suicides of the Swiss Order of the Solar Temple (1994), or the later 1997 suicides of Heavens Gate in California (this latter case highlighting themes similar to Aum, where members increasingly came to fear 'space aliens' and where the final group suicide was embraced by members as the way to move to 'the next level' (Urban 2000). All these groups and cults appeared to be waiting for the end of the world, and the violence unleashed by Aum and McVeigh seemed to point to a clear break with earlier forms of terrorist violence, to the extent that neither was linked to a public statement of demands or even responsibility, suggesting that for whoever was behind these attacks, violence was meant to 'speak for itself'. Both also seemed driven by a logic of excess, seeking to bring about a maximum number of deaths, and the theme of 'Apocalypse' or 'end of the world' seemed to capture the absence of limits that appeared to characterize these attacks.

However, a closer exploration of the violence of McVeigh and the Aum sect suggests the need for a more nuanced analysis. What is striking about both these attacks is less their 'religious' dimensions than their debt to popular culture. McVeigh appears far more embedded within a secular culture of anti-governmentalism and conspiracy, with his preoccupation with UFOs and implants, than within any religious motivation; while Aum's subway attack of 1995 seems to follow the pattern of a year earlier when judges were killed, with violence being directed at those perceived as a threat, from within or without. Aum's members were highly educated, and while McVeigh and the world he seems linked to were not, both were concerned with hidden forces at work, from the presence of aliens to the possibility of accessing magical powers. The Aum case in particular highlights what may be an increasingly problematic status of embodied experience within modern, virtual capitalism. While on the one hand the middle classes attend gyms and fitness classes in an effort to control their lives and remake themselves, authors such as Iida highlight the significance of pain as a mode of embodiment and of self-construction in a culture where the boundaries and meanings of selfhood seem increasing open to flux and flow. The importance of pain in Aum's practices can be understood as a search to recover a lost integrity or wholeness of self through a search for limits. In this case, ascetic practices associated with experiencing pain and limits blur into practices of inflicting pain upon others, and it is possible that this played an important role in the increasing recourse to violence as a medium of control within the sect. It was this recourse to violence against internal threats that framed the response to those outside the sect seen to be a threat, first the judges who would determine a land planning application, and later the central government.

This dynamic suggests that instead of religion leading to violence, we may in fact be encountering its opposite, namely a process where an increasing fascination with violence as a mode of embodied experience leads to religion, whether in the form of the priesthoods of Christian Identity or the scientist occultism of the Aum sect. This dynamic may alert us to patterns of experience that are becoming increasingly significant in the context of contemporary globalization, a relationship between violence and experiences of revelation of hidden worlds. This may be highly relevant to an increasingly central dimension of contemporary violence: the search for the extreme, and the increasing association of violence with death.

7

Violence, the Mask and the Extreme

Beyond the Rational Actor Paradigm

The themes we have explored thus far point to transformations in violence that we need to understand. The violence of the revolutionary students we encountered in Chapter 4 was always accompanied by communiqués and claims of responsibility, and to a significant extent corresponds to the political violence model proposed by the sociologist Charles Tilly, who defines terror as 'a political strategy to extract resources and increase power'. For Tilly, terrorism is one of a range of actions that 'employ violent means of claim making' (2003: 13). From this point of view violence is a tool or instrument, to be taken up or put down, within an epistemology of actors *using* violence. This captures important dimensions of cases where 'elites', to use the term proposed by Crenshaw (1981), embrace violence as a strategy to 'awaken' the masses or to destroy the credibility of those in power, as we saw with Irgun in Chapter 2. But it is important that we recognize that the rational actor approach, framing violence as an imposition of a cost–benefit choice upon an opponent, offers no conceptual distinction between to 'employ violence' and 'to kill'. Violence is understood as to 'inflict damage on others' (Tilly 2003: 4) or even to 'administer damage' (Tilly 2003: 17). Killing is approached as an example of a lethal contest, where what is at stake is 'using harm to reduce or contain the others' capacity to inflict harm' (2003: 104). Death is reduced to being in a state of a reduced capacity to inflict harm.

But it seems that there is some sort of shift at work in the forms of terror that we encounter today. In Chapter 6 we saw McVeigh convicted of the mass murder of 168 people in 1995, killing non-combatants on a scale not seen before. Such killing was amplified by the 11 September attacks of 2001, and in both cases these killings were not accompanied by any of the warnings or the claims of responsibility that typically accompanied attacks in earlier periods. To that extent this violence seemed to break with theories of the rationality of terrorism, summed up by the widely repeated phrase, 'terrorists want a lot of people watching, a lot of people listening, not a lot of people dead' (Jenkins 1975: 158). McVeigh's attack and the building he destroyed seemed to be a harbinger of bin Laden's attack six years later, and here, clearly, the aim of these actions was to kill as many people as possible.

The rational actor model of terrorism understands violence essentially as a medium of communication. Its principal target is a government or similar power-holder. From this perspective, the main relationship at stake in terrorism involves the violent actor on the one hand and the power-holder on the other. This leaves two areas of violence largely unexplored. The first is violence as an *experience*. This is evident in the language used by rational actor theories that speak of 'employing violence' as opposed to 'being violent'. In Chapter 4 we saw the way actors seek to transform themselves through violence, from the 'gut check' of the students of the Weather Underground to the beatings members of the Japanese United Red Army administered to each other. Chris Hedges (2003) speaks of the 'seduction' of violence and explores the way war 'is a force that gives us meaning', but such experiential dimensions remain unexplored by theories that approach violence as something to be 'administered' rather than lived. The rational actor model also leaves a second area largely unexplored, namely the relationship between the authors of violence and their *victims*. The rational actor theory does not offer an insight into whether the authors of violence take pleasure in imposing suffering on others, or why violence increasingly appears to take on dimensions interpreted as 'apocalyptic'. There are shifts at work in contemporary violence that highlight dimensions best described as horror and excess. Engaging with these opens out critical debates about violence: its personalization, the relationship between the hidden and the revealed, and the search for the extreme.

Violence, Ethics and Community

One way we can begin to approach the experience of violence is to explore its place in communities. This highlights the extent that violence is not simply a means to break down order. Violence can also produce order, as for example in the case of urban gangs, where fighting and defending borders produces order in worlds of disorder, producing internal hierarchy and loyalty through the violence of external competition (McDonald 1999). Violence plays a recurring role in building community identities, in particular in strongly integrated communities structured in terms of oppositions between 'us' and 'them' (McDonald 1999). This form of violence occurs frequently in military barracks, boarding schools, fraternities and sporting teams. Joining such groups often requires the shedding of previous identities and loyalties, involving rituals which demonstrate acceptance of the power of the fraternity to determine one's fate. This transition is often associated with shedding one's clothes, accepting a status of vulnerability, being tested by physical violence, and emerging from the process as a fully-fledged member of the community. Groves *et al.*'s (2012) analysis of initiation or hazing in sporting teams in the United Kingdom notes the persistence of these themes: alcohol, nudity, humiliation, physical and psychological abuse leading to violence and at times injury. These initiation rituals involve 'breaking down' former selves that are then rebuilt by the leaders of the team. A considerable number of university students have died as a result of such rituals – one US study pointing to over 400 deaths or serious injuries involved in college-based hazing over the period 1900–90 (Nuwer 2002).

Violence thus plays a significant part in community cultures. The French sociologist François Dubet (1992) argues that the more a community is integrated, the more important will be community-sanctioned violence that often takes the form of deviance from dominant social norms, constituting the group and loyalty to it. The 'bar brawl', for example, was for a long time a tolerated form of violence, a kind of popular leisure that involved release and freedom from the constraints of daily life. This 'drinking violence' combines a dimension of social protest (breaking free of imposed laws) with resistance to middle-class morality (Tomsen 1997). What is distinctive about this violence is that it is regulated by a community: weapons are not used and serious injuries or deaths rarely occur, older people or community leaders will often be on hand to step in if things get out of control, and the violence is framed by shared limits and a sense of 'fairness'. This is quite different from the violence that has become increasingly evident in bars since the 1980s, associated with the practice of 'glassing', where a glass or a bottle will be smashed to form jagged edges and then used as weapon. Almost unheard of in the 1940s or 1950s, in the 1990s 'glassing' attacks made up some 10 per cent of all assault injuries leading to admission to hospital in the United Kingdom, and in 75 per cent of these cases the glass used was thrust into the face of the victim (Shepherd 1998). This violence is radically different from the bar brawl with its ethos of the fair fight, relaxing violence and construction of a collective experience. The face is the sign and medium of individuality, and this is what glassing seeks to wound.

Honour, Respect and Singularity: The Hardman

The relationship between violence and community is central to anthropologist Allen Feldman's (1991) exploration of violence and its transformations in Northern Ireland. Feldman begins by exploring the violence associated with the 'hardman'. The hardman is a person who develops a reputation obtained through fights in pubs or on waste ground. The hardman fights with his fists, he stands up for his honour and that of his friends, family and community. The violence he engages in is regulated by norms, shaped by an understanding of what is right and wrong. The hardman fights fairly; he does not use weapons, but relies on his strength and skill. Through his violence he builds up and defends the reputation of his family, his street, his community and neighbourhood. This violence is structured in terms of the norms of honour and respect – he will defeat his opponent, but he will not dishonour him. This morality of violence is sustained by a working-class culture that understands and values the moral imperative of strength in a world dominated by the logic of the machine, at a time when deskilling meant that the machine was no longer a tool of creativity but an instrument of dehumanization.

Through his violence the hardman stands out, he gains a reputation; he is not reduced to being an appendage of a system of production. He achieves what contemporary urban culture calls 'respect' (Bourgois 1996; McDonald 1999). The hardman's violence is integral to being a man, to being a human being. For Feldman, it is a form of 'moral construction of the self through techniques of the body that set the body apart from others' (1991: 52). But this is achieved in a world where reputation is finite – in increasing his own reputation, the hardman diminishes that of the opponent he vanquishes. He strengthens the reputation of his community, his street or neighbourhood, while diminishing that of the defeated. As such, his community benefits from this violence: 'through the self-construction of the self in violence, the hardman came to signify the self-contained and autonomous singularity of his community' (Feldman 1991: 52). This moral violence would be radically transformed by the violence that emerged in Northern Ireland from the 1970s in the period that came to be known as The Troubles (Bairner 1999). This period witnessed the use of troops in policing, the collectivization of arrest (Hughes 2011), the development of militias, and the emergence of a radically new type of violence.

Masked Violence

The period referred to as 'The Troubles' in Northern Ireland (1963–85) saw the development of what has now become referred to more widely as 'low intensity warfare'. At its heart were strategies that had been pioneered in 'counter-insurgency' and 'counter-subversion' operations in Kenya, Malaya and Cyprus, as a generation of military leaders shaped by these conflicts were given responsibility for solving the problems of violence emerging in Northern Ireland. Advocates of low intensity operations argued that successful counter-insurgency was based on large amounts of 'low grade information' as opposed to small amounts of 'high grade information' (Kitson 2011: 73), and this objective led to new practices of collective arrest and detention, in which large sections of the population would be detained for questioning, but only a small proportion would eventually be charged with offences (for an overview of this model of counter-insurgency, see Newsinger 2001). This practice involved, as Feldman notes, a radical departure from the idea of individual responsibility for illegal acts. Feldman notes how such collective arrest, detention and interrogation came to play the role of a 'rite of passage', becoming an experience marking political maturity. As in other cases where collective arrest has been practised, such as Palestine, the experience of arrest and imprisonment often plays a key role in joining a militia, as these groups structure prison life, looking after a person in detention and continuing contact with them after they have been released (Bucaille 2006).

What is at stake here is not simply the development of militias. Feldman notes that the violence of these militias took on a new form, particularly evident in the large mural images of militia fighters that came to be displayed on walls throughout Northern Ireland during this period. What is striking is the extent that the fighters depicted in these murals are almost always masked. The painting on the wall could be of a generic person, but instead it is a masked fighter who is always depicted, with the mask and the gun at the centre of the image. Feldman explores the significance of such visual representations, above all when contrasted with traditional forms of violence associated with the hardman. We saw that the hardman asserts his selfhood through his body; he gains reputation and visibility and constructs himself as an individual through violence. The murals of militia fighters highlight something quite different, a transformation Feldman describes as the 'anonymous collectivization of violence' highlighted by the powerful visual association of the mask and the gun:

> In visual propaganda the mask has many more iconic functions than merely protecting individual identity for security reasons. Posters of masked paramilitaries holding weapons are statements about historical transformations and the construction of power. The masking of the agent of force, his depersonalisation, identifies this agency with the trajectories of history as generalized force... There is a reversal between the masking of the face and the display of the gun.
>
> (Feldman 1991: 53)

These murals are paintings, not photos. The artist responsible could create a generic image of a person holding a gun. During this period such generic political images were widespread, for example in the murals and posters produced during the communist periods in China and the Soviet Union, where generic heroic workers lead the challenge of creating socialism (see Landsberger 1997; Andrews 1994). These images circulated widely, with generic people symbolizing courage, determination, strength and solidarity, as revolutionary murals and posters celebrate their collective effort to create a new world. But in Northern Ireland there is almost never a generic face associated with the gun; instead, the gunman is masked. We encounter a similar pattern elsewhere, for example in posters and murals of Hamas fighters in the Palestinian territories, where once again the gun and the mask form the centre of the image. The pattern originally occurring on murals in Northern Ireland or in the Palestinian territories is now repeated in the visual representations of their fighters that militia organizations place on their Internet sites, with mask and weapon occupying the centre of the image.

Given that such images could depict a generic person, the issue at stake is not one of protecting anonymity. Something more important is happening. As Feldman underlines, in the case of the hardman, the fighter achieves visibility and individuation through violence. In the case of the paramilitary, the masked gunman seeks to avoid visibility, while it is the victim who is to be as visible as possible. In the shift from hardman to gunman, writes Feldman,

> the relations of visibility and invisibility that govern the relations of the agent of force to the object of force are inverted. The hardman attains visibility through the objectification of his own body. The paramilitary achieves political visibility by objectifying the bodies of others.
>
> (Feldman 1991: 54)

What does the mask hide? For Feldman, masked violence is performative: 'the absent face of the agent of violence is worn by the victim marked by violence' (1999: 54). It is the victim who is to be made visible through violence. This alerts us to a critical dimension of this type of violence, from Northern Ireland to Palestinian refugee camps: the placing of the body of the victim in public.

Masking as Social Practice

Sociologists and political scientists have generally paid little attention to masking as a form of social practice, leaving this instead to anthropologists.

Recent anthropological scholarship has focused in particular on the action of masking in Africa, especially in the context of increasing masked violence. Anthropological studies have traditionally underlined the role of masks as a form of social control – the presence of the mask often indicating the presence of a form of power. But the mask is also a vehicle for transformation, with masked performances being central to situations of transition from one state to another, evident in particular in the role of masks in rituals associated with marriage, initiation or death. Christian Kordt Højbjerg (2005) underlines that such passages from one state to another are generally associated with danger, and such critical situations call for forms of mediation to allow the passage to occur. Elizabeth Tonkin (1979: 244) understands the mask as a 'metaphor-in-action': 'since masks are themselves transformations they are used as metaphors-in-action, to transform events themselves or mediate between structures'. Kordt Højbjerg builds on this, arguing that the mask is an expression of paradox and ambiguity, where the act of covering conceals one identity while simultaneously revealing another (2005: 159).

In such cases, the mask is not primarily an object, but a medium of transformation and metamorphosis. The wearers of the mask inspire fear because they stand outside the social world of norms, obligations and reciprocity, and exchange of meaning. In African societies, the mask is a source of power because it gives access to 'another world', that of the ancestors (Argenti 2006). In such cases, the fact that the mask conceals identity is of secondary importance; in fact the identity of the wearer is most often known. What is significant is that the mask is both a metaphor and a vehicle for a particular type of power. Nicolas Argenti's exploration of masking practices in Cameroon is particularly evocative. He explores ritual dances evoking the experience of being captured and taken as slaves, dances where bodies re-enact being manacled together, being consumed and annihilated through cannibalism. The place of the mask in these rituals, he suggests, is linked to undomesticated and anarchic violence, to the unfettered appetites of slave traders in the pre-colonial and early colonial eras. The practices of masking that Argenti explores evoke traumatic events not present in stories and myth, but which are recreated somatically through dance. The violence and trauma of enslavement still cannot be spoken, but it has not been wiped from the culture of these descendants. Instead this is present in dance, where the mask is a medium to access embodied memory.

To explore what might be at work in such masked dances, Argenti draws on the work of the philosopher Jean-François Lyotard (1990), who emphasizes the paradoxical silence associated with experiences of traumatic shock, arguing that such trauma is 'encrypted', or 'entombed', within the subject.

Far from being a mere absence, writes Lyotard, this crypt or tomb will come to influence the conscious life of the person, but only later:

> Something... *will make* itself understood, 'later'. That which will not have been introduced will have been 'acted', 'acted out', 'enacted' [in English in the original], played out, in the end – and thus re-presented. But without the subject recognizing it. It will be represented as something that has never been present... understood as feeling fear, anxiety, a threatening excess whose motive is obviously not in the present context. A feeling... which therefore necessarily points to an elsewhere.
>
> (Lyotard 1990: 13)

In these cases, the mask is associated with access to, or an irruption of, a hidden world. This world is experienced somatically, in embodied experience that stands outside language, by evoking embodied experiences of fear, anxiety and 'threatening excess' that are unintelligible within the present as time and place. Above all, these analyses suggest a link between masking and excess, a dimension that appears increasingly central to extremes of violence, from the Nazi death camps through to the massacres that have taken place in countries such as Colombia, Rwanda or Burundi.

We Can Destroy Your Souls

Certain dimensions of violence are imperative to recognize, both intellectually and ethically. Intellectually, because they highlight in extreme forms dimensions that may also be present in more prosaic cases. Ethically, because they underline the extent to which certain forms of violence seek to destroy the very humanity of the victim. This lay at the heart of the Nazi death camps created during the Second World War. As the political philosopher Hannah Arendt argued, the violence exercised in the camps set out to annihilate the humanness of its victims as rights-bearing judicial persons, as moral persons and as differentiated individuals, creating instead the 'living dead' (Arendt 1951/2009: 441–3). The camps did not serve any economic, strategic or military purpose; indeed they diverted much needed resources from the war effort. Far from being a form of instrumental violence, the camps manifest a form of violence that, as Etienne Balibar (2009) notes, sets out to demonstrate the total power of those who yield it, an objective that he argues extends to the wider paradigm of terrorist violence. The aim of such violence, he argues, drawing on the work of the philosopher Simone Weil, is to reduce whoever is subject to it to the status of a 'thing' or an object. The death camp, underlines Balibar, sets out to demonstrate the total impossibility of resistance, smashing in the process what philosophers from Hegel onwards have called the 'dialectic' of conflict, where conflict is a medium through which the self and the other are constituted. Balibar argues that the destruction of this relationship destroys the complementarity that exists between life and death, one that makes possible the chain of generations and the formation of communities. The destruction of all capacity to resist and the obliteration of any sign of assertion of the self involve a rupturing of the very idea of life, and with it the cyclical experience out of which emerges the possibility of memory and community. In its place, Balibar argues, drawing on the work of the Italian philosopher Giorgio Agamben (1998), we are left with 'naked life', where life is reduced to only a physical state, one where death becomes preferential to life.

This analysis helps us to understand another form of violence that is otherwise difficult to comprehend, namely the violence exercised upon victims in torture and interrogation, where seeking information plays so little a role (Huggins *et al.* 2002). The practices we encounter in the death camps alert us to the fact that rather than a means of seeking information, in torture and interrogation something quite different is happening, signalled by the philosopher Richard Rorty:

> the worst thing you can do to somebody is not to make her scream in agony but to use that agony in such a way that even when the agony is over, she cannot reconstitute herself. The idea is to get her to do or say things – and, if possible, believe and desire things, think thoughts – which later she will be unable to cope with having done or thought. You can thereby ... unmake her world, by making it impossible for her to use language to describe what she has been.
>
> (Rorty 1989: 178)

Camp survivor and philosopher Primo Levi points to the horror of such destruction in the practice of 'Sonderkommandos' (special squads) in the Nazi camps (Levi 1986/1989: 36ff). In these squads inmates were responsible for preparing and disposing of the bodies of the dead, before they in turn were killed. The Sonderkommandos not only had better living conditions, but they were allowed to take goods and food from those arriving at the camps and use it for themselves (Brown 2010). As Levi argues, this system was not primarily one of saving manpower and resources (the whole camp system constituting an irrational waste of such resources). The practice of involving victims in the process of preparation and disposal of those executed aimed at shifting the burden of guilt to the victims, in the process destroying any innocence that could be associated with the experience of victim. It was a message Levi describes in the following terms: 'We, the master people, we are your destructors, but you are no better than us: if we wish, and in fact we do wish, we are capable of destroying not only your bodies but also your souls, just as we have destroyed our own' (Levi 1986/1989: 37). The Nazi use of the Sonderkommandos was a means of making the victims complicit in their own destruction, and in the process to make it impossible for them to use language to describe what they have been.

Strange Bodies

Dimensions of these practices recur in other examples of extreme violence. The South American country of Colombia witnessed ongoing conflict and war for much of the twentieth century, a violence that has continued into the new millennium (Cabrera 2005; Waldmann 2007). We encounter something of what is at stake in this violence in accounts of witnesses to a massacre that took place in 1997, and recorded by the Colombian anthropologist María Victoria Uribe (Uribe 2004). In this massacre a group of men in camouflage arrive at a village and force all the villagers to assemble in the town square. Names are read out from a list that has been established with the help of a *sapo* (an informer, literally a *toad*), whose face is hidden by a ski-mask and who stands silently in the square, pointing out people who fail to step forward when their names are read out. The *sapo* who has supplied these names to the militia is an unknown member of the village, accusing those named of secretly supporting or collaborating with other militias, thus sealing their fate. The existence of *sapos* among them means that the villagers have to avoid not only any form of involvement supporting one militia or another, they must avoid expressing any opinion at all to a neighbour who may be, or may become, an informer for a militia. The path to survival becomes to see nothing, to hear nothing, to say nothing. The threat of death is no longer only present in combat zones in the mountains; it becomes a part of everyday interaction between neighbours.

This violence captures a key dimension of contemporary armed conflict: competing militias do not principally use their military strength to fight each other, nor to ensure the loyalty of the population in the territory they control. Rather, as observers of contemporary war underline (Kaldor 2001), such violence is increasingly directed at terrorizing a population. In this case, the violence directed at these populations aims at destroying not only the community, through its use of the *sapo*, it also denies any possibility that victims or survivors might understand the reasons for killings that take place. Refusing to offer a reason for killing appears increasingly to be integral to practices of massacre that seek to reduce the victim to the status of an animal. This is starkly illustrated in the massacre recounted by Uribe. Here masked militias enter a village, but their camouflage uniforms do not indicate which militia group they are from, or indeed if they are government forces. The villagers do not know who has entered the village, only that the village is encircled and they must gather at the town centre:

> One does not see them. The moment one hears that a group of paramilitaries is coming, or that the army is coming, or anyone, one doesn't wait to see. You don't really know whether they are coming to chat with you or kill you.
>
> (Uribe 2004: 94)

This uncertainty is amplified by the extent to which members of different militias (who may be linked to right-wing paramilitaries, the left-wing FARC or to drug cartels) may change their loyalties. A group of masked men may come to a village one year linked to FARC, but these same men may return the year after, having shifted their loyalties, arriving this time as a paramilitary group linked to a drug cartel. In the massacre described by Uribe, after the *sapo* has made his identifications, the people named are taken to the village slaughterhouse where pigs and other livestock are killed. They are kept there during the day, and in the evening the process of torturing and killing begins. Uribe quotes the account of a woman who was not on the list of people selected for killing, but who lives near where the killings took place:

> I live a block away from the municipal slaughterhouse, the official slaughterhouse of the town. And every night my sons and I would watch, I saw it, people passing with their hands tied behind their backs and their mouths gagged. When they gave the order to shut down the lights and turn off the power station, they would start to kill, torture them first, and then kill them. They shouted for help. But as you will understand, in this country the one who commands is the one with weapons or he who has the power to send the armed killers. So we were impotent, and all the good people of the town were impotent before these criminals. And we were at their mercy for five days, without anyone's help ... We locked ourselves in early in order to know nothing. One would look at them go by with people, but we would act as if we knew nothing.
>
> (Uribe 2004: 93)

Those on the list are interrogated, often posed questions that appear arbitrary, and, based on their responses, they are either killed or released. Uribe quotes a person who had been released in this way, and who while awaiting interrogation had asked one of the young executioners what he felt when confronted with victims pleading for their lives. The young militiaman had answered:

> No, nothing happens, it's like ... with hens ... An animal is a living being, it has life ... So when one kills them, when one is going to eat [comérselas] them, you will take their life away. So then, a human being is the same; it has life just like

an animal. So killing a human being, a person, is like killing a hen. So it's just like killing an animal.

(Uribe 2004: 94)

The practices of massacre in Colombia illustrate a further dimension of contemporary extreme violence, evident in the extent that this often involves manipulation of victims' corpses after death. There is a certain structure to these manipulations: often what belongs inside will be placed outside – the foetus of a pregnant woman will be cut out and placed on her midriff; a cut will be made under a man's chin, and the tongue pulled though it to be exhibited like a necktie. What belongs outside will be placed inside: the penis of a dead man will be cut off and placed in his mouth, testicles cut off and stuffed in the mouth, a rooster killed and placed where a foetus had been. At other times, the order of the body will be reversed, top to bottom: in the 'flower vase' the head, arms and legs will be cut off, the thorax emptied of its contents, and the limbs shoved in, protruding like the flowers from a vase (Uribe 1990: 175). In more recent massacres, the top part of the body of the victim is thrust head first into the ground, the torso and legs protruding as a flower. Thus manipulated, the bodies of the dead are left in public places, to be found by relatives or inhabitants if they return to the area. This violence, as Uribe (2004) notes, is often linked to expelling populations.

There is a very stark contrast between this violence and the violence Feldman explores in Northern Ireland. He describes a conversation he was part of with a group of IRA members, who had beaten up a person who had behaved badly towards a woman. The issue was whether a punishment of beating was enough, or whether he should be shot as well. In response to Feldman's question as to why a shooting was necessary, the answer was 'Because people forget' (2003: 60). In this case punishment involved the victim being snatched from a street or pub, being tortured as part of an interrogation, witnesses called, and then a punishment meted out. The type of wounding and the weapon used (ranging from small pistol to sawn-off shotgun) depended on the crime being punished. Other crimes, such as petty theft or forming a romantic liaison with a British soldier, would be punished by tarring and feathering in a public place. Such violence is intelligible to both those involved in meting it out as well as to the victims; it is structured by a logic of proportion, and can be seen as a form of brutal community regulation.

The violence meted out upon unarmed peasants in Colombia is radically different, and alerts us to a critical dimension of extreme violence. Such violence seeks to transform its victims into animals: their torturers constantly refer to their victims as different domestic animals, in particular birds; the terms used for the killing are those used for the preparation of animals – slaughter as opposed to kill, while different forms of killing and body mutilation are referred to in the language of domestic food preparation. Killing and torture often take place in the village slaughterhouse, while the exercise of taking villagers to the site of their execution has much in common with the ways animals are herded:

> Feminized and faunalized, victims are assimilated to the domestic sphere: they become susceptible to being penetrated, eaten and tamed. In this way they are dehumanized, and the slaughter, dismemberment, and vivisection of their bodies becomes a licit act.
>
> (Uribe 2004: 91)

The effect of such violence, insists Uribe, is to destroy the capacity of actors to create meaning: 'Identities, traditions, beliefs, and a sense of belonging disappear from view, leaving only the bodies of abominable strangers.' In such a situation, Uribe argues, social structures or the competition for power and resources cease to matter: 'In these contexts, it doesn't matter whether war is between true alterities or between equals, because the question of Otherness or selfness has lost most of its meaning' (2004: 95).

This type of dehumanization extends to the violence engaged in by regular armies. United States troops during the early years of the Iraq War posted pictures to an Internet site where digital images of mutilated Iraqis could be traded for access to pornographic images (Glasner 2005). In one such image, a smiling group of soldiers are gathered around an incinerated person, with the caption 'cooked Iraqi' (this picture remains widely available in the public domain). In another, a decapitated head is placed next to its body, while a soldier squats and rubs the tousled hair, smiling at the camera. Hundreds of such images were posted to the Internet. The British historian Joanna Bourke (2000) recounts a case from the Vietnam War that echoes the postmortem manipulations we encounter in Colombia, where American troops sat the body of a recently killed Vietnamese upright, placed a pair of wraparound sunglasses on the head, a lighted cigarette in the mouth, and a 'large and perfectly formed piece of shit' on the head. The officer recounting this story says that he should have been outraged to encounter such a manipulation, but he describes instead a feeling of pleasure:

> I pretended to be outraged, since desecrating bodies was frowned on as un-American and counterproductive. But it wasn't outrage I felt. I kept my officer's face on, but inside I was…laughing. I laughed – I believe now – in part because of some subconscious appreciation of this obscene linkage of sex and excrement and death; and in part because of the exultant realization that he – whoever he had been – was dead and I – special, unique me – was alive.
>
> (Bourke 2000: 3)

What is happening here is very different from accounts of 'administering violence' or being a 'purveyor of coercion'. We referred above to Hedges' reference to the 'seduction' of violence, where horror and excess combine:

> The seductiveness of violence, the fascination with the grotesque – the Bible calls it 'the lust of the eye' – the god-like empowerment over other human lives and the drug of war combine, like the ecstasy of erotic love, to let our senses command our bodies. Killing unleashes within us dark undercurrents that see us desecrate and whip ourselves into greater orgies of destruction. The dead, treated with respect in peacetime, are abused in wartime. *They become pieces of performance art.*
>
> (Hedges 2003: 89; emphasis added)

This transformation becomes evident in the ways that the bodies of the dead become souvenirs rather than the homes of lives that were lived by human beings. The historian John Dower's interviews with former troops in the Pacific during the Second World War describe the practice of harvesting body parts as souvenirs from killed Japanese troops (Downer 1987: 61), while Japanese skulls were used as ornaments to decorate military vehicles (1987: 64). Today we recoil in horror from such stories, but in 1944 *Life Magazine* published a photo as 'picture of the week' of an attractive woman posing with a Japanese skull sent to her by her fiancé serving in the Pacific (*Life Magazine*, 22 May 1944: 35). The skull had been autographed by her fiancé and 13 other friends. Dower observes that such practices of collecting body parts appeared to be limited to the bodies of Japanese soldiers, suggesting that this was unthinkable in the context of the European war against Germany or Italy: the humanity of dead Italians or Germans was recognized in ways that the humanity of dead Japanese, or 60 years later, that of the 'cooked Iraqi', was not.

Aphasic Violence

The French sociologist Daniel Pécaut (2000), also a Colombia specialist, underlines the destructuring effect of being subjected to extreme, yet unpredictable, violence. Villagers' day-to-day lives remain shaped by the boundaries of territory, by rivers and streams, fields to cultivate and trips to market. But in the context of such violence, the boundaries of territory become immaterial, defined less by geography and more by the potential of threat. And while village life remains structured by the rhythms of seasons and land, time is increasingly experienced as fragmented, where random events can irrupt, seeming so portentous and disconnected from any understandable human agency that they take on dimensions of myth (Pécaut 2000: 140). And at the level of personal subjectivity, while persons subjected to extreme, random and arbitrary violence maintain sufficient continuity of selfhood to speak in the first person and narrate experiences, their very subjectivity appears fragmented by multiple and contradictory frames of reference. The experience of the victims is one of an overloaded imagination: 'every situation is evaluated on the basis of "what might happen", every event seems, despite all appearances, "to have been foretold"' (Pécaut 2000: 148). Here Pécaut captures what may be central to the imaginary associated with violence, terror and the extreme: on the one hand an imaginary that is overloaded and full of 'representations', charged with foreboding that everything has been foretold, that everything has a significance; but on the other, a world experienced as a state of chaos, an entanglement of events, one that denies the possibility of what Pécaut calls 'unity of perception' (2000: 148). This leaves people living in social worlds where the experience of time is fractured, where the medium term has ceased to exist. Temporality is experienced as being torn between the short-term calculations needed to survive and a kind of vast temporality that shapes a world that actors seem powerless to influence: a time of myth (2000: 140). This fracturing of time evokes the experience Khosrokhavar (2005) describes in Palestine, where actors are no longer able to project themselves into the future, and where political temporality collapses into a fusion of the immediate and the finality of death.

Pécaut reports on a series of interviews he undertook with people involved in militia killings (2000: 145). What emerges in these accounts, of members of government-backed paramilitaries as well as of the FARC, is the absence of any reference to vision or goals that would justify such extreme violence. None of the actors speaks about their violence in terms of a vision of a transformed society. Instead the violence appears as *aphasic*, as marked by the inability to use language. In such aphasic violence, action appears to triumph over language, action is its own justification, requiring nothing more than itself, leading to a type of identity among the killers where existence is experienced only in the pursuit of action.

These massacres highlight more general processes associated with the experience of extreme violence. In Colombia, terror destroys the capacity to construct a unified perception and a discernible axis of conflict, in a way close to the violence of death camps that seek to destroy the capacity to create meaning and to produce a relationship with the other. Extreme violence, argues Pécaut:

> is experienced as an entanglement of events, or prosaic short-term calculations, as a parade of sufferings. Neither the protagonists not the victims have principles of identity, much less utopian commitment at stake in the midst of the terror.

This absence of the imaginary determines even the perception of politics, which is reduced to relations of force or to utilitarian transactions. The institutionalizing potential of the political has disappeared.

(Pécaut 2000: 148–9)

Pécaut's analysis points to a kind of oscillation, where actors find themselves dissociated from their world but also locked within patterns of hyper-charged meaning, a pattern explored by Michel Wievorka (2009) in terms of forms of subjectivity associated with violence. Wieviorka distinguishes between what he calls a 'floating subjectivity', where actors find themselves unable to experience themselves within social relations and conflicts, and what he calls a hyper-subject who experiences a world charged with portent and meaning (2009). In the cases explored by Pécaut we encounter a kind of oscillation, where involvement in extreme violence is experienced on the one hand as banal and without meaning, and on the other as inevitable. For both the victim and the perpetrator, extreme violence smashes the ability of the actor to hold together space, time and subjectivity: both are unable to construct narratives of self that are located in place and oriented towards the future.

Intimate Killing: Unmasking the Other

Pécaut's exploration of extreme violence points to a 'hypertrophic' imagi-nary that dilates out of control, one where hidden meanings are everywhere, where every object and event conceals something of greater significance than what is at first revealed, evoking and amplifying themes we encoun-tered when exploring conspiracy theory in Chapter 6. The theme of hidden meaning, present in conspiracy and so central to the forms of extreme vio-lence explored by Pécaut, alerts us to one of the most significant dynam-ics present in contemporary violence and terror, namely violence which removes the mask and exposes what is hidden. Such violence is increasingly associated with the body of the victim.

The anthropologist Arjun Appadurai (2006) points to this when he argues that contemporary violence manifests a surplus of rage and an excess of hatred, evident in the extent that such violence involves violation and deg-radation aiming at destroying both the 'body and being' of the victim (2006: 10): maiming, torturing, disembowelling women, hacking and amputating the limbs of children, sexualized humiliation of every type. What is par-ticularly significant, he argues, is that this rage and excess often takes place among former friends and neighbours, alerting us to a critical dimension of extreme violence: its *intimacy* (2006: 47).

This is evident in several ways. First, such violence involves violation and degradation of the body, in particular focusing on the sexuality of the person being killed. Second, such violence increasingly occurs between people who live shared lives. The paradigm case of such violence, insists Appadurai, is 'ethnocidal' (2006: 2). He suggests this occurs in contexts where newly generated large-scale identities, that have replaced older identities linked to village or clan, are themselves rendered uncertain by the flows of globalization. Violence, he argues, offers a response to such uncertainty. It targets those most perceived as threatening the purity of the community, those who represent a threat of contamination or danger:

> Islamic fundamentalism, Christian fundamentalism, and many other local and regional forms of cultural fundamentalism may be seen as a part of an emerging repertoire of efforts to produce previously unrequired levels of certainty about social identity, values, survival and dignity. Violence, especially extreme and spectacular violence, is a mode of producing such certainty.
>
> (Appadurai 2006: 7)

Paradoxically, argues Appadurai, such violence is not directed against large minorities, but against small minorities that do not represent any real threat to national unity. These small minorities, he argues, 'remind these majorities of the small gap which lies between their condition as majorities and the horizon of an unsullied national whole, a pure and untainted national ethnos' (2006: 8). Small minorities, argues Appadurai, are the source of a sense of *incompleteness* that in certain cases 'can drive majorities into paroxysms of violence' aimed at expunging the minority and achieving the purity of nation and ethos (2006: 8). In eradicating difference experienced as contamination, extreme violence under conditions of globalization aims at securing a state of completeness, 'a complex response to intolerable levels of uncertainty about group identities' (2006: 88). In such cases, the persons who embody the most significant threat to purity and homogeneity are not those who are most different and distant, but those who are are most close and most similar to the majority. It is fakes and counterfeits who represent the greatest threat, because they claim a share in identity while in reality they represent a threat of contamination.

Faisal Devji (2005) notes a similar pattern of violence in sectarian massacres in Pakistan. Typically involving massacres in mosques, those killed are not those who are most different from the members of the dominant group responsible for the massacres, such as the Ismali sect or Christian minorities. Instead the victims are members of the Shia' minority, those who are most similar to the dominant Sunni groups, and who have a long history of interaction, ranging from intermarriages to involvement in each others' public rituals. This pattern of violence also mirrors contemporary forms of racism, where racist violence is not directed at those who differ most from majority groups, but targets instead those who are most similar, people who live in the same suburbs, who are integrated and assimilated, who live the same lives (Wieviorka 1995: 78). In Nazi Germany, the Jewish population was largely assimilated and rightly considered themselves to be as German as anyone else. Nazi violence, with its labels, tests of nationality and creation of ghettos, was not a response to difference: it set about creating it, in the process seeking to deny the very humanity of its victims.

Liisa Malkki's (1995) study of massacres in the African country of Burundi, based on interviews among Hutu refugees in camps in Tanzania, equally underlines the extent to which killing aims at removing the mask of the other. In the spring of 1972, the Burundi army, under the control of the minority ethnic Tutsi population, began massacres of the majority ethnic Hutu population in response to what was regarded as a Hutu uprising. Some estimates suggest at least 100,000 people, or 3.5 per cent of the population, were killed within a period of a few weeks (Lemarchand and Martin 1974: 5). What is striking, apart from the horror, is the extent to which the killing aimed at destroying not simply physical persons but also symbolic systems of meaning. Malkki's respondents describe atrocities that echo the horror of violence in Colombia, in stories of mothers forced to kill and eat their babies, of a father forced to drown his daughter, or, in an account reminiscent of the Sonderkommandos, of men lined up and forced to kill the person standing next to them, after which they in turn would be killed by the next person in the line (Malkki 1995: 91).

This violence involves much more than killing – otherwise bullets would be chosen as the most efficient way to kill, above all in the case of violence organized by armed forces. This violence aims at destroying worlds. When the aim was not to kill a large group but a smaller number of individuals, women were killed by focusing on the sex of the body: penetration through the vagina, attacking the womb and above all the protective link between mother and child. The killing of men would often focus on the head and the brain, or forms of killing when the anus, linked to the status of unclean, is connected to the head (Malkki 1995: 90ff). And as we have seen in the case of informers in Colombian villages or the Sonderkommandos in the Nazi camps (who in both cases will eventually suffer the same fate as those they identify or dispose of), in these massacres the victims are denied the status of victim, but instead made to kill their own friends and families, or in the often recounted cases of pregnant women forced to eat part of their unborn children, they are forced to kill their future. These massacres are frequently associated with spaces of security, with victims forced into houses or churches that are then set alight. In these cases of extreme violence, the victims are stripped of what their executioners regard as the mask of humanity, as violence sets out to transform its victims into 'something less than human' (Malkki 1995: 93).

In the cases explored by Malkki, a constant concern of those committing the massacres is the difficulty in detecting who is really Hutu and who is really Tutsi. In this case, it is *the act of killing and mutilating that establishes for certain the ethnicity of the victim*, in a way similar to the violence explored by Feldman in Northern Ireland: 'the ethnicity of the body is built in its dismemberment and disfigurement. Violence constructs the ethnic body' (1991: 64). Through such violence, argues Malkki, 'bodies of individual persons become metamorphosed into specimens of the ethnic category for which they are supposed to stand' (1995: 88). This is particularly evident in the language used by the survivors, where both victims and their executioners are never named, but always described as Hutus and Tutsis, even in those cases where the survivor knows the names of those killed and those killing, many of whom grew up in the same villages, attending the same schools and churches, often intermarrying.

Extreme Violence

These are not simply isolated events or aberrations, but point instead to what amounts to a type of violence which, as the Italian sociologist Consuelo Corradi argues (2007), requires new theoretical categories. Normal violence can be understood as transgressing a norm, or integrating a community, or when cars are burnt in a riot, as making a claim. However, in this chapter we encounter something else. Extreme violence, as Corradi argues, does not transgress norms, it transgresses taboo, it crosses the boundary delineating what is human and what is not. Extreme violence, from this perspective 'does not belong in any way to the ordinary' (Corradi 2007: 96), something described above by one of Malkki's interviewees in Burundi who describes the violence witnessed there as 'against the laws of God' (2005: 91). The extraordinary practices associated with such killings and the importance attached to manipulations of bodies following death suggest that extreme violence is a medium connecting the actor with something that stands beyond and outside the humanity that he no longer experiences himself sharing with his victim, a victim unmasked by violence that destroys their self, their body and their world.

These dimensions underline what we can call the 'performativity' of violence. As we saw in Chapter 2, the term 'performative' originates in the work of the British philosopher of language John Austin, who explored what he called 'performative' utterances, forms of communication that do not simply describe the world, but change it, examples being the act of naming a ship or stating 'I do' in a wedding ceremony: these phrases bring about a new state of affairs, they are acts of transformation (Austin 1976: 40). The violence we have explored in this chapter is performative in a similar way. It does not simply aim at producing a change in behaviour of another person, nor is it a simple medium to communicate a claim. The violence we encounter in this chapter sets about making and unmaking worlds. The complexity and the tensions present in such radical violence may offer us insight into one of the most disturbing forms of violence and that appears increasingly associated with globalization: the violence of the martyr.

8

The Martyr

Suicide/Martyr

The years following the attacks of 11 September 2001 have seen a significant increase in suicide or martyrdom violence. A comprehensive data set compiled by Assaf Moghadam (2009) identifies 1,857 suicide attacks from December 1981 through to March 2008. While the number is relatively low in the 1980s and during the first half of the 1990s (averaging around seven per year internationally), it increases to some 530 different attacks in 2007 (2009: 48), a pattern Moghadam describes as constituting a 'global rise' of suicide attacks. Half of these attacks took place in Iraq following the US-led invasion of 2003. However, it would be wrong to regard this development as uniquely linked to Iraq: while concentrated in Iraq, Afghanistan, Israel and the Occupied Territories, Sri Lanka and Lebanon, suicide attacks have occurred in over 30 countries (Moghadam 2009: 50). One of the key characteristics associated with this violence is the high level of deaths and injuries caused. Moghadam's data set points to some 20,600 people killed and at least 48,000 injured in these attacks. There is clear evidence that the death rate involved in suicide attacks is significantly higher than in other forms of attack (Brym and Araj 2006). The intent is clear: suicide attacks aim at more than inflicting damage; they aim at bringing death.

The challenge is to understand the significance of this violence. Popular accounts often refer to 'fanatics' or 'lunatics' (for an overview, see Reuter 2003), but the obvious question is why killing oneself was not part of earlier periods of terrorist violence. The frequent answer to this question is to attach the term 'religious' to the term 'fanatic', as if religious ideals in some way explain the recourse to suicide. Not infrequently, popular suggestions propose that it's the promise of limitless sex in paradise that motivates such killings. Christopher Reuter's (2003) analysis of the profile of the 11 September attackers highlights the inadequacy of such accounts. He notes that the leader of the attack insisted in his last testament that no women should be at his funeral, and any woman involved in preparing his body for burial should wear gloves, lest she inadvertently touch him, while others involved in the 11 September attacks watched pornography on pay-per-view television while staying in a motel (Reuter 2003: 8). This suggests that attitudes to and experiences of sex among suicide bombers may well reflect the diversity we encounter across the population as a whole, a conclusion supported by psychiatrist Marc Sageman's analysis of the profiles of 172 identifiable individuals involved in al-Qaeda networks, demonstrating marriage rates corresponding to their population, characteristics of age, nationality and education (Sageman 2004). Recurring images of sexually frustrated religious fanatics may be more explainable in terms of popular forms of racism combined with a Western history associating religious devotion with sexual renunciation, rather than with any real attempt to understand what is at stake in such violence. Another cluster of analyses, this time more associated with academic discourse than the popular media, highlights the rationality of suicide attacks, framing these in terms of the cost–benefit calculations of organizations (Stern 2007).

The categories of analysis used across these debates diverge. The term 'suicide' tends to be associated with the idea of fanatics and extremists, or paradoxically, with an emphasis on 'strategic logic'. It is often used in opposition to the term 'martyr', a term seen to imply legitimacy to the cause being died for, or to accord religious significance to the death. As is often the case, the choice of descriptor implies an analytical framework conferring meaning on the term used. In this case, the choice of term can also imply a location on a spectrum of attitudes towards this violence. The option taken in this chapter is to explore this violence using the term 'martyr'. This is not, as we will see, to attach any religious significance to this form of killing. Instead it takes as its beginning point a dimension captured in the very term itself. The origins of the word 'martyr' lie in the Greek word *martyros*, or 'witness', the term originally referring to a person giving witness in a legal dispute. The death of the martyr is not a simple suicide, an act of killing the self, nor even killing the self as a *means* to kill another; it is a form of witness, an act of communication that constitutes a public event and a public experience (for an overview of martyrdom as witness in early modern culture, see Brietz Monta 2005). This public and communicative dimension will emerge as crucial to understanding contemporary forms of martyrdom, and as we will see in the next chapter, to its emergence as a global form of violence.

Social and Cultural Contexts

The emergence of suicidal violence is closely associated with particular social and cultural contexts. In Chapter 5 we saw suicide attacks emerge in the second Intifada. Our analysis of this development highlighted a shift from violence linked to civil organizations to more personalized violence, much more focused on death, which came to characterize the second Intifada. This shift seemed linked with the closure of other possibilities as the uprising faced defeat. But defeat itself does not explain suicidal violence. Many groups and struggles have been crushed by more powerful military forces and not given rise to this form of violence.

Other conflicts have witnessed the development of suicide attacks. The most well known is the case of the *tokkōtai*, known outside Japan as 'kamikazi', widely regarded as fanatical pilots determined to destroy themselves and their planes in attacks on Allied forces during the dying days of Imperial Japan. Anthropologist Emiko Ohnuki-Tierney's analysis of the diaries of the *tokkōtai* does not reveal a group of hateful, death-obsessed people determined to die to uphold the honour of the emperor, but very often sensitive students, who to a significant extent are immersed in a culture of Western romanticism, principally moved by cultural forms of nationalism, in particular those symbolized by the fragile and ephemeral beauty of the cherry blossom, which came to serve as a symbol of the *tokkōtai*, painted on their planes and waved by well-wishers as the planes took off (Ohnuki-Tierney 2004). These diaries highlight personal introspection and anguish, not a search for honour at any cost. Significantly, as Ohnuki-Tierney observes, not a single officer from Japan's military academies volunteered for these missions, which they recognized were meaningless in terms of the Japanese war effort (2004: 15). Equally, Ohnuki-Tierney highlights the extent of coercion involved in these missions, where 'volunteers' had little choice but to carry out what was demanded of them.

Such cases suggest the recent growth of suicidal violence demands of us more than a recourse to national stereotypes. It also demands that we understand the ways violence and its meanings can cross borders and shift between conflicts. The first suicide attacks that later became a model for subsequent ones, involving a video testament before death, did not occur in the Intifadas, but in Lebanon. And these attacks were not undertaken with any reference to religion, but by members of secular leftist political parties. While framed within a discourse of secular nationalism, the structure of this martyr violence, as the sociologist Farhad Khosrokhavar (2005) argues, demonstrates a great debt to the *Basiij* brigades that emerged in the Iran–Iraq war. Indeed, he argues that a qualitatively new form of suicidal violence emerged in that war, shaping the violence that would emerge in Lebanon and later in Palestine. To understand contemporary martyrdom violence demands some understanding of these mutations. They point to new forms of visibility and witness associated with death, as well as to wider forms of violence against the self, from self-immolation to self-starvation. But before exploring these, we need to understand the ways dominant paradigms of violence have approached the question of the martyr.

New Fanatics

Influential authors promoting the 'new terrorism' thesis, such as Walter Laqueur (1999), emphasize what they see as the pathology of contemporary terrorists, considered as people attracted to sects and cults and likely to engage in extreme forms of violence and fanaticism. For Laqueur, the intensity of such violence indicates that social and political explanations are inadequate, with the violence pointing to 'issues of personality and personality disorders' (1999: 94). Discussing the Aum Supreme Truth we explored in Chapter 6, Laqueur affirms 'the murkier the political purpose of terrorism, the greater its appeal to mentally unbalanced persons' (1999: 40). For Laqueur, 'Marx, Muhammad and Armageddon' all become sources of what he calls the 'new fanaticism' (1999: 79). For Laqueur there is an evident parallel between groups such as the Heaven's Gate suicide cult (where members killed themselves in California in 1997 believing that they would be met by a spaceship and taken to heaven) and suicide attacks in Lebanon or Palestine. All these groups manifest a similar, basic characteristic:

> rational calculations do not apply. Sheiks acting as gurus for extreme Muslim or Arab groups, and who declare that they love death and welcome it with the joy of a bride at the arrival of a bridegroom, will not be deterred, nor will sectarians convinced that a saving remnant will remain. The fallen will be taken to heaven in a *markabah*, or by special messengers sent by Allah, or in a spaceship. A few deranged individuals can be found in many religions, and while they may in the past have engaged in group suicide, they could, if they had access to weapons of mass destruction, prefer a deed aimed at others.
>
> (Laqueur 1999: 264)

It is this toxic combination of cult-like groups, deranged individuals and the availability of increasingly powerful weapons that, Laqueur argues, forms the destructive potential of the 'new fanaticism', a phenomenon that he sees as being shared by members of the Aum sect, Californian suicide cults, and by suicide bombers in Palestine and Lebanon.

Rational Actors

Given the pervasive impact of such analyses, proponents of the rational actor thesis are attempting to humanize the terrorist by emphasizing the rationality of his or her action – the terrorist is not a fanatic, they argue, but someone like you and me. Terrorism from this perspective involves rational action, namely action directed towards a goal and based on an analysis of costs and benefits. Some of the most ambitious attempts to develop such analyses have been undertaken by political scientists: for example, Robert Pape (2005) and Mia Bloom (2007).

Pape (2005: 10) distinguishes two kinds of terrorist violence: *demonstrative terrorism*, which seeks publicity for a cause; and *destructive terrorism*, which seeks to coerce opponents through inflicting real harm on a target audience. Suicide terrorism, he argues, is the most deadly form of destructive terrorism, a contention supported by Moghadam's (2009) data discussed above. Pape argues that when we examine suicide actions, we encounter a specific type of conflict and a specific logic of action. He contends that such actions are not the product of religious fanaticism, as the 'new terrorism' thesis suggests, but instead reflect an older motivation: nationalism. Every suicide campaign over recent decades, he argues, has at its core a struggle for national independence, its central objective being to coerce what is regarded as a foreign government to remove occupying military forces, whether in Sri Lanka, Palestine or Kurdistan. What is more, he argues that such attacks are rational, given that in each case suicide campaigns are undertaken against democratically elected governments, who will eventually experience electoral consequences if sufficient pain is applied to their populations. For Pape, a suicide campaign is an attempt by an organization to make an occupying population suffer to the point that they will eventually withdraw. Such 'coercive violence', he argues, mirrors states' calculations when deciding to commit air power to a military conflict. This contention is reflected in the titles of Pape's key books, *Bombing to Win* (1996) (where he examines states' use of air power in modern warfare) and *Dying to Win* (2005) (where he analyses the development of suicide violence). For Pape, both the air power of states and the suicide violence of organizations manifest the same dynamic:

> By threatening to harm civilians, the coercer seeks to raise the costs of continued resistance above the target state's value for the territory at stake. If the threat is

sufficiently great, the target state will abandon the territory to preserve its greater interest in protecting the populace.

(Pape 1995: 17)

In this analysis, 'coercion is the paramount objective of suicide terror', with both suicide terror and aerial bombardment being examples of 'coercive instruments that can be understood with a theory of the rationality of coercion and responses to it' (Pape 2003: 345).

Mia Bloom (2007) also adopts a rational actor model, but rather than look to the rationality of coercion and responses to it, she locates suicide bombing within a theory of organizational competition. Bloom's departure point is the premise that political organizations are in competition with each other to gain power, resources and supporters, hence the logic driving organizations to suicide actions is best understood in terms of 'political dynamics and organizational motivations for outbidding' (2007: 84). A key dimension of Bloom's analysis lies in a distinction between the individuals involved in suicide actions and the organizations that are the source of that action. The individuals, she suggests, tend to be young, impressionable and 'easily manipulated' (2007: 86), and may often have a personal grievance such as the loss of a family member, being 'individuals who perceive that their lives have little significance otherwise' (Bloom 2007: 88). While terrorist organizations may seek to project an image of themselves as fanatics who count no costs, this she contends is part of their strategy of presentation. The reality is that suicide actions are a strategy used to break a stalemate and to increase what she terms the 'market share' (2007: 19) of the organization concerned. In the case of Palestinian groups, she contends, 'multiple organizations are engaged in competition and use violence to increase their prestige' (2007: 19). In the case of suicide bombing, 'the organizations that use this tactic reap multiple benefits on various levels without incurring significant costs' (2007: 76), each operation involving only the sacrifice of one person, after which many more will offer themselves as a result of the one who dies.

The key to this dynamic is organizational competition: 'all of the bombers are first and foremost members of organizations that train them, select their targets, buy their explosives, issue orders for when to launch an attack and try to convince the larger population that their cause is just' (2007: 85). A rational actor model, she argues, can also explain the decision of individuals to become suicide bombers: 'the individuals who perpetrate suicide attacks have social, cultural, religious, and material incentives. These include spiritual rewards in the afterlife, the guarantee of a place with God for the attackers' families, celebrity, and even cash bonuses' (2007: 85). For Bloom the key to understanding suicide actions lies in organizational competition in a context where other forms of violent action have failed to produce results.

Beyond Individuals versus Organizations

These are important analyses, and without doubt highlight the role of organizations as supporters of martyrdom violence. But attaching primary importance to organizational calculations tends to mean that the person who dies and kills takes on secondary importance. Bloom's description of such people as 'easily manipulated' (2007: 86) or 'individuals who perceive that their lives have little significance otherwise' (2007: 88) accords little agency to the candidate for a suicide mission: according to her, they are acted upon rather than actors.

In the case of Palestinian bombers, there is relatively clear data available that contests this 'easily manipulated' image. Most have a level of education higher than the average of the population (Yom and Saleh 2004), a pattern also replicated by the data compiled on 461 individual suicide bombers by Robert Pape (2005: 211). Once we begin to explore more closely the personal histories of these bombers, it becomes clear that, in a majority of cases, it is the person seeking to become a bomber who approaches an organization to ask for assistance with a 'martyrdom mission'; the initiative originates with the potential bomber rather than the organization itself. Nicole Argo's study (cited in Hafez 2006) of 15 failed Palestinian bombers (thus available for interview) indicates that the majority had no experience with violent organizations or even violent conflict with Israeli forces. Half volunteered for their mission, while the others were recruited by family members or friends. Once deciding on their mission, 20 per cent had begun within a week, and 80 per cent within a month. The conviction necessary to become a suicide bomber, argues Argo, is not the result of organizational priming. Indeed, several in Argo's sample changed organizations once it became clear that another organization could better facilitate their action.

This, however, is not at all to deny the importance of organization. If we turn to the United Kingdom, there is ongoing debate about the extent that those involved in the London bombings of 2005 may have had connections with al-Qaeda networks (House of Commons 2006), but there is relatively clear data regarding overall patterns of jihadi-related violence in the United Kingdom, where between 2001 and 2009 over 200 people were imprisoned for planning or attempting to undertake terrorist-related violence. An analysis of some 120 people convicted for jihadi-related offences in the period indicates that 68 per cent had no identifiable links with terrorist-related organizations, 14.5 per cent had a connection with al-Qaeda networks (Simcox *et al.* 2010: ix), although the proportion of persons connected with these networks increased to 30 per cent in cases where the attempted action involved higher levels of co-ordination and planning, evident in eight major plots that took place during this period, such as an attempt to produce a bomb to blow up a shopping centre or an attempt to detonate a device on transatlantic flights (Simcox *et al.* 2010: ix).

In these major plots, the data highlights connections that extend beyond the framework of the nation state, either in the form of organizational contacts or travel that may involve contact with 'training camps'. But in the majority of cases of people convicted of terrorism-related offences, these contacts do not exist, and where they do, while they certainly play a role in *facilitating* access to knowledge and techniques of violence, it is not evident that they help us understand the *origins* of the path into violence. The relatively clear evidence available indicates that the al-Qaeda network did not have a 'recruitment' strategy, much less 'operatives' (Devji 2005). Rather than al-Qaeda or similar organizations being involved in the active 'recruitment' of potential members, the pattern appears to be the opposite, with individuals seeking to establish contact with such groups (see, for example, the court statement by the person who pleaded guilty to the attempt to bomb Times Square in May 2010, who describes deciding to leave the United States and 'figure out a way to get to the Taliban' (United States District Court, Southern District of New York 2010: 21). And in the United States or the United Kingdom, there is no evidence that organizational competition can meaningfully be considered as the source of the search for extreme violence.

Studies of the Palestinian experience itself caution against regarding organizational competition as the source of suicide bombing. Brym and Araj (2008) point to significant inter-organizational *co-operation* in support of suicide bombers, while Pedahzur and Perliger (2006) conclude that suicide attacks are sustained principally by networks of co-operation rather than by organizational competition. This suggests that too excessive an emphasis on organizational competition as the driver of suicide action may highlight the limits of using North American and European models of competitive democracy to understand dynamics of action in very different situations. Again analysing Palestinian data, Hafez argues those presenting for suicide operations are best understood as volunteers, 'not brainwashed victims of opportunistic organizations, nor were they manipulated victims that were fooled by calculating terrorists' (2006: 50). Taking this into account shifts our focus from organizational strategies to the social and cultural processes and embodied experience at stake in the act of volunteering for death. And this takes us back to the emergence of the martyr brigades, the *Basiij*, in the Iran–Iraq war.

Death Becomes the Goal: The Democratization of Martyrdom

On 11 February 1979, Ayatollah Rubollah Khomeini returned to Iran and assumed power after months of bloody protests by a broad coalition of groups opposed to the Shah's regime (Bayat 1998). But within a year the new Islamic Republic found itself engaged in a bloody conflict with Iraq that would last from 1980 to 1988, a conflict threatening the existence of the regime itself (Bayat 1998). It was in this period of dire peril and mass mobilization of military forces that a new brigade was formed, the *Basiij* (Mobilization) Brigade, to be made up of young volunteers who would walk through minefields to clear the way for Iranian fighters to engage with Iraqi troops (Brown 1990). The Brigade's founding myth lies in the story of a young boy who decided to use his body as a last line of defence early in 1980, tying several grenades to his belt and throwing himself under an advancing Iraqi tank (Gruber 2012). His story was taken up by the state, with a massive mural constructed in Tehran, Iran's capital (Gruber 2008). Like the *tokkōtai*, this Brigade was not primarily of strategic importance. But it would become central to the state's efforts to constitute and mobilize an Islamic population. Mystical themes of self-loss and self-annihilation in love (Abrahamian 1992; Rahnema 2000) were increasingly mobilized by the revolutionary state in a new discourse celebrating martyrdom as the union of citizen and nation, lover and beloved, servant of God and God (Varzi 2006: 47).

Farhad Khosrokhavar's (2005) interviews with Brigade members show these candidates for martyrdom experienced the revolution as not only threatened by Iraq, but also betrayed and threatened by Iranians themselves who had failed to live up to its possibilities. This sense of betrayal was not only attached to others. While many young men joined the *Basiij* for the social advancement it offered (such as a guaranteed place at university), many demonstrated what Khosrokhavar calls a morbid religiosity (2005: 90), very different from the revolutionary period where religion was linked with utopian images of the future Islamic society. The collapse of utopia and an increasing realization that the hoped-for Islamic society was impossible involved a sense of being a 'foreigner in the world' (2005: 90) experienced as a state of increasing distress. *Basiij* culture, argues Khosrokhavar, was increasingly shaped by guilt and sin, and this came to define the relationship with the body itself:

> The body of the Iranian martyropath was affected by a deep feeling of sinfulness...If the body was to be purified, it must rid itself of its blood. Similarly, the subject had to part from his body if he was to redeem his sins.
>
> (Khosrokhavar 2005: 100)

Death was not simply a way to kill the other, but also to purify the self. Khosrokhavar argues this martyrdom is very different from classical martyrdom in Shi'a history. In Shi'a religious tradition the martyr is a person who fights for their faith and is prepared to lay down their life. Death is a consequence of action, not the goal. In the case of the *Basiij*, death became the goal. In traditional religiosity, the martyr is a special person chosen by God. But in this period, martyrdom becomes a form of self-realization that anyone can potentially achieve – rather than an extraordinary event, martyrdom had become 'democratised' (Khosrokhavar 2005: 90).

Living with the Dead: The Macabre

The cultural transformations at work during the Iran–Iraq war highlight what Hans Joas (2003) calls the 'dynamics of violence'. One of the most striking developments associated with this period was the emergence of an aesthetic that became increasingly evident in art, posters, museums and television – an aesthetic of the macabre, manifest in an extraordinary focus on images of dead bodies and horrible mutilations. War culture itself appeared focused on death, in stark contrast to the earlier decade shaped in the period leading up to the revolution, with its hope of social transformation and new beginnings (Bayat 1998). Faced with this material, the first reaction of an observer is incomprehension. What sense can we make of what seems a society-wide obsession with death? One view is put forward by Osama bin Laden, who states: 'Being killed for God's cause is a great honour only achieved by those who are the elite of the nation. We love this kind of death for God's cause as much as you like to live' (Lawrence 2005: 56).

This affirmation was repeated by one of the 2005 London bombers, who asserts in his final video testament 'We love death the way you love life' (Middle East Media Research Institute 2006). From this perspective, Islam is represented as a religion that is focused on death, while Western culture is centred on life, enjoyment and pleasure.

Putting aside such claims, there is none the less clear evidence of a culture of the macabre emerging in Iran during its war with Iraq (Butel 2002). But this is not historically unique, nor in any way limited to Muslim majority societies. Such a broad engagement with death also characterizes different periods of Western culture, in particular the late medieval period (Sekules 2001: 106ff). Here we also encounter a culture of the macabre, one that involved images of the dead, the emergence of funeral art and decorated tombs, new rituals of burial, as well as an extensive didactic literature on *Ars Moriendi*, the 'art of dying'. The American art historian Paul Binski (1996) suggests a link between the rise of this culture of the macabre and the birth of a new modern subjectivity. He argues that the practices of can-onization of saints that developed during this period meant that the living were able to shape the world of the dead, while new practices of prayer for the dead allowed the living to 'colonize paradise ahead of time'. The new forms of tombs were not primarily symbolic, as we understand them now, but were instrumental – the prominent display of a grave meant that the person buried there could continue to watch over the community, affirming dynastic and territorial continuity. The *Ars Moriendi*, detailing works of art depicting the experience of death (see Reinis 2007), offered the possibility of thinking about and controlling one's own death, while the culture of relics with its veneration of body parts and blood represented a 'pilgrimage of the mind' (1996: 125). Brian Repsher (1999) argues that this new cultural focus on death involved an emerging form of spiritualism focused on the person and his/her action, reflecting a psychology of anxiety integral to a new cul-ture of self-construction and self-examination (1999: 201).

Somewhat unexpectedly, these historical analyses link the emergence of a death culture with a new sense of individuality, and suggest possible ways of thinking about the rise of the macabre in post-Revolutionary Iran. For Binski the key to understanding the macabre is the opposition between *intactness* and *decay*, an opposition highlighting a new cultural awareness of instability and contingency. The French sociologist Eric Butel (2002) takes up this analysis, and uses it to explore the extraordinary production of images of death during the Iran–Iraq war. He argues that this development is not an expression of a Shi'a tradition of veneration for the dead, but is better understood as pointing to a new concern about the *corruption* of the body that itself points to a deeper social transformation:

> the body carries within itself the *mal de vivre* of the new individual...not as a regression, but as one of the necessary and unavoidable phases in the progressive conquest of freedom...the explosion of the macabre in Iran is not a question of a conjunctural antimodernization...Rather it involves a fundamental and painful rupture with traditional society.
>
> (Butel 2002: 313)

Butel is arguing that an experience of social and political corruption is expe-rienced in terms of bodily corruption, highlighting a tension between intact-ness and decay. This is equally central to Khosrokhavar's (2005) analysis of the emergence of martyrdom violence in this period. He argues that the martyr is a person who is no longer located within and shaped by a com-munity, but is better understood as a person shaped by a strong longing for individuation yet at the same time by a powerful experience of this desire being blocked (2005: 49). The future martyr longs to assert him/herself as an individual, as a person possessing dignity and capable of realizing his/her ambitions. But at the same time this person no longer believes that s/he will ever be able to realize these ambitions, their hope for a future has collapsed. This, argues Khosrokhavar, leads to a very real form of suffering that can only be overcome through the *desire for life becoming transformed into a desire for death*. As a result, he reverses the understanding of the relationship between martyr and organization proposed by Mia Bloom: for Khosrokhavar it is the future martyr who needs, and uses, an organization like the *Basiij* or Hamas in order to make the transition successfully from life to death (2005: 50). This pattern has also emerged in other contexts, with Philip Bobbitt pointing to studies of Pakistan, where there too, candidates for death care little about what organization they join (2008: 52).

Pictures of the Dead: Constituting Subjects in Public

The *Basiij* deaths suggest a new type of martyr. In the classical meaning of the word, loss of life is accepted, but is not the goal; in religious terms, the loss of life is decided by God. During the Iran–Iraq war, a radically new type of martyr emerged for whom death becomes the point of self-realization (Khosrokhavar 2005). The self-image of the *Basiij*, in particular of those who actively sought death, was one of guilt and impurity, of lost hope in a revolution betrayed by a corrupt society (Khosrokhavar 2005). The *Basiij* fighter experienced himself as a foreigner in a contaminated world, and, according to Khosrokhavar, has a self or ego that can only be realized in death. The world is so impure that both self and other are guilty, and only the death of a martyr can purify this. But the martyr does not die alone. Death serves two purposes: it purifies the martyr and it punishes evil. The martyr does not die alone, but takes the world with him or her. In the process, the martyr becomes a 'somebody' (Khosrokhavar 2009: 45).

Roxanne Varzi's (2006) exploration of youth and martyrdom in post-revolutionary Iran underlines the crucial role played by the state media in this development. She explores the way the revolutionary state set about constructing mystical violence. In the immediate period following the revolution, the only face allowed within public spaces was that of Khomeini, in a cult of the personality where the difference between him and the hidden Imam, a religious saviour figure important in popular Shi'a religiosity (see Amir-Moezzi 2011: 133ff), became increasingly blurred. The state mobilization of the population for the war involved a massive media presence of new images, namely the faces of the young who died. These were posted on walls, painted on buildings, printed on banknotes (Varzi 2006). Television played a key role in this new culture of martyrdom. Each day film from the warfront was driven 12 hours to Tehran to be broadcast as *Revayat-e Fath* (Witness to Glory) on state television (Varzi 2006). This broadcast did not focus on strategy and battles, but on individual fighters preparing to die. The aim was not to film a war, but to film faith (Varzi 2006: 79). One of the main producer/directors of these films describes the types of images he was seeking in the language of contemporary television, with its primacy of personal experience:

> If we were to merely show a large number of people sacrificing themselves, emphasising numbers rather than the uniqueness of the individual, it would decrease the value of martyrdom, so we show individuals.
>
> (Varzi 2006: 93)

In a post-revolutionary period images of martyrs flooded cities and grave-yards. These were not abstract images of martyrs in general, but specific images of particular persons who had died. It was as if through dying it was possible to achieve public visibility as an individual person in the new public space. A poster from the period, produced by the Ministry of Islamic Guidance, has photographic images of two men who have died at the front, the text beside them reading 'I am choosing death in order to build life' (Varzi 2006: 82). One of the film-makers describes what was at stake:

> The front was the place to experience life, because death is life's biggest experi-ence. Khomeini told us the spirit of Islam is in this war. The war front was the best place to practice faith. It takes sometimes seventy years on the mystical path to come close to transcendence. The front is an expressway to heaven.
>
> (Interview cited in Varzi 2006: 84)

These themes are not an expression of traditional culture. War as an 'expressway to heaven', with its emphasis on speed, arrival and results, is part of modern culture, not a traditional mystical experience. But this debt to modern culture extends well beyond the war films produced during this period. Varzi cites one of the most extraordinary, a description of martyr-dom offered by the Ministry of Islamic Guidance in Shiraz, which attempts to explain martyrdom through referring to the American comedy movie *Men in Black*: 'Remember the last scene, how they move away from Earth and become very, very small, well, that's what it's all about' (cited in Varzi 2006: 84).

The importance of the *Basiij* martyr brigades does not lie in their strategic significance, but in their place within the reconstruction of Iranian society and culture. Again, what is critical is not mass deaths, but individual experiences of faith leading to death. To capture this, as Varzi argues, an image is essential. The experience of faith leading to death is above all an individual experience, hence the critical importance of *a visual record where the individual is represented*. In such cases, the photographic image of the martyr does not simply tell a story, it is *constitutive* of the act of martyrdom as witness. *Without the image there is no martyr*: 'martyrdom is meaningless without memorialization, and memorialization is not possible without a photograph' (Varzi 2006: 62). In Iran's war cemeteries a photographic image on the headstone marks the grave of every martyr, while on its reverse is the image of Khomeini.

A 'theatre of death' (Varzi 2006: 63) was created that would outlast the war. It would become the very centre of the revolutionary state's reconstruction of society. Varzi summarizes this new mode of constituting subjects: 'the space of death needs two things in war-era Iran: a martyr and a photograph' (2006: 62). The Iranian case underlines the importance not only of images in the construction of public space, but in constituting modes of experience. *The image makes possible the individuation central to death as self-realization.*

The Martyr's Video

The first *Basiij* martyrdom actions were undertaken in 1980. This mode of violence spilled into Lebanon, with suicide attacks including truck bombs being used against the American embassy (Pape 2003) and military barracks housing US marines and French troops, killing over 300 (Kushner 2003: 386). In April 1985, a 16-year-old girl, a member of the secular Syrian Social Nationalist Party (a party wanting to create a Greater Syria made up of Lebanon, Palestine, Jordan and Syria), blew herself up in an attack in South Lebanon (Ricolfi 2006: 87), while later that year, a member of the Lebanese Communist Party undertook a similar attack (Mickolus 2009: 502).

These events introduce another significant transformation to the practice of martyrdom. A young woman who undertook an early attack worked in a video store in Beirut, and was the first person to put together a final testament on video about her martyrdom. She addresses the camera, dressed in the red beret and military-green fatigues that is the SSNP uniform. She captures many of the themes that would occur in later martyr testaments:

I am the martyr...I am 17; I am from the South. Southern Lebanon. The occupied, oppressed South, the South of resistance and revolution...I am from the South of the martyrs, the South of Sheikh Raghab Harb [founder of Hezbollah, assassinated in 1985]...the South of the hero Wajdi al-Sayegh...May your joy burst forth on the day I die, as though it was my wedding day...I hope that my soul will join those of the other martyrs and will rebound like thunder on the heads of the enemy soldiers...I am not dead; I am still living amongst you; I am singing, dancing and fulfilling all my ambitions, I am filled with joy at being the embodiment of heroism and martyrdom...do not weep for me...be happy and laugh, because there are still living people to give you hope for liberation...I am putting down roots in the land of the South, and making it stronger with my blood and my love. I am going towards death so as not to have to wait for it...My last wish is that you call me 'the bride of the South'.

(Quoted in Khosrokhavar 2005: 148)

We can see here that a sacred death is not necessarily the same as a religious death. Khosrokhavar points to key themes in this video: the transformation of sadness to joy, the struggle against the oppressor, the identification of the martyr's death with marriage and the call to celebrate this new and lasting union. Blood and death are central as well: the blood of the martyr will make the land fertile, giving it new life, transfusing life into a community facing potential 'moral and physical destruction' (Gruber 2012: 81). In the words of the Iranian revolutionary thinker Ayatollah Mutahhari, martyrdom is a 'tranfusion of blood into society, especially into a society suffering from anemia' (Gruber 2012: 81). For Khosrokhavar, such shedding of blood is 'thaumaturgical', a form of magic: when blood spurts from the body and feeds the soil, it gives new life not simply to the land but also to those fighting the forces of evil. Through death the martyr can achieve immortality, physically becoming part of the land and the struggling people. This same theme emerges several months later in the video of a young member of the Lebanese Communist Party referred to above: 'Now, I am departing my country, in body only; I will still exist in the souls of all the honest patriots in Lebanon' (Khoury and Mroué 2006: 189). This young woman and young man were both members of leftist and nationalist political parties. Both refer to themes that would become prominent in later martyr testaments, in particular the images of a wedding feast, the martyr as bride or groom, blood making the soil fertile, living forever in the hearts and souls of the people. Neither makes any reference to religion.

Ross Birrell (2005) argues such deaths draw on a culture where gift exchange plays an important role. He points to the importance of 'potlatch', a type of giving explored by the anthropologists such as Marcel Mauss and Georges Bataille, where giving takes place within a system of honour, and where the giver will give so extravagantly as to cause his own destruction, but in the process secure his honour: through, for example, holding a wedding feast that will ruin his family financially (see Mauss 1950/1990: 3). Within the culture of gift exchange, those invited to accept such gifts are obliged to repay in kind, or be dishonoured. The young woman who made the first martyrdom video calls on all Lebanese people to join in her wedding celebrations. In the case of a wedding, the honour gained by the extravagance of the celebration does not belong to the bride or groom, but to the parents who host the event. A similar theme is evoked in the video of the young man who addresses his parents at the end of his testament:

> As for you, the dearest and finest mother and father in existence, my beloved brothers and sisters: my wish for you is not to mourn and wail, but rejoice and dance as you would do at my wedding, for I am the proud groom of martyrdom, and that is the happiest wedding I could hope for.
>
> (Khoury and Mroué 2006: 189)

This would become a recurring theme in such videos, the recurring image of the martyr's death bringing about a new world, a community of celebration in just the same way as a marriage.

Erasing Time

These young people videotaping themselves were not the first martyrs, but they were the first to begin their testaments with the phrase 'I am the martyr...', a phrase that has been repeated constantly since. Analyzing these videos, the Lebanese film theorist Jalal Toufic (2002) suggests that the phrase 'I am the martyr (name of speaker)...' may be one of the most important innovations and legacies of the Lebanese civil war. The person, he suggests, is in fact saying 'I am dead'. The martyr has no future, 'his or her timeline has stopped' (Toufic 2002: 79). But on the other hand, their communications are full of references to eternal life, to experiencing immortality in and through the nation. Khosrokhavar (2005) explores this temporal experience, and suggests that the bomber's action is situated simultaneously in a radical present and 'outside' of time.

In Chapter 5 we examined the case of a young woman who in 2003 exploded a bomb in a restaurant in Haifa following the death of her brother, killing herself and 21 others (the circumstances of this bombing are discussed in Pedahzur 2005: 148ff; Graham 2004: 192; Hafez 2006: 49). In her final testament she states that she knows that the bombing will not bring about change, but then she goes on to say 'let the whole world be erased' (in Levi-Barzilai 2007). This suggests a temporal experience where the act of bombing collapses time into the point of destruction. This may help explain the preference for bombing in such actions: bombing produces a death where everything and everyone disappear at once. The temporality of the 'medium term' is destroyed. For the bomber there is only the 'now' and 'eternity' – there is nothing in between (Khosrokhavar 2005). The temporality of political action, of campaigns, hopes and disappointments, compromise and negotiation is erased as time collapses into the instant of destruction.

Violence Against the Self: Grammars of Embodiment

French sociologist Olivier Grojean (2006) argues that to understand martyrdom we also need to locate it within wider patterns of violence against the self. He notes that self-directed violence in fact takes many forms, from self-mutilation and hunger strikes to self-immolation or explosions. The range of social actors who engage in violence against the self is also wider than we might first imagine. Self-mutilation, such as sewing lips together, is not uncommon among asylum seekers; in one action in Australia in 2002 some 60 people sewed their lips together as a protest against their detention as illegal immigrants (Goldsmith 2002), while in 2007 Bolivia prostitutes sewed their lips together in protest against legal brothels being closed, with others engaging in a hunger strike as part of the same campaign (*The New York Times*, 25 October 2007). The hunger strike emerges as one of the most common forms of violence against the self, from early-twentieth-century Britain and the United States suffragettes fighting for women's right to vote (Peel 1997) to India or Northern Ireland (Mulcahy 1995). During the period 2000–03 over 100 Kurdish prisoners died following hunger strikes in prisons in Turkey (Anderson 2004).

One of the most significant forms of violence against the self is self-immolation. In the 1960s in Vietnam several Buddhist monks burned themselves alive in public places as a protest against what they regarded as persecution of Buddhism by the South Vietnamese government (Biggs 2005: 173). In that same decade several Americans burnt themselves alive as protest against the Vietnam War, including in 1965 a Quaker and pacifist who burnt himself to death directly outside the Pentagon office of the Secretary of Defence (King 2000). In the late 1960s and early 1970s some 30 people killed themselves in a similar way protesting the communist regimes of Poland, Czechoslovakia and East Germany (Cechova-Vayleux *et al.* 2010). Such practices continue into the new millennium. In 2003 a campaign against the declaration of the leftist Peoples' Mojahedin of Iran as a terrorist organization and the arrest of its leader in France led to hunger strikes and self-immolations in France and the United Kingdom (Henley 2003). Beginning in 2009, press reports describe a series self-immolation deaths of Tibetan monks protesting Chinese rule; in 2011, a Chinese government spokesperson is reported as describing these suicides as 'terrorism in disguise' (Branigan 2011). In Tunisia in December 2010 a fruit-vendor set himself alight in front of the Governor's Building in a provincial city following an altercation with local officials. He later died of his injuries, but not before the event set off local and national protests, playing a decisive role in launching the social mobilization that came to be called the Arab Spring (Khondker 2011). In 2012, newspapers reported self-immolations of people outside taxation offices in Italy (Reuters 2012).

Violence against the self remains significant in a wide range of social contexts and conflicts. Grojean argues that these different actions involve what he calls a 'hermeneutics of the body'. At stake is:

> the way in which individuals construct their relationship to the world, think of themselves, organize themselves and act in different places. How then does the body become a place, a moment and an object of commitment? How does a person sometimes make the transition from violence against others to violence whose aim is to destroy both the other and the self?
>
> (Grojean 2007: 108)

This means that to understand violence directed towards the self we must locate it within wider social relationships. Grojean argues hunger strikes are, above all, attempts by persons to *contest a judicial or political status* either attributed or denied to them by the state. Once we begin to examine the experience of hunger strikes, a clear pattern of contesting a status that is ascribed or denied does in fact emerge: women denied the status of voters; migrants denied the status of refugees; persons treated as criminals demanding the status of political prisoners; persons seeking recognition of their nationality; persons contesting the attribution of the status 'terrorist'. In applying violence to their own bodies, these actors contest the state's monopoly of power over them, while at the same time claiming the status of victim. In such cases, violence against the self is associated with a position of relative weakness, in particular within the political system (Siméant 1993; Mouchard 2002). Most important, the hunger strike is a form of *public* suffering: 'the suffering body bears, in the very exposure of its suffering, the embodied mark of faith that both leads to such suffering and makes possible enduring such suffering' (Roux 1997: 133).

Grojean observes that there are significant parallels between the hunger strike and self-immolation, reflecting the fact that the majority of people who set themselves alight survive the event (2006). While this violence does not contest an ascribed or denied status, the act of self-immolation is a public event that addresses an authority (for an overview of this practice, see Biggs 2005).

This is particularly evident in the *location* of acts of self-immolation, almost always in proximity to centres of authority: outside the Pentagon office of the Defence Secretary; outside the United Nations building; outside the Vatican; in Beijing's Tiananmen Square; outside government offices, as in Tunisia in 2011. To this we need to add the significant development of self-immolation as a form of protest against conditions in marriage, a pattern evident in self-immolations in countries such as Iran, where the practice is overwhelmingly carried out by women (over 80 per cent), the majority being young, this form of violence against the self being linked to conflict within marriage and family (Ahmadi 2007).

The violence of hunger strikes and self-immolations has several dimensions. It seeks to project guilt on to the adversary; it appeals to public opinion; and in the case of collective actors it reinforces the unity of the group. Exercising violence on one's own body is a means of contesting the control of a dominant actor. This violence is also embedded in a temporality. While directed against the self, it is also directed towards a political power, and located within a temporality of negotiation. It is a form of sacrificial violence that involves gradation and does not exclude time from the relationship with those in power.

Violence against self that also seeks the death of the other, however, highlights very different meanings. First, this violence does not aim primarily at demonstrating the guilt of the enemy, it aims at killing the enemy. Second, its temporality is radically different. This violence is not constructed within a temporality of negotiation. Political time is obliterated, hence the importance of the explosion as a way of killing. Exploring different modes of embodiment present in these forms of violence, Grojean suggests that we can contrast what he calls the *'status-body'* as a mode of embodiment addressing the modern nation state, and another form of embodiment that he refers to as *'truth-body'*, where embodiment is associated with an assertion of a non-negotiable truth (2006: 170). While the status-body can be the basis of collective forms of action, what Grojean terms the *truth-body* involves a highly individualized form of action: the actor destroys his/her own body in an act of self-realization.

Such *individuation through death* is central to Khosrokhavar's (2005) analysis of the martyr, and recurs in the constant references to individual transformation in the martyr testaments, where the new community imagined in the marriage celebration is achieved through the act of love and singularity of the 'bride' or the 'groom'. This personalization may be critical to the globalization of martyrdom pointed to by Moghadam (2008). What we have encountered in this chapter is a form of death framed by a temporal experience closely associated with the explosion, and what Khosrokhavar argues is a type of action highlighted above all by the reference to the wedding feast, and which we saw would later emerge in the Palestinian Intifada: a form of dying and killing where the martyr's act of love would bring into being an otherwise *impossible community*. Unable to be achieved through life, this community, argues Khosrokhavar, can only be brought into existence through death. What is striking in the period that has followed, however, is the way that this imaginary of violence has detached itself from this theme of community, a theme that we find completely absent in attacks such as the London bombings of 2005. This suggests a further mutation at work in the dynamics of violence, one associated with its separation from communities and its increasing association with mediated experience and the Internet.

9

Mediatizing Violence: From Snapshots to the Internet

In the period since the Iran–Iraq war and the early videos produced in Lebanon discussed in the previous chapter, the visual has become increasingly central to violence, from Internet postings of beheadings and other atrocities to the filming of martyrdom, with Khosrokhavar arguing that jihadists experience the world as an 'immense platform' where violence allows them to occupy centre stage (2009: 45). But this importance of the visual extends beyond the violence generally regarded as terrorism. For example, digital images and their circulation were central to the violence visited upon prisoners at the Abu Ghraib prison in Iraq from October 2003. This chapter sets out to explore this increasing mediatization of violence, a dynamic involving both its globalization and personalization. Drawing on Brian Axel's study of radical Sikh activists (2002, 2005) we explore a grammar of experience that we can call 'sublime', where powerfully opposed emotions collide, and where violence may be associated with limit experiences linked to horror. These transformations suggest changes in what constitutes violence as such. While social scientists long believed that the rise of the media and technology would be associated with an increasingly rationalized society (Habermas 1970), what we seem to be encountering instead points to the increasing presence of the occult in violent imaginaries. Today's imaginary of violence may be less associated with programmes, goals and organization, instead being increasingly present in images connecting places and domains of experience in ways that we are only now beginning to understand.

Terror and Image: A Rhetoric of Power

It is increasingly evident that images are not primarily a means of *recording* violence. As with the martyrdom videos explored in the previous chapter, images play a central role in *constituting* violence. David Grindstaff and Kevin DeLuca (2004) explore this through an analysis of the video produced by the executioners of a Jewish-American journalist kidnapped while in Pakistan on assignment in 2002. In this video he is made to confess to being an American, to being Jewish, to his family having close connections to Israel. None of the information he is forced to recount on film is new or not already in the public domain. In that sense, it is clear that his torture was not concerned with eliciting information. Instead it seems closer to the account of torture we considered in Chapter 7, where we saw the philosopher Richard Rorty (1989) argue that torture is not primarily about eliciting information, but the use of violence to force people to feel and desire things that they will later be unable to cope with having thought or desired. For Rorty, the aim of torture is to oblige the victims to destroy their world, to make them deny all that makes them who they are.

In the case of the kidnapping and torture of this journalist, the confession was filmed and posted on the Internet. For Grindstaff and DeLuca, the action of posting the victim's 'confession' on the Internet involves 'the illegitimate appropriation of the victim's voice...The tortured body, emptied of its own world, stripped of its own agency, is thus transformed into a rhetoric of power' (Grindstaff and DeLuca 2004: 308). There is a visual grammar at work here. As the journalist reads his confession, the film produced by his torturers cuts away to images of Palestinians suffering in the Occupied Territories, including a well-known image of a father and son as they were killed in crossfire in Gaza in 2000. The juxtaposition of the confession with images of suffering Palestinians is a form of visual assertion that one is responsible for the other. The narrative ends, the victim falls silent, then once again images occupy the screen: planes dropping bombs, images of injured and dead children. Once again the juxtaposition proposes a logic of cause and effect. The video moves to black, and then refocuses on the journalist, now lying prostrate, his head pulled up by the hair. Two arms grab the head and cut through the throat, decapitating him. The head is then held up by the hair, occupying half the screen, while in the other half there is a montage of images: celebrating children, a person praying, and again pictures of wounded and dead. The video then focuses in on the head, while a series of demands in the name of a group calling itself the 'National Movement for the Restoration of Pakistan Sovereignty' scroll across the screen, demands which include that the United States deliver F-16 fighter planes to Pakistan (Grindstaff and DeLuca 2004).

Held up to the camera while the text scrolls, the victim's 'head mutely announces the demands and in its muteness testifies to the power of the group making the demands' (Grindstaff and DeLuca 2004: 305). The executioners transform the body 'into a text that testifies to the truth of their power, the truth of their grievances, the truth of their worldview' (2004: 305). The self-styled 'national movement' responsible for this kidnapping and torture had not been heard of before or since this event. The 'movement' comes into existence only through the violence that possesses and destroys its victim's body, an operation that demonstrates a 'frightening freedom of referential activity' (2004: 309), one that allows a small group to claim to be a national movement. Significantly, the images of suffering proposed are completely decontextualized. The suffering of Palestinians is presented as a truth, one that not only justifies the execution of a Jewish-American journalist, but also a demand for the delivery of F-16 fighter planes to a military regime that presumably the 'national movement' despises. Not a single image in the visual montage refers to Pakistan: instead they are offered as images of the oppression of a generic Muslim.

This torture and beheading highlights the increasing centrality of the visual to contemporary violence. Working within a Foucauldian tradition, Allen Feldman (2005) suggests that the increasing visualization and aesthetization of violence is best approached as a phenomenon that developed throughout the twentieth century. He considers Walter Benjamin's analysis of cinematized Nazi political rallies, with massive crowds and awe-inspiring light shows, as important points in this process. For Benjamin, the fascist political rally was a form of theatre that 'incorporated the individual spectator into a virtualized corporate body of sovereignty', combining a politics of suggestion and an aesthetic of mass consumption (Feldman 2005: 215). Feldman argues that such visualization continues today, taking as an example the US-led invasion of Iraq of 2003. This invasion was based on a model of warfare known as 'Shock and Awe', a form of attack that seeks to mobilize such overwhelming force that an opponent will not seek to resist (for the original statement of this strategy, see Ulman and Wade 1996; for a critical evaluation of its use in Iraq, see Sepp 2007). More than simply a military tactic, Feldman argues that the 2003 invasion of Iraq was 'an exercise in war as visual culture for the consumption of the televisual audience' (2005: 217), where the power of visual experience 'constructs the crowd, the polity, as both cinematic object and as a mass spectatorship' (2005: 216). The importance of the visual in the Iraq War extends well beyond the model of war for a televisual audience, a reality highlighted by another circulation of images, namely the thousands of digital photos taken by troops, among which figured most notoriously those taken by guards at Baghdad's Abu Ghraib prison.

Abu Ghraib: Pornographic Violence, the Public and the Private

In Chapter 1 we opened out the debate about transformations of war and the implications for the question of violence. This involved introducing the classical sociological account of war, contrasting with this with contemporary arguments proposing the emergence of what have been called 'New Wars' (Kaldor 2001). Protagonists of this view argue that war is less and less organized by states, and increasingly involves a wide range of actors, from warlords, families, criminal groups and even individuals. This argument is countered by a more classical theory of war, which considers war as the activity of uniformed specialists, working in bureaucratized organizations, clearly separated from the rest of the population (Giddens 1987; Malešević 2008).

Embedded within this debate is a question that is rarely confronted directly, namely what is constituted as public and private violence. As we saw in Chapter 1, for Giddens, military personnel are specialist purveyors of the means of violence (1987: 230), a specialization signalled by the uniform. When putting on a uniform a person steps into a function or role. Significantly, when developing this argument, Giddens offers a parallel with the prison:

> Within the army as an organization, the uniform has the same implications for disciplinary power as in carceral settings of other types, helping strip individuals of those traits that might interfere with routinized patterns of obedience. The uniform indicates to the civilian population the distinctiveness of the military figure as the specialist purveyor of the means of violence... This has become such a universal feature of the nation-state that it is perhaps difficult to see how novel it is.
>
> (Giddens 1987: 230)

From this perspective, violence is 'depersonalized', something separate from the subjectivity of the actors – this proposition is at the centre of the instrumental accounts of violence that form the basis of 'rational action' approaches to violence. This fundamentally approaches violence as a *public* experience, similar to the ways that people act out roles in organizations.

This is called into question by the developments that took place at the Abu Ghraib prison in Iraq (for an overview, see Greenberg *et al.* 2005). From 2004, digital photographs taken by American military personnel serving as guards at the prison began to circulate widely in the United States. These consisted of hundreds of photographs as well as videos of Iraqi prisoners being subjected to torture and degrading violence. Elizabeth Dauphinée notes that almost all of the prisoners who subsequently testified about their experience at Abu Ghraib specifically refer to the experience of being filmed or photographed. She argues that taking images was part of the violence, not simply a matter of a visual record (2007: 147). The response of many people when confronted with these images is captured by US Senator John McCain, a Republican presidential candidate and a victim of torture in

Vietnam, when asked to compare the events at Abu Ghraib with his experience of being tortured: 'I was never subject to sexual humiliation and degradation' (Stolberg 2004: A19, cited in Zurbriggen 2008: 311).

McCain points to the fact that sexual humiliation and degradation were central to the violence at Abu Ghraib, and this evokes the increasing importance of intimacy to violence that we explored in Chapter 7. The sworn statements of many of the victims (taken for legal purposes) recount being forced to masturbate while being photographed, or being subjected to gender inversion through being forced to wear women's underwear. Gourevitch and Morris (2008: 232) note the extent that pornography was consumed by the jailers, while Faisal Devji observes that many of the practices that took place at Abu Ghraib were modelled on pornographic material that the torturers were consuming (Devji 2008: 151), and which were staged specifically for photographs (Gourevitch and Morris 2008: 195). Devij suggests (2008) that through these acts the torturers integrate the victims into their own fantasies, posing their victims to simulate pornographic images, from piled naked bodies (evoking images of mass graves) to anal penetration with various objects (a constant theme in victims' statements; see Danner 2004). In other cases prisoners were manacled naked in stress positions, with women's underwear spread across their faces, in others hooded men were forced to masturbate together. One guard describes seven naked prisoners being piled on to each other in a pyramid as 'just another crazy night' (Gourveitch and Morris 2008: 197). Another describes one of these sessions as mixing 'work and play' (Gourevitch and Morris 2008: 196), and refers to photography that took place as 'happy snaps' (Gourevitch and Morris 2008: 196). Many events, such as the piling of naked prisoners into a pyramid, are described by guards as 'staged' specifically for photographs to be taken (Gourveitch and Morris 2008: 197). Photography was central to the experience of those subjected to this violence, one prisoner describing the guards as 'taking photographs as if it were a porn movie' (Danner 2004: 236). Hundreds of these images are widely available in the public domain, a sample available at http://www.salon.com/2006/03/14/introduction_2/.

There is now an extensive literature attempting to understand these events, and this wider debate is beyond the scope of this book. But the type of violence is significant, and questions we have explored in earlier chapters highlight several themes that recur in the debate about Abu Ghraib. One attempt to make sense of this violence, proposed by Feitz and Nagel (2008: 209), draws on Milgram's (1974) study that we examined in Chapter 3, where volunteers inflicted what they believed to be extreme pain on 'students' because they were told to do so by a person in a white coat. Other arguments point to socialization, and to Zimbardo's Stanford Prison Experiment (1972), where undergraduates were given the roles of prisoners and guards, also discussed in Chapter 3, with Zimbardo emphasizing the socialization that occurred when volunteers adopted the roles of guard and prisoner. Both Milgram and Zimbardo point to what Randall Collins (2008) calls 'situational dynamics', and this appears to be a key dimension of what occurred in Abu Ghraib. But what happened also seems beyond these analyses. The primary relationship in Milgram's study was between the volunteer and the authority figure instructing him or her to increase the voltage that 'students' would be subjected to. There was no direct relationship with the 'victims' of the electric shocks in Milgram's experiment, and certainly no evidence of sexualization of torture. The fundamental relationship Milgram was exploring, obedience, was between volunteer and authority figure, not volunteer and victim. Zimbardo (2008) discusses the events at Abu Ghraib directly and argues that these manifest the socialization evident in his earlier prison roles experiment. He proposes that the violence of the guards can be explained in terms of the validation of a 'higher authority' that sanctioned the roles and actions at Abu Ghraib (2007: 226). He echoes Giddens, arguing that uniforms, costumes and masks all promote anonymity and reduce personal accountability, with uniforms being a tool to achieve 'deindividuation' (2008: 219).

But such socialization into roles is in question at Abu Ghraib. Studies of the lives of the guards point to a widespread ignoring of many of the requirements of military roles: pets were kept, uniforms often not worn, alcohol consumed on duty, and practices differentiating ranks such as saluting often not followed, while sexual relationships took place between people of different ranks (Danner 2004: 133; Devji 2008: 151–2). Rather than a socialization into roles, at Abu Ghraib these roles seemed to disappear and the socialization associated with military discipline appears largely absent. Above all, neither the 'obedience' nor 'socialization' theses offer any insight into the two dimensions that appear at the centre of the Abu Ghraib events: sexual humiliation and the visual recording of violence.

At Abu Ghraib, photographs were a means of creating an experience. The camera is part of a pornographic imagination to the extent that it is, as Feldman argues, a 'penetrative device' that appropriates 'the psyche, sexuality and gender identity of the hooded Iraqi detainee' (Feldman 2005: 220). This appropriation extends beyond death, evident in practices of photographing dead bodies. In one such image a female guard poses for a photograph by the corpse of an Iraqi detainee. She is bending down, her head next to that of the dead prisoner as she holds open the bodybag, smiling at the camera and giving a 'thumbs up' signal (one of these widely circulating images is reproduced in Zimbardo 2008: 410). The references to 'crazy nights' and 'happy snaps' alert us to the fact that the photos were consumed and circulated among military colleagues and friends primarily for recreation purposes. This practice fractures the separation of public and private embedded in the idea of the uniform and the modern military. The circulation of such images points, as Devji argues, to the way the 'act of photography breaks up the public and collective identity of the military by introducing within it a strictly private and even civilian desire' (Devji 2008: 151–2). The images transform public and professional events into personal ones. This blurring is signalled by the extent to which the guards occupy a similar pose in hundreds of the photos (looking directly at the camera, smiling, thumbs up signals) that they might adopt in holiday snaps taken at markets and other tourist locations. These photos highlight the shift away from obedience and depersonalization associated with the classical theory of the military, to the increasing *private and intimate* dimensions of violence, dimensions explored in Chapter 7.

Media Nightmares

The image is not only increasingly central to the act of violence, it is at the centre of the flows that constitute the globalizing forms of jihadi violence that have emerged since the 11 September attacks of 2001. When we start to explore jihadi websites or personal accounts leading to engagement with violence, what is striking is the extent that accounts centre on the experience of images. And these are not simply the accounts of minor actors. No less a figure than Osama bin Laden, when explaining the processes leading up to the attacks of 11 September, described this in terms of watching a videotape aired by al-Jazeera Television in October 2004:

> God knows it did not cross our minds to attack the towers but after the situation became unbearable and we witnessed the injustice and tyranny of the American–Israeli alliance against our people in Palestine and Lebanon, I thought about it. And the events that affected me directly were that of 1982 and the events that followed – when America allowed the Israelis to invade Lebanon, helped by the US sixth fleet. In those difficult times many emotions came over me which are hard to describe, but which produced an overwhelming feeling to reject injustice and a strong determination to punish the unjust. As I watched the destroyed towers in Lebanon, it occurred to me to punish the unjust the same way (and) to destroy towers in America so it could taste some of what we are tasting and to stop killing our children and women.
>
> (*The Guardian*, 30 October 2004, Reuters translation, available at http://www.guardian.co.uk/world/2004/oct/30/alqaida.september11)

What is striking here is the reference to a personal experience of watching television, as opposed, for example, to an account of personally knowing victims. Bin Laden describes this experience as producing emotions that are 'hard to describe', the source of an 'overwhelming feeling' that, according to this interview, is at the origin of the decision to destroy the World Trade Center towers in the United States in 2001. Faisal Devji argues that the place of media images in the contemporary jihad is so important that the global jihad should be less regarded as a phenomenon emerging out of Islam, but should instead

> *be seen as an offspring of the media,* composed as it is almost completely of pre-existing media themes, images and stereotypes. Like the murderous Freddy, in the Hollywood horror film *Nightmare on Elm Street*, the jihad appears simply to bring to life and make real the media's own nightmares.
>
> (Devji 2005: 88, emphasis added)

There is now a significant degree of evidence to support this contention. During the inquest into the 7 July 2005 bombings in London, evidence was tendered consisting of texts sent between two of the bombers in the days leading up to the attack. In these texts they communicate with each other through adopting the personas of characters from the 1980s television action series, the *A-Team*. At one point in their exchange they jokingly dispute who had the right to use the catchphrase of one of the television characters with a fear of flying:

> Wat kina bullshit flex r u on now. I say we aint getting on no plane, fool. Now get sum.
> Hahahahahahahahaha.
> Fuck u bitch, dats my line ... Now lets get dis right, I aint getting on no plane! fool! I aint getin on no plane! Fool!
> No bullshit doctor! fix it!
> I aint getin on no plane! Murdock tel dis fool.
>
> (7julyinquests.independent.gov.uk/evidence/INQ10516-47.pdf)

These exchanges suggest more than communicating in a way to avoid detection, as these young men banter and joke with each other, adopting characters and catch-lines from Hollywood popular culture. In another case, in 2006, a man in the United Kingdom was convicted of terrorism offences linked to acts committed using an Internet persona based on the fictional spy James Bond, calling himself Terrorist 007 (http://www.washing tonpost.com/wp-dyn/content/article/2006/03/25/AR2006032500020. html, accessed 30 March 2010). During legal proceedings it emerged that a man convicted for attempting to blow up a transatlantic flight through a concealed 'shoe bomb' was referred to by his co-conspirators as 'Van Damme', the name of a well-known action hero actor (Silber 2012: 34). These young men clearly appear at home in a Western media culture, integrating this into their own actions.

Other dimensions of global media culture also appear reproduced within the jihad. Images of suffering become deterritorialized and decontextualized, removed from any specific context so that they become stereotypical, as in the montage of images produced by the kidnappers discussed at the beginning of this chapter. Generic suffering plays an important role in the contemporary humanitarian movement, which relies heavily upon television, focusing on images of suffering that while personal (in particular the suffering of children), are decontextualized. From this perspective, one suffering child – who remains nameless, disconnected from family and location – is the equivalent of another (McDonald 2006). In the jihad not only is suffering made generic, but so too are the places of jihad, separated from local histories and meanings. Devji notes that these become significant only to the extent that they are in the news:

> reduced to caves and ruins, the towns and villages occupied by the jihad lose their own histories and become nothing but news, to enjoy their being in a state of immediacy. And once their particularity is destroyed, the very roots eradicated, these blasted habitations and their former occupants are transformed into universal figures. They become Muslims as such, people whose particular histories have suddenly disappeared to become part of the universal history of Islam ... What makes Islam universal, then, is the forging of a generic Muslim, one who loses all cultural and historical particularity by his or her destruction in an act of martyrdom.
>
> (Devji 2005: 94)

Violence, Personalized Responsibility, Repetition

Images and mediated experience emerge as central to the bombing of London's transport system that took place in 2005. Two of those involved in these attacks released video testaments (Khan 2005; MEMRI 2006), and what is striking about these videos is the absence of anything that we might regard as 'social data', such as references to work, neighbourhood, family, ethnicity, race, poverty or inequality – themes we saw in Chapter 3 as being central to classical debates about the causes of terrorism. Rather than poverty or racism, the video testaments speak above all about 'mediated experience', the *world experienced through the media*. One begins with an appeal to the 'Muslims of Britain', but does so without reference to any experience they may be living. Instead the key reference point is reality experienced via television:

> Oh Muslims of Britain, you, day in and day out on your TV sets, watch and hear about the oppression of the Muslims, from the east to the west. But yet you turn a blind eye, and carry on with your lives as if you never heard anything, or as if it does not concern you. What is the matter with you that you turn back not to the religion that Allah has chosen for you?
>
> (MEMRI 2006)

The testament does not make a single reference to suffering or racism experienced in the north of England where its author lived. Instead what is described is the oppression of Muslims as encountered through the medium of the television. The importance of such mediated experience occurs in other ways as well. The *Report of the Official Account of the Bombings*, about the London bombings (House of Commons 2006: 17) notes that members of the group were involved in paint-balling. Such activity is part of popular culture, typically involving going into a new location, dividing up into teams that compete with each other, with the exhilaration of role-playing amplified by the tensions generated through simulated combat. But in this case the dynamic was different, as we see in an account of this group offered by a person who claims to have been a member of the group:

> Before we would leave the house we would reflect about what was happening in Palestine, what was happening in Chechnya, or other places around the world where Muslims were affected ... people would get emotional, they would get fired up, they would get stirred up ... Nothing was said before, they were presented as 'this is what's happening in Palestine, this is what's happening in Chechnya'. No one was looking for recruits, or funds or gifts, nothing like that ... [They were] standard images, people being mutilated, people being shot, people being oppressed, people at checkpoints for hours on end, people crying, etc., etc.
>
> (Unnamed member of paint-balling group,
> BBC Radio 4 2006)

If this is an accurate account of these events, it suggests that watching extreme violence was followed not by discussion, but by physical exertion. The sociology of encounters with extreme violence may offer us some insight into what is happening here. The German sociologist Bernhard Giesen argues that such encounters involve a transformation, with the person seeing such violence changing from being an *observer* to being a *witness* (2005). A witness takes on responsibility for the events that s/he sees. Such a dynamic emerges as central to the video testaments, as we see in another key passage:

> Your democratically elected governments perpetuate atrocities against my people and your support of them *makes you responsible, just as I am directly responsible* for protecting and avenging my Muslim brothers and sisters.
>
> (Khan 2005, emphasis added)

What we see here is a statement of *shared responsibility*: the responsibility of the perpetrator and that of the person responsible for protecting and avenging the victims. This video also alerts us to something important about the form this responsibility takes, evident in the way the author expresses himself in the first-person singular tense as 'I am directly responsible', underlining a type of *responsibility experienced in the first person*. This mode of personal experience potentially offers us some insight into the type of violence that flows from it, namely the relatively weak *collective dimensions* of such violence. This may help us to understand why contemporary jihadi violence does not possess anything like the organizational imaginary that we encountered in Chapter 4 with groups such as the Red Brigades or the Weather Underground, who set about creating clandestine organizations. The personal form of responsibility motivating it may explain why such a high proportion of jihadi violence takes the form either of individuals acting loosely together, or the increasing extent to which individuals act alone. In such cases, violence is not the collective action of an organization, but an expression of personal responsibility.

This form of responsibility is echoed in an alleged video testament tendered in evidence in the trial of another young person convicted of terrorism offences in the United Kingdom in 2008:

> You know, I wanted to do this myself, for many years I had dreamt of doing this, you know, but I didn't have no chance of doing this. I didn't have any means. But thank God Allah has accepted my duas [prayers] and provided me a means to do this.
>
> (Transcript available at
> http://news.bbc.co.uk/2/hi/uk_news/7330367.stm,
> accessed 10 January 2010)

In this case, the organization (here a group of friends) is an instrument to achieve what appears as a very personal goal. The would-be martyr *uses* an organization rather than *builds* one. This helps us to understand the lack of debate about programmes and shared objectives – within such a personalized mode of responsibility, such things associated with more organized

forms of action are largely irrelevant. The would-be martyr does not consider him/herself to be alone, but the conception of action is deeply personal. As a result, s/he is only able to imagine that others will come after
him/her and *do the same thing*. This is the basis of the frequent references
to 'waves of martyrs' that recur in video testaments. The temporality and
imagination of action is one of *repetition*. Indeed, in one alleged martyrdom video tendered as evidence in the United Kingdom in 2008 where
the person was subsequently convicted of terrorism offences, the person
declares:

> You know, I only wish I could do this again, you know come back and do this
> again, and just do it again and again until people come to their senses and realise,
> you know, don't mess with the Muslims.
>
> (Transcript available at
> http://news.bbc.co.uk/2/hi/uk_news/7330367.stm,
> accessed 10 January 2010)

Such highly personalized responsibility is equally evident in the transcript
of the police interview released to the media in 2010 of a woman convicted
of attempting to murder a Member of Parliament in the United Kingdom
(http://www.guardian.co.uk/uk/2010/nov/03/roshonara-choudhry-poli
ce-interview). According to the record of the interview, this young woman
dropped out of university close to the point where she would have completed her studies, encountered a radical preacher over the Internet, and
watched hours of videos of suffering people in Iraq and Palestine. When
asked if she had spoken with anyone about what she was learning, her
reported response was that she didn't speak with anyone, 'because nobody
would understand'. Her interview describes her as taking up prayer, but
not at a mosque or in the community, but alone in her room. She declares
that she had no previous experience of involvement in anti-war activism
or involvement in an anti-war organization. Indeed, in the transcript of
the interview she describes a school visit to Parliament several years earlier, when one of her classmates criticized a Member of Parliament for supporting the Iraq War. She describes her own response to this event as being
embarrassed and wanting her classmate to stop talking.

She describes her response to the violent images she witnessed and the
preacher to whom she listened was to purchase knives, one of which she
used to stab a Member of Parliament who had voted for British involvement in the Iraq War. Her action *mirrors* the violence she opposes: 'if he
could treat the Iraqi people so mercilessly, then why should I show him
any mercy?' Once again, what is striking about this trajectory is the extent
it signals a mode of *individualized responsibility*, the product of a mediatized

encounter with violence, one where responsibility is constructed in the first person. When asked 'what made you get these strong feelings that you've obviously got now', she responds

> When I realised that I have an obligation to defend the people of Iraq and fight on their side, that's when it changed my mind and also just like the death tolls and the civilian, like casualties, and the pictures from the prisons.
>
> (http://www.guardian.co.uk/uk/2010/nov/03
> /roshonara-choudhry-police-interview)

What we encounter in this interview is the same structure of shared responsibility that emerges in the earlier video testaments of the London bombers. This involves a statement of personalized responsibility that mirrors the responsibility imputed to the other, whether that be commuters ('your government'), or to a Member of Parliament involved in voting for the deployment of troops. Mediatized violence produces responsibility shared between the violent actor and his/her victim.

What we see here is a public sphere where violence is the source of shared responsibility. However, the videos of the London bombers are very different from the early videos that emerged in Lebanon, which we discussed in Chapter 8. Those video testaments were full of references to the martyr as bride or groom, to death being a marriage feast that would bring the community together, to blood fertilizing the soil and giving life to the nation. In such cases, death brings into being an impossible community (Khosrokhavar 2005). Strikingly, in the case of the London bombers, there are no references to grooms and marriages, to the renewal of community through the death of the martyr, while equally no references to building the type of organization that characterized terrorist violence in the 1970s. What we encounter today suggests more an imaginary of *repetition*, where others will come and do the same, or where the same person imagines themselves 'coming back' and repeating the same action again and again.

The Hidden and the Revealed: Conspiracies and Dreams

In these video testaments, it is the extremity of the violence that removes any doubts about who is responsible. Any refusal to accept this is interpreted as an act of hypocrisy, as a deliberate attempt to conceal reality (Devji 2005: 102). Those who disagree or fail to embrace the jihad are not simply uninformed, they are *hypocrites* who fail to act on what they know to be right, an accusation at the centre of the criticism directed towards Muslim leaders:

> go to your so-called knowledgeable people and ask them why are they hiding this knowledge from us. It is acceptable for them to play [unclear] with the Ummah, which means deception? Can they lie about Islam and mislead us just because they fear prison? Is this what these great scholars of the past did? Our so-called scholars today are content with their Toyotas and semi-detached houses, they seem to think their responsibilities lie in pleasing the Kuffar instead of Allah, so they tell us ludicrous things like you must obey the law of the land.
>
> (Khan 2005, author transcript)

What emerges in these video testaments is a view of the world shaped by the hidden actions of those in power, whether religious leaders or those in government.

As well as the two video recordings, the House of Commons *Report of the Official Account of the Bombings* notes that one of the bombers left a written testament (House of Commons 2006: 19). At the time of writing only a redacted section of this testament had been released (http://7julyinquests. independent.gov.uk/evidence/docs/INQ9365-12.pdf). However, specialists suggest that it is modelled on one written by 'Suraqah al-Andalusi' (Devji 2008: 67–8; the pseudonym of a British man believed to have died during the US bombardment of al-Qaeda positions at Tora Bora in Eastern Afghanistan in 2001 (Casciani 2009). According to the House of Commons *Report*, Suraqah al-Andalusi 'appears as something of a role model' for the London bomber (House of Commons 2006: 19).

Stories of al-Andalusi's life were published and circulate widely on the Internet (see, for example, http://www.islamicawakening.com/viewarticle.php?articleID=713&pageID=233&; accessed 30 March 2010). These accounts spend a great deal of time describing his personal discovery of the jihad, where again we encounter the central place of mediated experience. Al-Andalusi is described as a young Muslim searching for meaning, who comes across an audio cassette called *In the Hearts of Green Birds*, a collection of stories of miraculous events associated with martyrs who died in the Bosnian war of the 1990s (see Kohlman 2004). He is searching for something missing from his life; a sense of incompleteness is central to his experience of selfhood. The accounts make no reference to shared social experiences or solidarity produced through shared struggle, motifs that recur in accounts of coming to class consciousness, for example. There is no encounter with groups or even individuals. Instead the jihad is encountered through an audiotape, in this case a collection of martyr stories of Europeans who had gone to fight in Bosnia in the 1990s. The Internet-based accounts of al-Andalusi's life suggest that after hearing this cassette he comes to a realization that makes sense of his own experience of emptiness and disconnection, and this leads to the decision to embrace jihad. While constructed very much in terms of the modern individual's search for meaning, al-Andalusi's search is not grounded in a social context. Meaning is found in audiotapes and videos, not in neighbourhood, community or workplace.

These accounts describe al-Andalusi uncovering a hidden reality, one that lies beneath the visible and the everyday. He comes to realize that many Islamic scholars are hiding the truth, defending man-made social systems (democracy), while gradually realizing that his search will mean becoming 'a stranger to this world'. His path is just as much a search for knowledge as for jihad. It is on this path that al-Andalusi discovers a thinker who helps him to go beyond appearances and finds the world that is hidden:

> He finally came to understand that to adhere to this path means that you are to be a stranger in this world. He read a book by Sheikh Abu Muhammad Al-Maqdisi [a Palestinian-Jordanian, widely regarded as one of the most influential thinkers behind the al-Qaeda current; see Allawi 2007: 238] and was amazed by one of the Sheikh's arguments: *'Two worlds exist: the apparent world and the world of the unseen. Actions done in the apparent world are rewarded in the world of the unseen despite sometimes no change being brought about in the apparent world.'* This statement quelled any of the remaining doubts in his heart about his chosen path.
>
> (Azzam 2003: 126, emphasis in original)

This whole account is structured in terms of the opposition between an apparent world and the world of the unseen. Echoing the ancient Greek philosopher Plato, it is the world of the unseen that is the real world, opposed to the visible world, which is a world of corruption and one where attachments bring with them the threat of contamination. This opposition is structured in terms of the opposition between the *ordinary* (al-Andalusi's childhood is described as being brought up as *nothing out of the ordinary*), and a reality that extends beyond this to be truly *extraordinary*. This same opposition of *hidden and revealed* recurs in video testaments of the London bombers, with the real world hidden by a conspiracy of Muslim leaders and the government. This is associated with a call to engage in a personal search for hidden knowledge: 'If you have any doubts or reservations about this and the other jihadis then I strongly suggest you research them, check the Islamic history, the books are very widely available' (Khan 2005).

These themes of a hidden reality were very much part of popular culture in the period leading up to the end of the millennium, and by no means restricted to jihadist milieux. One such example is *Shadows in Motion*, a video widely circulating during the years before the attacks on London, that purports to reveal a conspiracy dating back to the eleventh century, claiming to unmask an alliance between Jews, Freemasons and a secretive organization known as the Illuminati, responsible for actions ranging from the Crusades to the Iraq War, and who are now seeking to consolidate their control of the world through mechanisms such as the United Nations, the New World Order, and identity cards – the only defence against these plotters being Islam. There is nothing religious about such conspiracy theories; they are a product and expression of contemporary popular culture, the basis of a whole market of airport fiction.

In Chapter 6 we saw the importance of conspiracy theory in the world out of which Timothy McVeigh, the convicted bomber of the Federal Building in Oklahoma, emerged. Conspiracy theory is not fundamentally a set of ideas, but more a 'structure of feeling', a form of emotion flow that is a significant expression of contemporary globalization. Kathleen Stewart captures important dimensions of this, describing it as a social world made up of:

> the networked world of system and power, the constant shock waves that never quite wake us from the dream world of late capitalism but replicate states of anaesthesia and obsession. The always already replicated, the simulacra, coupled with the suspicion that something is hiding the REAL behind the curtain ... a cultural politics awash in inchoate yet palpable structures of feeling that are themselves peppered with the occasional shock of half-recognition that there is something going on. The sure knowledge (and experience) that everything is connected and merging – a seduction, a moving toward and within – coupled with the guilty pang, the moment of terror when something whispers in our ear that the interconnectedness is all controlled by a dark and monolithic Other and we are in it, no exit.
>
> (Stewart 1999: 13)

The 'structure of feeling' evoked here is similar to the sublime, the co-presence and mutual reinforcement of opposed emotions, such as fear and fascination, exhaustion and exhilaration, certainty and the unknown, or immortality and monstrosity (Mellor 1996), suggesting a form of transcendence evoking the European Romantic movement (Weiskel 1976). In such a world, Stewart argues,

> everything is connected and the connections are uncanny. There are moments of déjà vu, moments when the sense of overdetermination is palpable. Conspiracy theory lays a claim to a threshold state of consciousness where you are at once connected to the concrete tangible detail and projecting into a future, a higher

knowledge, a leading edge, seeking an order behind the visible. It moves between the realms of story and event, the official and the unofficial story, the fantasy and the reality, the subject and the object: caught up in the nervous oscillation of no-man's land, it finds itself fascinated by transformation, encounter, risk.

(Stewart 1999: 17)

The structure of conspiracy is one of power revealed and power concealed. As Sanders and West argue, conspiracy's structure is close to that of the occult, and this alerts us to the importance of a phenomenon linked to conspiracy theories, namely 'occult cosmologies'. Such cosmologies are organized in terms of two separate realms, where 'there is more to what happens in the world than meets the eye', and where 'power operates in two separate yet related realms, one visible, the other invisible; between these two realms, however, there exist causal links, meaning that invisible powers sometimes produce visible outcomes' (Sanders and West 2003: 17). As structures of feeling rather than collections of cognitive propositions, conspiracy and the occult can be understood as a form of global structure, an 'ideoscape of suspicion' (Sanders and West 2003: 15).

Significantly, the world of conspiracy theory is one where 'the new' appears to be absent: the same plotters recur, today's yielders of hidden power are the same as those who have yielded power for centuries, even millennia – hence the recurring role of the Iluminati. *Shadows in Motion* purports to uncover a plot that has lasted over 1,000 years, while many jihadist websites refer to hidden networks of power that take the form of a global conspiracy to destroy Islam (Brachman 2008: 82). Véronique Campion-Vincent (2005) points to the parallels between conspiracy theory and forms of knowledge such as esotericism, knowledge pertaining to hidden domains from astrology to spiritualism, all of which 'function' in terms of analogy, where understanding the presence and action of hidden relationships in one domain serves as a model to understand others. Here the aim is not to understand or invent a future, but to find the hidden actors at work in the past and who are also present today. There is not the exhilaration of imagining a new world; instead it is the breathless experience of recognition in the shadows. Conspiracy theory not only offers a key to understand hidden realities, it offers the prospect of control, where the fascination of entering a no-man's land of risk is matched by the exhilaration of discovery and powerful experiences of déjà vu, where pre-existing and hidden forces are not so much seen as felt. Life is lived in a threshold state, on a dangerous edge of revelation and discovery, but also of being swallowed up and annihilated by the immensity of it all (Stewart 1999).

The structure of the known and the unknown, the hidden and revealed, also recurs in the importance of dreams within the jihad. Faisal Devji (2005) underlines the importance of such dreams and visions, while Hafez (2007: 157) points to the importance of dreams to the jihadi culture of martyrdom, where stories of dreams recur in the biographies of volunteers for suicide missions. In such cases, martyrs appear in dreams to tell future candidates of the joyful and wonderful experience of dying as a martyr, where communication with the dead affirms the importance of martyrdom. Iain Edgar (2007) equally underlines the place of dream interpretation within the culture of the jihad, evident in the important place of dreaming in the jihadi movement in Kashmir, where jihadists claim that Mohammad appears in dreams to announce the elevated spiritual status of martyrs to their family members.

The Performativity of the Martyr: Death and the Internet

Martyrdom and its association with the Internet is not unique to the culture of the jihad. It also plays a central role in the global network of radical Sikhs calling for an independent Khalistan or Land of the Pure (Shani 2005; Baixas and Simon 2008). Unlike many nationalist movements, these Sikh militants are not fighting for the creation of a state or country that existed in the past, and has now been incorporated into some other state. The origins of Sikhism date from the fifteenth century in what is now the Punjab area of northern India bordering Pakistan, and while Sikhism played an important role in the history of the Punjab, a state by the name of Khalistan, as a Sikh homeland, has never existed. The 1980s and 1990s witnessed the emergence of movements within this region demanding the creation of a new Sikh state to be called Khalistan, and this movement developed extensive support from global networks of the Sikh diaspora. Indeed, to a significant extent this movement is a product of that diaspora, with the Internet playing an increasingly important role. Brian Axel (2002, 2005) notes that what is striking in the Internet sites created by such radical Sikh groups is the extent to which these are saturated with images of death, mutilations and martyrs allegedly killed and tortured by Indian security services.

What is at work within this diaspora, argues Axel, is not an imaginary centred on place, but one that works through *temporality, affect and corporeality*. Within this imaginary, *the body of the martyr is the medium through which a global experience is constituted*. This, argues Axel, occurs in particular through the temporality constructed via visual images of the martyr, where pre-death and post-death images are found juxtaposed on Internet sites. The pre-death images consist of photos that are taken of the martyr-to-be in his best clothes, posing with a sword or AK-47. The aim of these images is to convey a sense of purity, but alone these photos simply convey people dressed in their best ceremonial clothes. However, the meaning of the image changes when it is juxtaposed with an image of the broken body following torture and death. These images reveal a temporal grammar. As Axel argues, the clean, whole body takes on a new significance as a *pure body* as a result of its subsequent destruction.

The *purity of the past is made real in the present* via the broken body of the martyr. Through these images an idealized period of the Khalsa, the time of the birth of the Sikh nation, does not simply remain in the past, nor is it turned into a kind of nostalgia for a bygone age. The death of the martyr brings the purity of the Khalsa *into the present*: 'the image of the tortured body reproduces, animates and makes actual ... the time before that *must have been* in order for a Sikh diaspora to emerge in the present' (Axel 2002: 424, emphasis in original). The mutilated body of the martyr makes possible an identification with what its supporters *'have not experienced* and *cannot imagine'* (Axel 2005: 146, emphasis added). This, argues Axel, is at the centre of what he terms the specific 'productivity' of the Internet, its ability to allow a 'fleeting moment of connection between the not-lived and lived' (Axel 2005: 144).

Images of the dead are equally pervasive in the global culture of the jihad, from jihadi literature of the 1980s to today's websites which are bursting with stories of death and dying, narrated in terms we have encountered, such as the opposition between intactness and decay, purity and being out of place in the world. These are full of stories of miraculous events, stories of fallen martyrs who do not decay, of the smell of flowers emanating from their dead bodies as a sign that they are in the presence of God (central to *In the Hearts of Green Birds*, the collection of martyr stories discussed above). The ease with which such images and, increasingly, film can be circulated has seen a new emphasis on the face of the corpse, where these will be photographed as smiling, an indicator that the martyr has seen God or an angel at the moment of death (McDonald 2011). Increasingly on jihadi websites we encounter close up film of dying itself, where martyrdom is less a religious event than part of a global culture of reality television (Devji 2005). Death is the bridge between the hidden and the revealed (McDonald 2011), where the lived and the not-lived meet (for a wider analysis of the place of death in the culture of the jihad, see Khosrokhavar 2009).

The critical relationship between death and communications technologies we encounter here is not unique to today. Erik Davis (1998) points to the close association between the emergence of the telegraph in the 1840s in the United States and Spiritualism, the movement of communication with the dead. The telegraph involved communication with unseen agents through short sounds and long sounds similar to knocking on a surface, and Davis notes that the early spiritualists claimed to be in contact with the dead who also manifested their presence through knocking. This reference to communications technology was evident in the title of the most popular spiritualist newspaper of the period, the *Spiritual Telegraph* (Stolow 2004). For Davis, the telegraph made possible communication with unknown others, and played an important role in the emergence of the type of gothic imagination that sustained spiritualism in nineteenth-century America (1998: 73). This was an imagination of dread and interest in dark and mysterious forces associated with the occult (Stolow 2004). It was also associated with experiments involving magnetism, believed to be a 'celestial telegraph' that would also allow communication with the dead (Cahagnet 1855). Stolow (2004) argues that that the telegraph, making possible communication with unknown others, played an important role in the emergence of a gothic imagination with its themes of presence and absence, visibility and invisibility, the ordinary and the extraordinary. At the heart of this imagination, he argues, is a tension between desire and dread, anticipation and horror.

Extraordinary Violence

These patterns may help us understand the surprising absence of reference to the *strategic* meaning of death in the culture of the jihad. The extensive images and discussion of martyrs are almost never accompanied by a discussion of what was achieved through the death (McDonald 2011). This is because the significance of death does not lie in the day-to-day or the mundane. Instead, death is located within a domain of experience that is perhaps best described as 'extraordinary' (Giesen 2005). Practices associated with the Internet and witnessing images of extreme violence together transform experiences of suffering into experiences of victimhood, and in the process constitute a public. But this is far removed from the images of the public sphere proposed by philosophers such as Jurgen Habermas (1989), who regards the public as constituted through dialogue and assessing the validity of arguments. It is equally striking how little interest the culture of the jihad expresses in the lives of those who suffer, apart from their condition of suffering. This may help us to understand why violence appears disconnected from other forms of action such as building political organizations or other imaginaries of social transformation, but is more shaped by an imaginary of miraculous events (de Vries 2001). The jihadi encounter with violence is perhaps best understood as an example of what anthropologist Thomas Csordas calls a 'somatic mode of attention' (1993: 135).

The immediacy, intensity and unspeakableness associated with such violence suggest that insights associated with the sociology of trauma may be more appropriate to understand the dynamics at work:

> Traumas represent a moment of violent intrusion or conversion that consciousness was not able to perceive or to grasp in its full importance when it happened. They represent the rupture of the web of meaning, the break of order and continuity – a dark and inconceivable boundary that provides the framework for the constitution of meaningful histories but has no meaning by itself. Only later on, after a period of latency, can it be remembered, worked through, and spoken out. The traumatic memory reaches back to an act of violence that breaks down and reconstructs the social bond. Thus trauma, too, refers to a source that constitutes the social order but that has its own origin beyond and before this order.
>
> (Giesen 2004b: 113)

In the globlalizing jihad, a public sphere of witnesses is constructed through witnessing the traumatic violence that the victim suffers. This trauma is shared and incorporated through modes of embodied reception, involving a mode of experience that is best approached not within a framework of guilt, nor collective identity, but through a grammar of the sublime, with its strong association of powerfully opposed emotions of dread and fascination, elation and risk, one that flows easily into the contemporary culture of conspiracy, and which becomes amplified through contemporary communications technologies where experience and the void collide (Axel 2005). Within the global jihad, death is a 'point of self realization' (Khosrokhavar 2005) as opposed to a danger to be avoided. But to the extent we can access the experience of those who come to the jihad through mediated experience, what seems at stake appears different from the attempt to free oneself from guilt.

In the globalizing jihad, death appears to be located in a very modern experience, one where it is a 'dark and inconceivable boundary', a border in a world without borders, one that allows stories to be constructed but which, as Giesen suggests of trauma, one that 'offers no meaning by itself' (Giesen 2004b: 113). In the global jihad we encounter experiences of mediated violence locked within practices of repetition, where threshold states of anxiety and release are linked by bodily practices and associated with the search for hidden meaning, in a dynamic of exhaustion and exhilaration, in moments of uncanny connection and déjà vu, in a flow between fantasy and reality, in a nervous oscillation of captivation and dread. These practices underline the critical role of what Appadurai calls 'global scapes' (Appadurai 1996: 43) in the development of the jihad. They help us to understand the jihad's disconnection from engagement with concrete national realities, and why it manifests itself only through violence. The jihad does not appear as an *extension* of other forms of action, with violence being embraced when other forms of action fail. What is at stake here is not a secretive organization with an international reach, but global flows of media, image, affect, violence and imagination, one where the modes of personalized embodied experience associated with such flows shape the forms of responsibility and repetition constitutive of contemporary jihadist violence. This underlines the critical role that the social and cultural sciences have in understanding violence and terror in the twenty-first century, where violence increasingly seeks excess and rupture rather than organization and programme.

10

Conclusion: Beyond Terror?

Violence and Terror

We began this book with transformations that have become increasingly evident as the twenty-first century has taken shape. These centre on new concerns around security and public violence, and a new sense of vulnerability being evident across a range of areas, from a fear of immigrants to increasing rates of imprisonment, or the militarization of policing to the blurring of internal and external security, anxieties highlighted and literally 'concretized' in the construction of walls by states across different continents. For some authors these changes manifest a transition to a new authoritarianism (Crouch 2004), while for others they point to a mode of governance shifting from prevention to pre-emption (Massumi 2007), in an attempt to exercise power in increasingly complex and opaque societies. However they are interpreted, these cultural and political shifts became increasingly evident as justifications for war (Bobbitt 2008) and for the massive increase in military expenditure that took place during the first decade of the twenty-first century (SIPRI 2010).

These changes frame the context of this book. It set out to explore the changing forms of 'categorial violence' (Taylor 2011: 188) that have played such a critical role in these wider transformations. It is important to recognize that the actual number of events classified by courts and police as 'terrorist violence' has been far fewer over recent years in countries such as the United States or the United Kingdom when compared with earlier periods of social upheaval such as the 1970s (see the Global Terrorism Database 'data rivers' at http://www.start.umd.edu/gtd/features/GTD-Data-Rivers.aspx). None the less, terrorist violence has taken on a central role in the politics and culture of these and many other countries. It has been the source of a new symbiosis between anxiety and securitization, and this arguably constitutes the great success of contemporary terrorism, which above all seeks to induce fear rather than achieve the political objectives that its authors appear unable to articulate.

169

This context has provoked a significant realignment of the social sciences. While 'Cold War warriors' (Ranstorp 2006) assert that states remain the principal actors shaping security and violence, others focus on the social and cultural processes at work in emerging violence. These debates have converged and collided around the issue of 'terrorism' that became so central to political and cultural life after the attacks of September 2001. For a time, the 'War on Terror' established itself as a global rhetoric, used by governments as diverse as China (Clarke 2007) or Russia (Russell 2007) when responding to threats they considered illegitimate. This has involved more general transformations in modes of policing, illustrated, for example, in the United Kingdom, where in the quiet rural county of Hampshire police are reported to have carried out over 4,000 stop-and-searches under anti-terrorism legislation during a four-month period in 2005 (BBC 2005). In this context it is not surprising that a wide range of observers and scholars have been reluctant to use the term 'terrorism', considering that in so doing they became complicit in or defined by a state strategy that they are not prepared to support.

Liberating Violence

Categorial violence can take on very different forms, from the assassination of political leaders to workplace confrontations or the violence emerging in demonstrations and occupations, as with the 'Black Bloc' violence associated with what came to be known as the 'anti-globalization' or global justice movement (Thompson 2010; Dupuis-Deri 2004). This violence involves not simply an 'objective' dimension relating to the social or political change that actors seek to bring about, it also involves a 'subjective' dimension where violence is experienced as an event bringing about self-transformation or even liberation. This emphasis on the liberating power of violence has had an important place in politics, culture and philosophy, from Robespierre's celebration of terror as the means to encounter 'great things' (explored in Chapter 1) to a more general belief that the oppressed can discover their authentic selves through violence, and that engaging in violence can free us from alienation or internalized oppression. This position was argued by the existentialist philosopher Jean-Paul Sartre, for whom violence involves:

> man re-creating himself... When the peasant takes a gun in his hands, the old myths grow dim and the prohibitions are one by one forgotten. The native cures himself of colonial neuroses by thrusting out the settler through force of arms.
>
> (Sartre 1961/2001: 18, 19)

Among early sociologists, Gorg Simmel was one of many intellectuals who longed for the outbreak of the First World War as a chance for the nation to reinvigorate itself (Joas 2003: 18). This understanding of violence as an instrument of self-creation and self-transformation has been central to wars of national liberation. For China's revolutionary leader Mao Zedong 'war is the highest form of struggle' (1936, in Schram 1999a: 476), an 'antitoxin which not only eliminates the enemy's poison but also purges us of our own filth' (1938, in Schram 1999b: 336). For Mao, war was a process through which insurgents could form themselves into an army and from there into a nation, themes echoed by Menachem Begin (whom we encountered in Chapter 2) in his autobiography *The Revolt*, when he affirms a core dimension of revolutionary violence: 'We fight, therefore we are' (1951: 26).

The idea of a new identity being forged by violence and war plays an important role in a wide range of national myths, rehearsed in history classes telling of heroic deeds performed in war and celebrated in the national anthems of many countries rejoicing in the nobility of war. One such example is Mexico, where the national anthem calls for a defence of the country, and with it national banners to be 'soaked in blood' and 'fields watered in blood' (http://www.presidencia.gob.mx/mexico/?contenido=15008#mexico_simbolos_himno; accessed 30 March 2010). The image of blood watering fields evokes the metaphors of martyrdom in Lebanon and Palestine we explored in Chapter 8, where the blood of the martyr gives new life to the land. Such national myths are celebrations of a collective where, through violence, individuals become one with a principle greater than themselves, at least at the level of the collective imaginary.

Given the pervasive role violence plays in public life and imaginaries, as Charles Tilly (2002) argues, there is little sense in defining particular groups or persons as 'terrorists', as if defined by a clear and unambiguous violent identity and programme that is in some way exclusive to them. This, and the extent that the term 'terrorist' is linked to the wider securitization of societies, has led many authors to focus on a critique of new forms of power, with little or no engagement with the changing nature of violence itself. This seems evident in significant currents within 'critical terrorism studies', where 'terrorism' ultimately becomes a product of the politics of labelling (Jarvis 2009). But while there may not be a category of actors that we can meaningfully call 'terrorists', in the course of this book we have, none the less, encountered violence as an event and process that transforms in ways that escapes the control of the actors involved, and in the context of such transformations, it does appear that violence can mutate into something that can be meaningfully called 'terrorism'. Such cases present a dimension highlighted in a statement widely attributed to one of the leaders of the Popular Front for the Liberation of Palestine in 1970: 'In today's world, no one is innocent, no one is neutral. A man [sic] is either with the oppressed or with the oppressor' (cited in Garrison 2008: 23). Central to such violence is the refusal to differentiate between combatants and non-combatants. In this book we have seen that this rejection of borders and of distinction between combatants and non-combatants not only defines terrorism, it may be emerging as one of the defining transformations of warfare in the twenty-first century.

The Deinstitutionalization of War

One of the most important transformations shaping the context of this book has been a transformation of war that became increasingly evident towards the end of the twentieth century. The most obvious dimension has been the end of the state's monopoly of war and the entry of new actors into new types of conflicts, with the majority of wars fought in the twenty-first century were not opposing two or more states (SIPRI 2010), but involving instead an array of actors from militias, warlords, criminal organizations, networks, families and even individuals. This development, first theorized as 'new wars' in the 1990s (Kaldor 2001), has continued into the twenty-first century. Early attempts to make sense of this transformation were particularly influenced by the forms of war that emerged as Yugoslavia broke up in the 1990s. Mary Kaldor, for example, argues that the new wars were less about taking control of a territory and rather involved killing those of a different identity. Appadurai's reflection on emerging forms of intimate violence (2006) that we explored in Chapter 7 arrives at the same conclusion. He argues that a new violence associated with globalization is emerging, one where majorities seek to obliterate minority groups experienced as in some way 'counterfeit'. Such violence, he argues, is driven by what he called a 'fear of small numbers' (2006).

These identity processes do indeed seem a critical dimension to contemporary violence. But the cases explored in this book have highlighted other changes at work, framed by a broader shift away from the clear separation of war and peace that played such a key role in the creation of modern society, and in the disciplines that emerged to make sense of this society, first philosophy and later the social sciences. This separation was reflected in the institutional arrangements that emerged from the Congress of Vienna of 1815 following the Napoleonic Wars, which saw a clear separation between peace and war and between civilian and military (Holsti 1991: 159), a separation still evident almost a century later in the First World War, a war in which estimates suggest as many as 90 per cent of those killed were military personnel (Chesterman 2001: 2). This separation framed ideas such as

Max Weber's assertion that it was the monopoly of legitimate violence that defined the state (Weber 1918/2008).

The great transformation at work over the twentieth century has been the collapse of this separation. The debate about 'new wars' involves an attempt to understand this. Early attempts pointed to transformations in the nature of those killed in wars, with Chesterman suggesting that in the wars of the 1990s as many as 90 per cent of those killed were civilians (Chesterman 2001: 2). Demographers and population specialists also engage increasingly with this question, proposing that the key to understanding the impact of contemporary war lies in the fact that deaths resulting from humanitarian crisis far surpass the actual numbers killed in combat. This is particularly the case today, as war in the twenty-first century is shifting to poor countries with weak infrastructure that are easily devastated and which themselves become the target of war (Lacina and Petter Gleditsch 2005). This pattern of population-wide death was clearly demonstrated during the Iraq War that began in 2003 (Roberts *et al.* 2004). These transformations suggest that war does not so much seek to kill enemy combatants as to destroy the capacity of societies to function, evident in examples of what urban scholars call 'urbicide', defined as violence that sets out to erase or 'kill' cities (Graham 2004, 2012). Such violence appears equally evident in terrorism as well, in the attacks on London's transport system, or New York City's Times Square or Twin Towers.

From a military perspective the meaning of war itself is changing (see Bobbitt 2008), with the emergence of the category 'unlawful combatants' leading to a blurring of civil and military detention of prisoners, and to an uncertainty around the meaning of war itself, highlighted by the Commission of Inquiry into military detention following the events at Abu Ghraib we explored in Chapter 9. That enquiry underlines what it calls 'a new kind of warfare': 'Today the power to wage war can rest in the hands of a few dozen highly motivated people with cell phones and access to the Internet' (Independent Panel 2004: 30). But this blurring of war and peace, combatant and non-combatant, goes beyond questions of the status of fighters or prisoners. What is at stake might be signalled by the events at Abu Ghraib. They do not simply point to a demilitarization of war (with the prisoners at Abu Ghraib not being classified as military prisoners of war), but to a demilitarization extending to military personnel themselves. At Abu Ghraib this was evident in the decline of the culture of ranks, uniforms and military discipline (see Danner 2004: 133; Devji 2008: 151–2), while the violence inflicted upon detainees suggests private pleasure, in particular through its association with cultures of the holiday photo and pornographic images. What occurred at Abu Ghraib may highlight what Devji terms a 'fragmentation and privatization of military life' itself (2008: 51).

Sociologists have pointed to processes of deinstitutionalization at work across wide areas of social life, as social interactions are organized less and less in terms of roles, rules and positions in organizations, and increasingly in terms of communications. This transformation forms the basis of contemporary management theory, which argues that successful organizations are based on values rather than rules, empowerment rather than obedience (Daft 2009). A similar transformation is at work in schools, as the sociology of education underlines that schools function less and less in terms of teacher and student *roles*, with learning and teaching being determined increasingly by the quality of *interactions* that take place (see, for example, Dubet 2002). Other sociologists argue that an older model of society based on bureaucracy, hierarchy and integrated organizations is being replaced by a new type of project-based capitalism (Boltanski and Chiapello 2005). Abu Ghraib leaves us asking whether the army itself is deinstitutionalizing, mirroring these wider social transformations.

Together these transformations signal the end, or at least the extreme fragility, of a model of classical military violence, one that we saw emphasized by the importance that sociologists such as Giddens (1987) attach to uniforms, depersonalization and obedience, and to a more general theoretical model that links the centralization of violence in the hands of the state (organized in terms of the obedience and rationality) to a long-term process of pacification of society. This association of violence with the exercise of authority was not only a proposition of sociologists as diverse as Elias (1976), Giddens (1987) and Bauman (1989), it was central to Milgram's (1965, 1974) experimental attempt to test how far people would inflict violence on the basis of obedience. The events of Abu Ghraib, as well as wider transformations we have explored throughout this book, highlight the need to shift to a new paradigm of violence, one that is no longer framed in terms of organization, depersonalization and a culture of obedience.

Between Organization and Movement

As we saw in Chapter 3 and again in Chapter 8, one of the ongoing debates within terrorist studies concerns the role of organizations. Today this debate focuses on whether al-Qaeda is best understood as an organization or something else. Bruce Hoffman (2008), for example, disputes what he calls 'the myth of grassroots terrorism' and affirms the role of 'al-Qaeda central' as an organization controlling and directing contemporary terrorist action. Others such as Marc Sageman minimize the role of organizations, arguing instead that contemporary terrorism, in particular the violence emerging in Western societies, is best understood as a dynamic emerging from 'a bunch of guys' rather than the plans and programmes of an organization (2008). Khosrokhavar (2009) proposes a path beyond this opposition, distinguishing between violence located within organized insurgencies in regions such as the Middle East, South Asia and North Africa, and the 'global movement' at the core of the violence emerging in regions such as Europe and North America.

The cases and themes we have explored in this book alert us to issues at stake in this debate. Organizations were clearly central to the groups and actors that emerged out of the student and nationalist movements. We saw in Chapter 4 the extent that the Italian Red Brigades developed an organization reflecting the bureaucracy of the Italian state, reminding us of the extent that such groups can be understood as mirrors of state power (Sommier 2008a: 196), a pattern equally evident, argues Khosrokhavar (2009), in the elitism and disregard for day-to-day life that characterizes al-Qaeda, mirroring the regimes in the countries where it implanted. But as we also saw in Chapter 4, the Red Brigades and the Weather Underground were *more* than organizations. In both cases members ended up living in group houses, when they worked they handed over their wages to their leaders, and in the case of the Weather Underground the organization played an increasingly important role in issues such as sexual partners.

This type of social organization has the potential to transform itself into a sect, a community that divides the world between pure and impure, saved and damned, true believers and apostates. In Chapter 4 we saw the extent to which such groups experience the menacing power of the outside seeping into the group itself, provoking a dynamic where violence turns inwards in efforts to 'purify' and 'reconstruct' members. An event that comes to exert particularly great pressure on such organizations is the attempted departure of members, interpreted as putting at risk not only the community but also the member who is leaving, who for their own good must be brought back to the group, even if by force. This dynamic played a key role in the transition to violence that we saw in the Aum sect in Japan (Chapter 6). In the case of the Red Brigades, as political violence seemed to no longer have any meaning, we saw violence turning inwards to purify the struggle. We also saw this dynamic at work in Chapter 4 with the Japanese United Red Army, where its increasing isolation saw the group turn on itself, using violence to purge members of bourgeois contamination, leading ultimately to deaths. This purifying dynamic equally emerged as a key dimension shaping the final period of the first Palestinian Intifada, where in Chapter 5 we saw fear of *Isquat* (falling) generate fear that kissing a girlfriend could lead to becoming a traitor (Bucaille 2004: 22), leading to the most extraordinary rumours of plots (Amireh 2003).

These nationalist and student struggles underline the centrality of an imaginary where the organization is experienced as the fundamental *vehicle of action*. But when we explore paradigms of violent action that have emerged with the twenty-first century, the situation appears to be significantly different. Rather than organization, the pattern we encounter tends to take the form of the *personal commitment*, often of someone who encounters a preacher or discovers a reality, frequently via the Internet, and then decides to undertake action. In Chapter 9 we considered the case of a young female university student in Britain found guilty in 2010 of attempting to murder a Member of Parliament because of his support for British involvement in the Iraq War. Such cases highlight an absence of prior experience of action or commitment and a process of transformation *unconnected* to local community, much less organization. This relative insignificance of organizational programmes and identity is not only a characteristic of societies such as the United States or Europe. In Chapter 8 we encountered studies pointing to similar processes at work among Palestinians (Khosrokhavar 2005) and in Pakistan (Bobbitt 2008: 52). Together these suggest that programmes and political objectives which groups use to differentiate themselves from each other (Bloom 2007) matter less and less in actual trajectories towards violence.

In the twenty-first century, rather than structured organizations we increasingly encounter networks that are 'fluid, independent and unpredictable entities' (Sageman 2008: vii), a transformation at the heart of the new sense of vulnerability associated with the impossibility of *prediction* (Massumi 2007). Rather than older forms of organization we encounter networks with little or no control from a centre. Voll and Voll (2010) consider the prevalence of this pattern among people convicted of terrorism-related offences in the United States since 2001. Rather than organizational cadres, the picture of those who have attempted to engage in such violence seems better represented by the case of a 20-year-old college student who moved from being a 'suburban teenager' to spending hours viewing online videos, participating in chat rooms and purchasing under-the-counter CDs 'almost excessively' before going on to create a stream of websites, blogs and postings, all spreading the call to 'fight jihad' (Hsu and Chandler 2010). Vol and Vol (2010: 14) describe this trajectory as 'self-defined'. Neumann and Rogers, exploring similar patterns in Europe, refer to such activists as 'self-starters' (2007: 85). Sageman refers to this phenomenon as being driven by a process of 'self-selection' (2008: 117) where individuals seek out similar people on Internet chat sites; while Javier Jordán, looking at Spanish evidence, encounters a similar pattern that he describes as one of 'grassroots jihadi networks' (2007). Rather than an older form of organization, such as we saw in Chapter 4, where members of the Weather Underground would follow directives from the 'Weather bureau' (up to the point of decisions around sexual partners), contemporary patterns of actual or attempted terrorist violence point instead to what Sageman describes as 'self-organizing clandestine networks' (2008: 114).

This 'bottom up' dynamic is not to deny the role of organized groups or networks in the planning and execution of violent attacks. The British data discussed in Chapter 8 (Simcox *et al.* 2010) clearly highlights the connection between organizational links and attempts at the most catastrophic violence. But even in these cases, the links with organizations appear tenuous, and the overall data available certainly emphasizes the need to break free of images of 'mafia' and integrated secret networks following decisions emanating from a central point. And while an 'international relations paradigm' may help us explore dilemmas of foreign policy, it is of little assistance in helping us understand why a 20-year-old becomes fascinated with images of jihad to the point of creating websites and attempting to join foreign fighters, nor why an individual would attempt to kill as many people as possible in an attack on Saturday night revellers in central New York City.

Grammars of Violence: Goals, Forms and Temporalities

Throughout this book we have encountered a wide range of violence, from torture and humiliation to explosions or theatrical violence. We have encountered cases where actors seemed in control of their violence (corresponding to the rational actor model), and transformations that simply cannot be explained by the intentions of the actors. To explore these meaningfully as embodied practice we need to construct analytical tools that allow us to distinguish between them, while at the same time recognizing that violence is a medium of relationship between an actor and a victim, an actor and the intended interlocutor (which may be a government), but also between the body and the self, and between the embodied actor and an imaginary. This book demonstrates that these are not simply 'academic' categories of relevance only to university seminars. Instead, they help us understand and respond to actual violence.

The work of the Turkish political sociologist Hamit Bozarslan (2004) can help us draw these together. He distinguishes between three kinds of violence: *rational violence* largely shaped by a vision of the future; *nihilistic/self-sacrificial violence*, where change is impossible and violence is a form of cleansing or purification; and *messianic violence*, where violence announces a radically new world (see Bozarslan 2004). These are not simply subjective states of violent actors, but have a direct impact on forms and organization of violence, and this framework helps us focus more clearly on the transformations of violence we have been exploring.

What Bozarslan calls *rational violence* corresponds most closely to the paradigm of violence that aims at constructing a new order. The focus of this violence is the political or social domain, and this violence is motivated by the idea that a new world is possible. This violence is particularly evident in anti-colonial struggles aiming at a change in political regime, where actors use violence to attempt to transform power relationships within or between societies. Bozarslan emphasizes that the authors of this violence are above all 'collective actors' – typically this will take the form of organized or militarized violence, and will be linked to creating collective identities. We encountered this imaginary of the army as central to the terrorist groups that emerged out of the student movement, from the Red Brigades to the Japanese United Red Army to the Weather Underground's imaginary of a 'people's war' and the inspiration they drew from wars of national liberation. This violence also possesses a *temporality*, one where change is believed possible within the lifetime of those involved in such violence. This violence involves *risk*, but risk is managed. The aim of violent action is not to die: the actors hope one day to live in a world created by their struggle. This action also possesses a logic of *scale*: as a means to achieve a greater goal, violence will increase to the extent required to achieve its goals. It largely corresponds to Jenkins' (1975) thesis that terrorist violence wants a lot of people watching, not a lot of people dead. Many theories of 'instrumental violence' consider it to be *strategic*, something that can be taken up or put down as circumstances dictate. But as we have seen throughout this book, this type of violence is much less stable than implied by such theories, evident in the ways that it mutates and turns inwards, escaping the control of the group seeking to use it. In the case of the Weather Underground, this dynamic was most evident at the 'War Council' we explored in Chapter Four, held after 'the people' failed to take up the group's call for war. We encounter here a dynamic that Wieviorka (1993) calls an 'inversion', as the group takes the place of the revolutionary movement that fails to appear.

Bozarslan's second kind of violence, that he terms *nihilistic/self-sacrificial*, emerges as more instrumental forms of violence fragment and decompose. We encountered such violence in Chapter Eight among the early *Basiij* brigades and the Palestinian martyrs. This violence, argues Farhad Khosrokhavar (2005), is fundamentally shaped by the *impossibility* of the new world, either in the form of the revolution in Iran or the nation in Palestine. In both these cases explosions play a key role: the first *Basiij* claimed as a martyr is a teenager reputed to have tied grenades to his belt and laid under an advancing

Iraqi tank (Gruber 2012), and the *Basiij* would walk over landmines, while bombs became the preferred method of attack in Palestine. In such cases, argues Khosrokhavar, the suicide bomber feels out of place in the world, is suffering, and is dismayed not only by the state of the world but also by their own responsibility for this. Khosrokhavar attaches a significant dimension of guilt to such violence, either as a failure to serve the revolution or guilt at the attraction that the power destroying their society exercises over them, a condition he describes as 'schizoid', evident in the attraction he contends that the Israeli way of life exercises over the Palestinians (2005). We saw a related phenomenon, pointed to by Pénélope Larzillière (2004) in the extent to which the body language of Palestinian militia members appears to mirror that of the Israeli military they oppose. In these accounts, the martyr knows that their death will not bring about the new world, instead death is experienced as breaking free from a world experienced in terms of corruption and lost hope. The paradigm of social transformation here is one where change cannot come about through living, but only through dying, evident in recurring appeals for the family to rejoice, and for lost unity to be recreated by the martyr's death in the metaphor of the marriage feast (Khosrokhavar 2005).

This metaphor extends well beyond the Iranian, Lebanese and Palestinian cases. The metaphor of marriage plays an important role in the practices associated with martyrs accepted for 'one-way missions' by Lashkar-e-Taiba in Pakistan, though in this case the images of marriage are drawn from Hindu weddings, despite that organization's professed 'anti-Hindu' orientation (Abou Zahab 2007). Such recurring images of the bride or the groom underline the extent that this path to martyrdom is profoundly personal, where death comes to be the only way to construct a coherent personal subjectivity in a world where both nation and selfhood are torn apart and corrupted (Bozarslan 2004). This theme emerges powerfully in Palestinian martyrs' testaments, in particular in descriptions where the bomber imagines their exploding body tearing apart those who have prevented the birth of the Palestinian nation, just as the Palestinian nation has been torn apart by settlements (see, for example, MEMRI 2004).

This violence involves *denouncing* a world that has become unbearable more than *transforming* it. It destroys temporality, in the act of the explosion the present and the final day of judgement are collapsed into the death event. This, more than efficacy, would appear to be the basis of the bomb as the weapon of choice, because the bomb allows the whole world to be erased in an instant. The intensely personal nature of this type of death also helps us to understand the low level of organization associated with it. The first examples of this kind of violence, which we considered in Chapter 5, took the form of individuals entering Israel in search of people to kill, their

victims being schoolchildren and old ladies. This is also evident in the cha-
otic and disorganized forms of violence engaged in by militias, where there
is little attention paid to the management of risk.

The changing role of the mask that we explored in Chapter 7 highlights
important transformations of such self-sacrificial violence. In Northern
Ireland, as we saw Allen Feldman argue, the mask anonymizes and collec-
tivizes violence, breaking with an earlier tradition of the 'hardman', where
violence was a path to achieve honour, reputation and singularity. The face
of the hardman is visible, while the face of the milita-member is hidden; it
is their victim that is visible, the body exposed for all to see. In the case of
Palestinian violence, the mask, as a metaphor of transformation, is removed
through death, and its removal can be understood as an act of individual-
ization. This also helps us to understand the practice of masking associated
with militias, evident on the websites of Hamas or the Jerusalem Martyrs
Brigade, where death brings about the removal of the mask, as though only
through death do we encounter an image of the true person (McDonald 2011;
Carneiro 2009). While the *Basiij* were not masked, as we saw in Chapter 8
they entered public space through the individual act of dying, via murals,
images in cemeteries and above all television. Death in this case meant the
passage from invisibility to visibility, where only through death does the face
of the individual martyr take on public visibility. This pattern remains central
to the culture of the wider jihadi movement that took shape in the 1990s (Roy
2004: 41), and is evident in the pervasive images of the faces of dead martyrs
on jihadi websites (McDonald 2011). Jihadi websites, when compared to the
websites of other violent groups such as gangs, demonstrate particularities
that highlight these patterns: the jihadi sites focus on individual members
more than group images; they accord great importance to the presence of
martyrs; and they record acts of violence while attaching little importance
to their outcomes (Weisburd 2009). To this we might add the incidence of
internet videos which suggest that once a fighter is wounded, the response
of those around that person is to film his/her death in extreme close up, to
the extent that it sometimes appears that filming the death is more important
than responding to injuries (McDonald 2011). This highlights once again the
centrality of the visual media to constituting martyrdom as an act of witness,
a theme that first emerged in the martyr brigades in Iran.

The third type of violence pointed to by Bozarslan, one that also recurs
in other analyses of terror, is *messianic violence*, understood as cosmic or
apocalyptic violence (see Cohn 1970). Here the actor experiences violence
as detonating an extreme event that will radically transform reality. This
understanding of violence features in Laqueur's (1999) argument concerning 'new terrorism' and Juergensmeyer's (2003: 148) 'cosmic war' thesis,
which we explored in Chapter 6. We considered two cases often presented

as examples of such violence: McVeigh's attack on the Federal Building and the Aum Sarin gas attack in Tokyo, both occurring in 1995. But once we began to explore these, the violence we encountered did not obviously correspond to an attempt to detonate an 'end of the world' event. Timothy McVeigh, as Michael Barkun (1997: 256) notes, read and recommended that others read the *Turner Diaries*, a fictional account of race wars threatening the end of the 'white race', while Juergensmeyer also notes the evidence suggesting that McVeigh appeared to take this novel seriously, in particular as an account of increasing government control (2003: 32). Barkun (2006: ix) notes that McVeigh had been involved in action protesting what he saw as government complicity in hiding the existence of UFOs and aliens from the American population. These authors all underline the extent to which the destruction of the Federal Building was located within a culture of conspiracy. The rambling teachings of the leader of Aum Shinrikyo, drawing on Nostradamus, Shiva as the God of War and Jesus Christ (Lifton 1998), certainly predicted an imminent end of the world, drawing upon the pervasive presence of 'end of days' themes in popular culture in the period leading up to the year 2000 (Wojick 1999). In the pre-millennium period, the 'end of the world' seemed to offer a framework to make sense of what appeared as a sequence of murder/suicide events, from Jonestown in 1978 to Waco in 1993. But in both McVeigh's and the Aum attacks, the violence is perhaps better seen as defensive. We saw in Chapter 6 that Aum members had released Sarin a year earlier when they felt threatened by an impending legal decision, and the Tokyo attacks were hastily organized along similar lines, as a response to an expected police raid. In the letter written prior to his execution, McVeigh presented his violence as a proactive response to a raid he believed was being prepared against Elohim City by the people he held were responsible for the deaths at Waco two years earlier (McVeigh 2001). It is clear that there is no sense that Osama bin Laden's speeches were in any way framed by a belief in an approaching end of the world (Lawrence 2005). The Apocalypse may be more important in popular culture than in contemporary terrorist imaginaries.

The models proposed by Bozarslan and Khosrokhavar offer key tools for the analysis of collective violence, highlighting the types of risk, the temporal frame, the extent of collectivity, the scale and extremity of violence and the forms of hope involved. Both place the subjectivity of violent actors at the centre of their analyses, not simply to explore what these actors feel or believe, but as a way of making sense of the form that violence itself takes. These authors open out more complex analyses of public violence, taking us beyond simple dichotomies of frustration versus strategy, and help us understand the ways that social worlds and personal subjectivities are constructed through violence, where dimensions such as risk, temporality, hope and scale play a decisive role in shaping violence and its accompanying organization. These analytical models help us consider what increasingly appears to be a new type of violence, disconnected from actual communities, one that is at the same time personal and global.

The Contemporary Experience of Violence: Global, Personal

The globalization of violence we encounter in contemporary terrorism involves both continuities and transformations. The continuities are evident in references to war and the rhetoric of 'I am a soldier' as those made by the people involved in the bombing of London in 2005 (Gilroy 2006) and in practices such as the video testament that we saw emerge in Lebanon in Chapter 8; in the importance of the explosion with its accompanying destruction of time, explored in Chapters 5 and 8. But equally important are transformations. The most obvious is the absence of any reference to community, previously highlighted by themes such as the wedding feast and the metaphor of bride and groom. When we explored the London bombings in Chapter 9, for example, we encountered no evidence suggesting that in dying the martyrs understood themselves to be a bride or groom bringing into existence a community that otherwise could not come to life.

Instead there appears to be a quite different mode of individuation associated with this death, *one that appears to be linked with forms of public sphere that have replaced community*. The clearest of these transformations is evident in the shift from observer to witness, associated with global flows of images of violence and suffering. This produces an experience of responsibility that we explored in Chapter 9 – 'You are responsible, just as I am directly responsible' – lived in the first-person singular: the grammar of this responsibility is a personal one. This personalization of responsibility is by no means limited to contemporary violent movements, but reflects more general patterns of action where roles and organizations are giving way to personal experience and networks (McDonald 2006).

This helps us to understand certain characteristics of the jihadi movement. While an experience of prior activism emerges as central to the transition to violence in the student movements we explored in Chapter 4, it is largely absent in the case of jihadism. The example of a young woman who moves from non-involvement (indeed, feeling 'embarrassed' when someone she knows criticizes a Member of Parliament) to attempting to kill a Member of Parliament who voted for the Iraq War seems to capture something that, while it may not be evident in every case, does suggest a pattern. Violence does not build upon an early life and experience of activism, rather it is a medium of *rupture*, of a break with an older life and identity. This helps us understand the over-representation of converts in networks associated with al-Qaeda (Roy 2004; Sageman 2004), and the extent that such conversion experiences may be unrelated to actual religious communities, associated instead with Internet-based preachers who often possess no religious training or grounding in religious traditions (Roy 2008). This highlights the more general pattern of jihadi intellectuals and leaders claiming religious authority while possessing no formal religious education (see Roy 2004).

What is striking about emerging globalized/personalized violence is the absence of any reference to the transformations it will bring about. Faisal Devji's work (2005) alerts us to this lack of connection to the everyday world. He argues that to the extent that action focuses on death, life and the problems associated with its transformation are not central issues. As a result, he argues, day-to-day life can continue largely unaffected by the commitment evident among contemporary jihadis. This, he argues, helps us understand the absence of 'identity' of this group, manifesting a very different configuration from sect-like groups. Normal day-to-day life can continue largely unaffected by jihadi commitment, because *this commitment is not focused on transforming day-to-day activities*. The distance from everyday life is reflected in the importance of martyrdom, where the martyr, not a social struggle, occupies 'centre stage' (Khosrokhavar 2009). This narcissim may be a more general characteristic of jihadism. It is suggested by the case of a person convicted of terrorism in the UK, who described to the court that while working in a supermarket he spent his time daydreaming about becoming either a model or a jihadi fighter (Githens-Mazer and Lambert 2010: 892), or in self-styled references to action heroes that we saw in Chapter 9. Hence, the relative absence of ongoing involvement in other forms of activism that might otherwise be understood as a 'precursor' to violence. Jihadi violence in that sense is best approached as 'extra-ordinary' in the sense developed by Giesen (2005) (see Chapter 9), as outside the mundane and day-to-day routine. It becomes possible for a person, with no previous experience of activism or involvement in attempting to bring about change, to pass directly to an attempt at extreme violence. The logics of gradation and scale, where violence is a medium of conflict with another social actor or authority, do not apply. This alerts us to what in Chapter 9 we saw Brian Axel call the 'productivity of the Internet', namely its ability to construct a 'fleeting moment of connection between the not-lived and the lived' (2005: 144).

In contemporary jihadi violence, the absence of images of a transformed world alerts us to a type of temporality. Khosrokhavar argues that the violence of the jihad is located within a modern anthropology of impatience, its focus on the 'dazzling event' of death reflecting an inability to focus on bringing about change through an entire life (2009). This absence of any reference to long-term commitment and transformation can be seen as a reflection of the temporal experience in complex, network societies, where there is no longer the culture of progress and orientation to the future that once sustained cultures and movements directed towards change. The temporality of globalization, suggests Hylland Eriksen, is captured by the soap opera. This combines accelerated drama with a lack of progression, as opposed to the narrative structure of popular media in the post-Second World War period, which tended to be slow and cumulative (2007: 142). This temporal experience that characterizes network society appears central to jihadi violence, evident not only in the absence of images of the future and its dissociation of violence from social transformation, but also in the *temporality of repetition* that emerges strongly in video testaments, evident in affirmations such as 'others will come and do the same', or even 'I would like to come back and do this again and again' that we considered in Chapter 9 (http://news.bbc. co.uk/2/hi/uk_news/7330367.stm; accessed 10 January 2010).

Within this broader imaginary, death is seen as a border event or limit experience, possibly the ultimate border in a network culture that seems to lack any limit. This may parallel the place of pain we explored in the Aum sect, where pain was a mode of embodiment that seemed to make life real. The place of death in the culture of the jihad signals its fascination with the extraordinary (Giesen 2005), a fascination amplified by its culture of the hidden and revealed, largely derivative of Western conspiracy theory and its breathless search for hidden plots and secrets in the shadows, and in its absence of any reference to the future. The constant circulation of images of death in the jihad underlines both its distance from day-to-day life and a cultural politics of repetition, both sustained by a mode of experience best understood in terms of the sublime, where intensified experiences of selfhood are discovered in the tension between fascination and horror, concealment and revelation, the proximity of the unexperienceable. In this world, truth is established by the extremity and excess of violence in ways similar to the dynamics we explored in Chapter 7, where, as Devji (2005) argues, any opposition or questioning is experienced as an act of hypocrisy. This highlights a mode of violence that is both globalized and personalized, characterized by excess and fascination, by a temporality of the present and repetition, and by its disconnection from the ordinary. This globalizing violence works through temporality, affect and corporeality, echoing the experience of Internet-based encounters with martyrs explored by Axel (2005).

This disconnection from the day-to-day might suggest that we are dealing with religious violence. But rather than see the origins of this phenomenon in religious texts or even traditions, the analysis proposed throughout this book has attempted to understand the social logics at stake in this development, where we have encountered themes cutting across each other, from the collapse of borders of experience in the world of peasants subject to random violence in Colombia to the models of personal responsibility and public sphere associated with the mediatization of violence. It seems clear that the power of contemporary violence and its association with awe and events that stand outside the ordinary may lead observers to suggest that this is a product of a religious impulse, that it is 'faith' that leads to violence (Dawkins 2006: 346). Whatever the merits of religious belief, this book has been arguing that today's violence is best not approached as the product of faith, but as a product of quite different transformations.

Beyond Terror

The theoretical discussion in Chapter 3 highlighted approaches to terror underlining political, social and situational dynamics. Political cycle analyses, associated with authors such as Sidney Tarrow (1989), emphasize the fragmentation and polarization of social movements as they decline, as part of the movement becomes absorbed into the political establishment, with those opposing this becoming radicalized and committed to fighting against what is perceived to be selling out. When we explored the student movement in Chapter 4 it appeared clear that the shift to terror emerged as hopes for wider transformation were fading, the dynamic at work in the dying stages of the movement, and this shift was also evident in Chapter 5 in the development of Palestinian violence, with the transition to terrorism emerging in the context of the crushing of the Intifada and the development of the Palestinian Authority. This political logic also seems to be present in the emergence of the global jihadi movement, where priority came to be given to global violence in part because of the failure or weakness of local/national movements associated with what Oliver Roy (1994) calls the 'failure of political Islam'.

We also considered social and cultural dynamics, in particular associated with the work of Michel Wieviorka (1993), who traces the transformation of militant groups as they embrace violence, exploring the way that their closure involves the development of sect-like dimensions, leading the terrorist to seek to take the place of the absent movement. In his more recent work, Wieviorka (2009) focuses on subjective experience as such, distinguishing between what he calls the 'floating subject', where the actor is unable to locate himself or herself within a social relationship and conflict, and what he calls the 'hyper-subject' where the actor finds himself or herself in a world hypercharged with meanings (2009). This analysis captures critical dimensions of the dynamic we have explored in the global jihad, where the fusion previously achieved by the sect gives way to a type of movement shaped by both forms of subjectivity that Wieviorka describes. This involves the impossibility of constructing an actual social relationship and conflict together with the hypercharged meanings associated with conspiracy theory and the extraordinary. The global jihad appears to manifest something of the oscillation that we considered in Chapter 7, in Daniel Pécaut's (2000) analysis of extreme violence in Colombia, where actors live in worlds no longer defined by geography but by the potential and reality of violence, and where events seem so unintelligible that they are experienced as portentous, at the same time both unintelligible and hypercharged with meaning. Wieviorka's focus on subjectivity and violence helps us understand something of the shift from the association of terror with sect-like organizations typical of an earlier period to contemporary forms of terror associated with mediated practices and an absence of identity and organization.

These dimensions converge to highlight the importance of the 'situational analysis' of violence proposed by Randall Collins (2008) that we explored in Chapter 3. Collins emphasizes the importance of face-to-face interactions to understanding transformations of violence, in particular in contexts such as protests, which he suggests involve what amounts to a 'dance' between protestors and police. Rather than approach violence as a strategy, for Collins it is an event that is a *co-construction of embodied actors*. This insight is of critical importance in attempting to make sense of contemporary jihadi violence, but in this case the 'situation' is no longer defined in terms of the physical co-presence that exists between protesters and police. In the 1990s, social scientists set out to explore emerging responses to *distant suffering* (Boltanski 1999), tracing both the rise of global humanitarian movements and the increasing presence of suffering in the media, in particular television. Today's jihadi movements alert us to a new phenomenon, the development of *distant violence*, and the complexity of the grammars of communication, action and embodied rhythms pointed to by Collins, today constructed through global violence. Such violence flows across the frontiers not only of states and institutions, but also the frontiers of personal subjectivities, creating new types of social space and social experiences.

It is clear that any response to violence and terror must involve policing and intelligence, disruption and prevention. However, looking back over the period of the War on Terror one cannot but be fearful of the extent it increased the global impact of groups such as al-Qaeda, presented as a dark and potent force, while at the same time amplifying the militarization of policing and a wider politics of fear. Researchers working across a range of countries (McPhail and McCarthy 2005) argue that the current recourse to paramilitary models of policing reverses the trend towards more negotiated forms of crowd control that had been emerging from the 1970s as a response to the violence of the 1960s. With Collins' emphasis on situational dynamics in mind, such studies highlight the potential in today's context of securitization for military models of policing to provoke military conceptions of protest, something that we saw in groups such as the Weather Underground and their 'people's war' against the police.

But beyond issues of policing, contemporary terrorism raises issues of wider patterns of action and social transformation. There may be a parallel between the anarchist terrorism that we considered in Chapter 2 and today's jihadi violence. As Michel Wieviorka (1993) argues, anarchists in the late 1800s made constant references to a workers' movement at a time when such a movement was a potential more than a reality. Significantly, anarchist terrorism disappeared as workers' movements developed and became institutionalized, to the point that what inspired fear and terror in the 1890s was only a memory in the 1920s. It is possible that the jihadi violence we encounter today may involve a similar process, that it may in part be understandable in terms of movements yet to be born. Khosrokhavar points to the rise of a cluster of movements within contemporary Muslim experience, from new forms of mysticism, new movements among Muslim intellectuals, feminists, artists and cultural actors (journalists, academics, film makers, writers and movie stars) that, he argues, focus on life and possess the potential to counter the narcissism and exhibitionism so central to the jihad's 'holy death' (2009: 331). These movements of renewal in contemporary Islam cannot exist in a vacuum, but can only thrive in a wider politics of constructing other forms of globalization and other responses to suffering and violence. Signs of this are evident in what has come to be known as the Arab Spring, combing social and religious mobilizations that have within them the potential to render jihadism anachronistic (Khosrokhavar 2012). To the extent that such movements create new ways of thinking about and experiencing new solidarities, they can play a role in countering the toxic effect of conspiracy theories that combine with cultural flows around violence.

At the same time the jihad alerts us to new global realities of responsibility, in particular the personalized forms of responsibility emerging in contemporary globalization (see Devji 2008). But, as Wieviorka's work suggests (2009), this is linked to a kind of subjectivity that oscillates between 'floating' outside social relationships and finding itself captured by hypercharged forms of portent and meaning. The jihad alerts us to both the way that sects and organizations have given way to global mediascapes, and to the way that war and violence are no longer contained within the frameworks established over the nineteenth century, and which have remained so important to sociological approaches to violence. While in the jihad we find new forms of responsibility, this responsibility translates into action that mirrors, and to a significant extent is constituted by, what it opposes, as is evident in the justifications that almost always take the form of 'your violence, my violence'.

The challenge that confronts us today is not simply to develop forms of policing and the disruption of terrorism that avoid irreparable damage to civic cultures. It is one of inventing new forms of responsibility for the other, grounded in actual social struggles, lives and temporalities, as opposed to the accelerated drama and repetition of jihadism. In that sense, jihadism may alert us not simply to the collapse of the separation of war and peace and to new grammars of violence, it may also alert us to the collapse of older cultures and representations of social change and justice. To respond to contemporary terror we have to find ways not simply to end the expansion of fear and our readiness to engage in war. We need also to create new ways of experiencing and living our responsibility for each other.

Bibliography

Abdo, Nahla (1991) 'Women of the Intifada: gender, class and national liberation', *Race and Class*, 32, 4, 19–34

Abou Zahab, Mariam (2007) 'I shall be waiting for you at the door of paradise: the Pakistani martyrs of the Lashkar-e Taiba (Army of the Pure)', in Rao Aparna, Michael Bollig and Monika Bock (eds) *The Practice of War: Production, Reproduction and Communication of Armed Violence*, New York: Berghan Books, pp. 133–59

Abou Zahab, Mariam and Olivier Roy (2004) *Islamic Networks: The Pakistan–Afghan Connection*, London: Hurst

Abrahamian, Ervand (1992) *The Iranian Mojahedin*, New Haven: Yale University Press

Agamben, Giorgio (1998) *Homo Sacer: Sovereign Power and Bare Life*, trans. Daniel Heller-Roazen. Stanford: Stanford University Press

Ahmadi, Alireza (2007) 'Suicide by self-immolation: comprehensive overview, experiences and suggestions', *Journal of Burn Care and Research*, 28, 1, 30–41

Alastuey, Eduardo (2005) 'La cultura del horror en las sociedades avanzadas', *Revista Española de investigations sociologicas*, 110, 53–90

Alexander, J. (2006) 'From the depths of despair: performance, counterperformance and September 11', in J. Alexander, B. Giesen and J. Mast (eds) *Social Performance: Symbolic Action, Cultural Pragmatics and Ritual*, Cambridge: Cambridge University Press, pp. 91–114

Allison, A. (2009) 'Pocket capitalism and virtual intimacy: Pokemon as symptom of post-industrial youth culture', in Jennifer Cole and Deborah Durham (eds) *Figuring the Future: Globalization and the temporalities of Children and Youth*, Santa Fe: School for Advanced Research Press, pp. 179–96

Amireh, Amal (2003) 'Between complicity and subversion: body politics in Palestinian national narrative', *South Atlantic Quarterly*, 102, 4, 747–72

Amir-Moezzi, M. A. (2011) *The Spirituality of Shi'i Islam*, London: Tauris

Amnesty International (2006) *Ambassador of Conscience Award: The Words of Nelson Mandela*, available at http://www.amnesty.org/en/library/info/ACT10/008/2006 (accessed 9 January 2010)

Anderson, P. (2004) 'To lie down to death for days', *Cultural Studies*, 18, 6, 816–46

Andrews, J. (1994) *Painters and Politics in the People's Republic of China, 1949–1979*, Berkeley: University of California Press

Appadurai, Arjun (1996) *Modernity at Large: Cultural Dimensions of Modernity*, Minneapolis: University of Minnesota Press

Appadurai, Arjun (2006) *Fear of Small Numbers*, Durham: Duke University Press

Arendt, Hannah (1951/2009) *The Origins of Totalitarianism*, Orlando: Harcourt

Arendt, H. (1963) *Eichmann in Jerusalem: A Report on the Banality of Evil*, New York: Viking

Argenti, Nicolas (2006) 'Remembering the future: slavery, youth and masking in the Cameroon grassfields', *Social Anthropology*, 14, 1, 49–69

Asad, Talal (2003) *Formations of the Secular*, Stanford: Stanford University Press

Atchison, Andrew (2010) 'Charles Manson and the family: the application of sociological theories to multiple murder', *International Journal of Offender Therapy and Comparative Criminology*, 54, 3, 1–28

Aust, Stefan (2008) *The Baader Meinhof Complex*, Oxford: The Bodley Head

Austin, John (1976) *How to Do Things with Words*, Oxford: Oxford University Press

Axel, Brian (2002) 'The diasporic imaginary', *Public Culture* 14, 2, 411–28

Axel, Brian (2005) 'Diasporic sublime: Sikh martyrs, Internet mediations and the question of the unimaginable', *Sikh Formations* 1, 1, 127–54

Ayers, B. (2001) *Fugitive Days: A Memoir*, Boston: Beacon Press

Azzam, Abdullah (2003) *The Lofty Mountain*, trans. Umm Salamah al-Ansariyyah and Shaheed Suraqah al-Andalusi. London: Azzam Publications

Azzam, Maha (2006) 'Islamism revisited', *International Affairs*, 82, 6, 1119–32

Bagon, P. (2003) *The Impact of the Jewish Underground upon Anglo-Jewry*, University of Oxford, M. Phil. thesis, available at http://users.ox.ac.uk/~metheses/Bagon.pdf (accessed 30 March 2010)

Bairner, A. (1999) 'Masculinity, violence and the Irish peace process', *Capital and Class*, 23, 125–44

Baixas, Lionel and Charlène Simon (2008) 'From protesters to martyrs: how to become a 'true' Sikh', *South Asia Multidisciplinary Academic Journal*, 2, available at http://samaj.revues.org/document1532.html (accessed 9 January 2010)

Bakker, E. (2006) *Jihadi Terrorists in Europe*, Clingendale: Netherlands Institute of International Relations

Balibar, Etienne (2009) 'Violence and civility: on the limits of political anthropology', *Differences: A Journal of Feminist Cultural Studies*, 20, 2/3, 9–35

Barkun, M. (1989) 'Millenarian aspects of "white supremacist" movements', *Terrorism and Political Violence*, 1, 4, 409–34

Barkun, M. (1994) 'Reflections after Waco: millennialists and the state', in James Lewis (ed.) *From the Ashes: Making Sense of Waco*, New York: Rowman & Littlefield, pp. 41–50

Barkun, M. (1996) 'Religion, militias and Oklahoma city: the mind of conspiratiorialists', *Terrorism and Political Violence*, 8, 1, 50–64

Barkun, M. (1997) *Religion and the Racist Right: The Origins of the Christian Identity Movement*, Chapel Hill: University of North Carolina Press

Barkun, M. (2006) *A Culture of Conspiracy: Apocalyptic Vision in Contemporary America*, Berkeley: University of California Press

Bauman, Z. (1989) *Modernity and the Holocaust*, Ithaca: Cornell University Press

Bayat, Asef (1998) 'Revolution without movement, movement without revolution: comparing Islamic activism in Iran and Egypt', *Comparative Studies in Society and History*, 40, 1, 136–69

BBC (2005) 'Are police misusing stop-and-search?', 23 October, available at http://news.bbc.co.uk/2/hi/uk_news/4365572.stm (accessed 10 January 2010)

Begin, Menachem (1951) *The Revolt: The Story of the Irgun*, New York: Steimatzky

Begin, Menachem (1978) 'Nobel Lecture', in Irwin Adams and Tore Frangsmyr (eds) *Nobel Lectures: Peace 1971–1980*, London: World Scientific Press, pp. 195–201

Bennett, H. (2011) 'Soldiers in the court room: the British Army's part in the Kenya Emergency under the legal spotlight', *The Journal of Imperial and Commonwealth History*, 39, 5, 717–30

Biggs, Michael (2005) 'Dying without killing: self-immolations, 1963–2002', in D. Gambetta (ed.) *Making Sense of Suicide Missions*, Oxford: Oxford University Press, pp. 173–208

bin Laden (2004) 'God knows it did not cross our minds to attack the towers', *The Guardian*, 30 October, available at http://www.guardian.co.uk/world/2004/oct/30/alqaida.september11, accessed 1 October 2007

Binski, Paul (1996) *Medieval Death: Ritual and Representation*, Ithaca: Cornell University Press

Birrell, Ross (2005) 'The gift of terror: suicide bombing as potlatch', in Graham Coulter-Smith and Maurice Owen (eds) *Art in the Age of Terrorism*, London: University of Southhampton/ Paul Holberton Press, pp. 96–113

Bloom, Mia (2007) *Dying to Kill: The Allure of Suicide Terror*, New York: Columbia University Press

Bobbitt, Philip (2008) *Terror and Consent: The Wars for the 21st Century*, New York: Penguin

Boltanski, Luc (1999) *Distant Suffering: Morality, Media and Politics*, Cambridge: Cambridge University Press

Boltanski, Luc (1993/1999) *Distant Suffering: Morality, Media and Politics*, trans. Graham Burchell Cambridge: Cambridge University Press

Boltanski, Luc and Eve Chiapello (2005) *The New Spirit of Capitalism*, London: Verso

Bourgois, Philippe (1996) *In Search of Respect: Selling Crack in El Barrio*, Cambridge: Cambridge University Press

Bourke, Joanna (2000) *An Intimate History of Killing: Face to Face Killing in Twentieth Century Warfare*, New York: Basic Books

Bowyer Bell, J. (1972) 'Assassination in international politics', *International Studies Quarterly*, 16, 1, 59–82

Box, M. and G. McCormack (2004) 'Terror in Japan', *Critical Asian Studies*, 36, 1, 91–112

Bozarslan, Hamit (2004) *Violence in the Middle East: From Political Struggle to Self-Sacrifice*, Princeton: Marcus Wiener

Brachman, Jarret (2008) *Global Jihadism: Theory and Practice*, London: Routledge

Bradley, S. (2009) *Harlem vs Columbia University: Black Student Power in the Late 1960s*, Chicago: University of Illinois Press

Branigan, T. (2011) 'Dali Lama's prayers for Tibetans "terrorism in disguise", China says', *The Guardian*, 19 October 2011, available at http://www.guardian.co.uk/world/2011/oct/19 /dalai-lama-prayers-tibetans-terrorism (accessed 10 January 2012)

Brietz Monta, Susannah (2005) *Martyrdom and Literature in Early Modern England*, Cambridge: Cambridge University Press

Brown, A. (2010) 'Beyond "good" and "evil": breaking down binary oppositions in holocaust representations of "privileged" Jews', *History Compass*, 8, 5, 407–18

Brown, Ian (1990) *Khomeini's Forgotten Sons: The Story of Iran's Boy Soldiers*, London: Grey Seal Books

Brown, Wendy (2010) *Walled States, Waning Sovereignty*, Cambridge, MA: MIT Press

Browning, C. (1992) *Ordinary Men: Reserve Police Battalion 101 and the Final Solution in Poland*, New York: Harper

Brym, Robert and Bader Araj (2006) 'Suicide bombing as strategy and interaction: the case of the second Intifada', *Social Forces*, 84, 4, 1969–86

Brym, Robert and Bader Araj (2008) 'Palestinian suicide bombing revisited: a critique of the outbidding thesis', *Political Science Quarterly*, 123, 3, 1–15

Bucaille, Laetitia (2004) *Growing Up Palestinian: Israeli Occupation and the Intifada Generation*, Princeton: Princeton University Press

Bucaille, Laetitia (2006) 'Israël face aux attentats-suicides: le nouvel ethos de la violence', *Cultures et Conflits*, 63, 83–99

Burns, J. and A. Cowell (2012) 'Militants plead guilty in plan to bomb London Stock Exchange', *The New York Times*, 1 February, available at http://www.nytimes.com/2012/02/02/world /europe/militants-admit-plan-to-bomb-london-stock-exchange.html(accessed 2 February 2012)

Butel, Eric (2002) 'Martyr et sainteté dans la literature de guerre Irak–Iran', in C. Mayeur-Jaouen (ed.) *Saints et Héros du Moyen-Orient Contemporain*, Paris: Maisonneuve & Larose, pp. 301–17

Byman, D. (1998) 'The logic of ethnic terrorism', *Studies in Conflict and Terrorism*, 21, 2, 149–69

Cabrera, Martha (2005) 'Exceso y defecto de la memoria: violencia política, terror, visibilidad e invisibilidad', *Oasis*, 11, 39–56

Cahagnet, Louis Alphonse (1855) *The Celestial Telegraph: or, Secrets of the Life to Come, Revealed through Magnetism*, New York: Partridge and Brittan

Caldwell, W. (2008) *1968: Dreams of Revolution*, New York: Algora Publishing

Cameron, G. (1999) 'Multi-track microproliferation: lessons from Aum Shinrinkyo and al Qaeda', *Studies in Conflict and Terrorism*, 22, 4, 277–309

Campion-Vincent, Véronique (2005). *La société parano: Théories du complot, menaces et incertitudes*. Paris: Payot

Capoya, E. and K. Tomkins (eds) (1975) *The Essential Kropotkin*, New York: Liveright Publishing Company

Carneiro, L. (2009) 'Dying to save us: multimediality in constructing mythical and religious narratives of Islamic fundamentalist martyrs', *Estudos em Comunicacao*, 5, 1–19

Capoya, E. and K. Tomkins (eds) (1975) *The Essential Kropotkin*, New York: Liveright Publishing Company

Casciani, D. (2009) 'Trio cleared of 7/7 attacks', *BBC World News*, available at http://news.bbc.co.uk/2/hi/uk_news/7507953.stm (accessed 30 March 2010)

Castells, M. (2001) *The Internet Galaxy*, Oxford: Oxford University Press

Catanzaro, Raimondo (ed.) (1991) *The Red Brigades and Left-wing Terrorism in Italy*, London: Pinter

Cavarero, Adriana (2008) *Horrorism: Naming Contemporary Violence*, New York: Columbia University Press

Chacón, Jennifer (2007) 'Unsecured borders: immigration restrictions, crime control and national security', *Connecticut Law Review*, 39, 5, available at http://papers.ssrn.com/sol3/papers.cfm?abstract_id=1028569 (accessed 30 March 2011)

Cechova-Vayleux, E., M. Briere, B. Gohier, J. B. Garré and S. Richard-Davantoy (2010) 'Self-immolation of the Soviet opponents in central Europe: suicidal behaviour or political protest?', *European Psychiatry*, 25, 1, 1352

Chartrand, S. (1990) 'Mideast tensions: Palestinian stabs 3 Israelis dead – revenge for Mosque melee seen', *New York Times*, 22 October 22 available at http://www.nytimes.com/1990/10/22/world/mideast-tensions-palestinian-stabs-3-israelis-dead-revenge-for-mosque-melee-seen.html?pagewanted=all&src=pm. accessed 20 March 2011

Chelkowski, Peter (2005) 'Time out of memory: Ta'ziyeh, the total drama', *The Drama Review*, 49, 4, 15–27

Chen, M. (2010) 'Alienated: a reworking of the racialization thesis after September 11', *American University Journal of Gender, Social Policy and the Law*, 18, 3, 411–37

Chenoweth, E. and M. Stephan (2011) *Why Civil Resistance Works: The Strategic Logic of Nonviolent Conflict*, New York: Columbia University Press

Chesterman, Simon (ed.) (2001) *Civilians in War*, Boulder: Lynne Rienner

Chomsky, N. (2011) *Deterring Democracy*, New York: Random House

Clarke, Michael (2007) *China's 'War on Terror' in Xinjiang: Human Security and the Causes of Violent Uighur Separatism*, Regional Outlook Paper No. 1, Brisbane: Griffith University

Clutterbuck, L. (2004) 'The progenitors of terrorism: Russian revolutionaries or extreme Irish Republicans?', *Terrorism and Political Violence*, 16, 1, 154–81

CNN (2001) 'Bin Laden says he wasn't behind attacks', 16 September, available at http://articles.cnn.com/2001-09-16/us/inv.binladen.denial_1_bin-laden-taliban-supreme-leader-mullah-mohammed-omar?_s=PM:US (accessed 10 March 2009)

Cohn, Norman (1970) *The Pursuit of the Millennium: Revolutionary Millenarians and Mystical Anarchists in the Middle Ages*, New York: Oxford University Press

Collins, R. (2008) *Violence: A micro-sociological theory*, Princeton: Princeton University Press

Connolly, W. (2005) *Pluralism*, Durham: Duke University Press

Corradi, Consuelo (2007) 'Identity and extreme violence: some elements for a definition of violence in modernity', in Alessandro Cavalli (ed.) *Issues and Trends in Italian Sociology*, Naples: Scriptweb, pp. 85–109

Crelinsten, R. (2009) *Counterterrorism*, Cambridge: Polity Press

Crenshaw, Martha (1981) 'The causes of terrorism', *Comparative Politics*, 13, 4, 379–99

Crenshaw, M. (1987) 'Theories of terrorism: instrumental and organizational approaches', *Journal of Strategic Studies*, 10, 4, 13–31

Crenshaw, Martha (ed.) (1995) *Terrorism in Context*, Philadelphia: Pennsylvania State University Press

Crenshaw, Martha (2000) 'The psychology of terrorism: an agenda for the 21st century', *Political Psychology*, 21, 2, 405–20

Crook, Bernard (2001) *Europe: An Encyclopedia since 1945*, London: Routledge

Crouch, Colin and Alessandro Pizzorno (eds) (1978) *The Resurgence of Class Conflict in Western Europe since 1968*, London: Macmillan

Crouch, Colin (2004) *Post-Democracy*, Cambridge: Polity

Csordas, Thomas (1993) 'Somatic modes of attention', *Cultural Anthropology*, 8, 2, 135–56

Cuninghame, P. (2011) 'Hot Autumn: Italy's factory councils and autonomous workers' assemblies', in I. Ness and D. Azzellini (eds) *Ours to Master and to Own: Workers' Control from the Commune to the Present*, New York: Haymarket Books, pp. 322–37

Daft, R. (2009) *Organization Theory and Design*, 10th edn, Mason: Cengage Learning

Danner, Mark (2004) *Torture and Truth: America, Abu Ghraib and the War on Terror*, New York: New York Review of Books

Darweish, Marwan (1989) 'The Intifada: social change', *Race & Class*, 31, 2, 47–61

Dauphinée, Elizabeth (2007) 'The politics of the body in pain: reading the ethics of imagery', *Security Dialogue*, 38, 139–55.

Davis, Erik (1998) *TechGnosis: Myth, Magic and Mysticism in the Age of Information*, New York: Three Rivers Press

Dawkins, Richard (2006) *The God Delusion*, London: Bantam Press

Dean, J. (1998) *Aliens in America: Conspiracy Cultures from Outerspace to Cyberspace*, Ithaca: Cornell University Press

de Grazia, E. (2006) 'The Haymarket bomb', *Law and Literature*, 18, 3, 283–322

Dein, Simona and Ronald Littlewood (2000) 'Apocalyptic suicide', *Mental Health, Religion and Culture*, 3, 2, 109–14

della Porta, D. (1992) 'Institutional responses to terrorism: the Italian case', *Terrorism and Political Violence*, 4, 4, 151–70

della Porta, Donatella (1995) *Social Movements, Political Violence and the State: A Comparative Analysis of Italy and Germany*, Cambridge: Cambridge University Press

della Porta, D. (2009) 'Leaving underground organizations: a sociological analysis of the Italian case', in Tore Bjorgo and John Horgan (eds) *Leaving Terrorism Behind: Individual and Collective Disengagement*, London: Routledge, pp. 66–87

della Porta, Donatella, Abby Peterson and Herbert Reiter (eds) (2006) *The Policing of Transnational Protest*, London: Ashgate

de Sade, D. A. (1787/2010) *Justine or the Misfortunes of Virtue*, London: HarperCollins

Devji, Faisal (2005) *Landscapes of the Jihad: Militancy, Morality, Modernity*, London: Hurst

Devji, Faisal (2008) *The Terrorist in Search of Humanity: Militant Islam and Global Politics*, London: Hurst

de Vries, Hent (2001) 'Of miracles and special effects', *International Journal for Philosophy of Religion*, 50, 41–56

Dillon, M. and J. Reid (2009) *The Liberal Way of War: Killing to Make Life Live*, London: Routledge

Dixon, P. (2000) 'Britain's "Vietnam Syndrome"? Public opinion and British military intervention from Palestine to Yugoslavia', *Review of International Studies*, 26, 99–121

Dollard, John, Leonard Doob, Neil Miller, O. H. Mowrer and Robert Sears (1939) *Frustration-Aggression*, New Haven: Yale University Press

Downer, John (1987) *War without Mercy: Race and Power in the Pacific War*, New York: Pantheon

Drake, Richard (1995) *The Aldo Moro Murder Case*, Harvard: Harvard University Press

Drake, Richard (1999) 'Italy in the 1960s: a legacy of terrorism and liberation', *South Central Review*, 16, 4, 62–76

Dubet, François (1992) 'A propos de la violence des jeunes', *Cultures et Conflits*, 6, available at http://conflits.revues.org/672?lang=en#entries (accessed 1 November 2012)

Dubet, François (2002) *Le Déclin de l'institution*, Paris: Editions du Seuil

Dudai, R. and H. Cohen (2007) 'Triangle of betrayal: collaborators and transitional justice in the Israeli–Palestinian Conflict', *Journal of Human Rights*, 6, 37–58

Dupuis-Deri, Francis (2004) 'Penser l'action direct des Black Blocs', *Politix*, 17, 4, 79–109

Durham, M. (1996) 'Preparing for Armageddon: citizen militias, the patriot movement and the Oklahoma City bombing', *Terrorism and Political Violence*, 8, 1, 65–79

Durham, M. (2007) *White Rage: The Extreme Right and American Politics*, London: Routledge

Durkheim, E. (2001) *The Elementary Forms of Religious Life*, Oxford: Oxford University Press

Eate, P. (2008) 'The replication and excess of disciplinary power in Sekigun and Aum Shinrikyo', *New Voices: A Journal for Emerging Scholars of Japanese Studies in Australia*, 2, pp. 153–78

Eckhardt, W. (1992) *Civilizations, Empires, and Wars: A Quantitative History of War*, Jefferson, NC: McFarland

Edgar, Iain (2007) 'The inspirational night dream in the motivation and justification of jihad', *Nova Religio: The Journal of Alternative and Emergent Religions*, 11, 2, 59–76

Eisenstadt, Shmuel Noah (1999) *Fundamentalism, Sectarianism and Revolution: The Jacobin Dimensions of Modernity*, Cambridge: Cambridge University Press

Elias, N. (1976) *The Civilizing Process: Sociogenic and Psychogenic Investigations*, Oxford: Blackwell

Elias, Norbert (1983) *The Court Society*, New York: Pantheon

Escobar, Edward (1993) 'The dialectics of repression: the Los Angeles Police Department and the Chicano Movement, 1968–1971', *Journal of American History*, March, 1483–514

Evans, B. (2010) 'Terror in all eventuality', *Theory and Event*, 13, 1, available at http://muse.jhu.edu/journals/theory_and_event/v013/13.3.evans01.html, accessed 30 March 2011

Falah, Ghazi-Walid (2003) 'Dynamics and patterns of the shrinking of Arab lands in Palestine', *Political Geography*, 22, 2, 179–209

Farrell, W. (1990) *Blood and Rage: The Story of the Japanese Red Army*, New York: Lexington Books

Farsoun, S. and C. Zacharia (1997) *Palestine and the Palestinians*, Boulder: Westview Press

Feitz, Lindsey and Joane Nagel (2008) 'The militarization of gender and sexuality in the Iraq War' in H. Carreiras (ed.) *Women in the Military and in Armed Conflict*, Wiesbaden: Verlag

Feldman, Allen (1991) *Formations of Violence: The Narrative of the Body and Political Terror in Northern Ireland*, Chicago: University of Chicago Press

Feldman, Allen (2003) 'Political terror and the technologies of memory: excuse, sacrifice, commodification and actuarial moralities', *Radical History Review*, 85, 58–73

Feldman, Allen (2005) 'On the actuarial gaze', *Cultural Studies*, 19, 2, 203–26

Fenster, M. (2008) *Conspiracy Theories: Secrecy and Power in American Culture* (2nd edn), Minneapolis: University of Minnesota Press

Fine, S. (1955) 'Anarchism and the assassination of McKinley', *The American Historical Review*, 60, 4, July, 777–99

Fleming, M. (1980) 'Propaganda by the deed: terrorism and anarchist theory in late nineteenth-century Europe', *Studies in Conflict and Terrorism*, 1/4, 1–23

Foot, J. (2007) 'The death of Giuseppe Pinelli: truth, representation, memory' in S. Gundle and L. Rinaldi (eds) *Assassination and Murder in Modern Italy: Transformations in Society and Culture*, New York: Palgrave Macmillan: 59–72

Foot, J. (2009) 'Contested memories: Milan and Piazza Fontana', in P. Antonello and A. O'Leary (eds) *Imagining Terrorism. The Rhetoric and Representation of Political Violence in Italy 1969–2009*, London: Modern Humanities Research Association, pp. 152–66

Forman, Geremy and Alexandre Kedar (2004) 'From Arab land to "Israel Lands": the legal dispossession of the Palestinians displaced by Israel in the wake of 1948', *Environment and Planning D: Society and Space*, 22, 6, 809–30

Franq, B. (1986) 'Les cellules communistes combattantes: Les deux figures d'une inversion', *Sociologie du Travail*, 4, 3, 458–83

Frisch, H. (2003) 'Debating Palestinian strategy in the al-Aqsa Intifada', *Terrorism and Political Violence*, 15, 2, 61–80

Galfré, Monica (2010) 'Left-wing armed struggle and political violence in 1970s Italy', *Twentieth Century Communism*, 2, 1, 114–40

Gage, B. (2009) *The Day Wall Street Exploded*, New York: Oxford University Press

Gambetta, Diego and Steffen Hertog (2009) 'Why are there so many engineers among Islamic radicals?', *European Journal of Sociology*, 50, 2, 201–30

Garrison, A. (2008) 'The theory and application of terrorism: a review of historical development', in B. Bowden and M. Davis (eds) *Terror: From Tyrannicide to Terrorism*, Brisbane: University of Queensland Press

Gentry, Caron (2004) 'The relationship between new social movement theory and terrorism studies: the role of leadership, membership, ideology and gender', *Terrorism and Political Violence*, 16, 2, 274–93

Gerges, Fawaz (2005) *The Far Enemy: Why Jihad Went Global*, Cambridge: Cambridge University Press

Gerges, Fawaz (2010) 'The transformation of Hamas', *The Nation*, 25 January, available at http://www.thenation.com/article/transformation-hamas# (accessed 20 November 2012)

Giacaman, R. and P. Johnson (1994) 'Searching for strategies: the Palestinian women's movement in the new era', *Middle East Report*, 186, 22–5

Giachetti, Diego and Marco Scavino (1999) *La FIAT in mano agli operai, l'autunno caldo del 1969*, Pisa: BFS Edizioni

Gibbs, N. (2001) 'Thanksgiving holiday in the post 9/11 world', *Time*, available at www.time.com /time/covers/1101011119/story.html (acccesed 10 January 2010)

Giddens, A. (1987) *The Nation-State and Violence*, Cambridge: Polity Press

Giddens, A. (2003) *Runaway World*, Cambridge: Polity Press

Giesen, Bernhard (2004a) *Triumph and Trauma*, Boulder: Paradigm

Giesen, Bernhard (2004b) 'The trauma of perpetrators', in Jeffrey Alexander (ed.) *Cultural Trauma and Collective Identity*, Berkeley: University of California Press, pp. 112–54

Giesen, Bernhard (2005) 'Performing transcendence in politics: sovereignty, deviance and the void of meaning', *Sociological Theory*, 23, 2, 275–85

Gilroy, P. (2006) 'Multiculture in times of war: an inaugural lecture given at the London School of Economics', *Critical Quarterly*, 48, 4, 27–45

Gitlin, Todd (1993) *The Sixties: Years of Hope, Days of Rage*, New York: Bantam Dell

Githens-Mazer, J. and R. Lambert (2010) 'Why conventional wisdom on radicalization fails: the persistence of a failed discourse', *International Affairs*, 86, 4, 889–901

Glasner, M. (2005) 'Porn site offers soldiers free access in exchange for photos of dead Iraqis', *OJR: The Online Journalism Review*, 20 September, available at http://www.ojr.org/ojr/stories/050920glaser/ (accessed 9 January 2010

Glynn, Ruth (2009) 'Writing the terrorist self: the unspeakable alterity of Italy's female perpetrators', *Feminist Review*, 92, 1–18

Goldsmith, B. (2002) 'Asylum seekers sew lips together', *The Guardian*, 19 January, available at http://www.guardian.co.uk/world/2002/jan/19/immigration.uk (accessed 28 April 2010)

Goodwin, Jeff (2006) 'A theory of categorical terrorism', *Social Forces*, 48, 4, 2027–46

Goto-Jones, C. (2009) *Japan: A Very Short Introduction*, Oxford: Oxford University Press

Gould, R. (1993) 'Trade cohesion, class unity and urban insurrection: artisanal activism in the Paris commune', *American Journal of Sociology*, 98, 4, 721–54

Gourevitch, Phillip and Errol Morris (2008) *Standard Operating Procedure*, New York: Penguin

Graham, Stephen (2004) 'Constructing urbicide by bulldozer in the occupied territories', in S. Graham (ed.) *Cities, War and Terrorism; Towards and Urban Geopolitics*, Oxford: Blackwell, pp. 192–213

Graham, S. (2012) 'When life itself is war: on the urbanization of military and security doctrine', *International Journal of Urban and Regional Research*, 36, 1, 136–55

Green, Sam and Bill Siegel (2003) *The Weather Underground: The Explosive Story of America's Most Notorious Revolutionaries*, Berkeley: The Free History Project

Greenberg, Karen, Joshua Dratel and Anthony Lewis (eds) (2005) *The Torture Papers: The Road to Abu Ghraib*, Cambridge: Cambridge University Press

Grindstaff, David and Kevin DeLuca (2004) 'The corpus of Daniel Pearl', *Critical Studies in Media Communication*, 21, 4, 305–24

Griset, P. and S. Mahan (2003) *Terrorism in Perspective*, London: Sage

Grojean, Olivier (2006) 'Les formes ultimes d'engagement du corps', *Quasimodo*, 8, 165–80

Grojean, Olivier (2007) 'Violence against the self', in Amelie Blom, Laetitia Bucaille and Luis Martinez (eds) *The Enigma of Islamist Violence*, London: Hurst, pp. 105–20

Groves, M., G. Griggs and K. Leflay (2012) 'Hazing and initiation ceremonies in university sport: setting the scene for further research in the United Kingdom', *Sport in Society: Cultures, Commerce, Media, Politics*, 15, 1, 117–31

Gruber, C. (2008) 'The writing is on the wall: mural arts in post-revolutionary Iran', *Persica*, 22, 15–46

Gruber, C. (2012) 'The martyr's museum in Tehran: visualising memory in post-revolutionary Iran', *Visual Anthropology*, 25, 68–72

Guidelli, Giorgio (2005) *Operazione Peci*, Rome: Edizioni Quattroventi

Gundle, S. and L. Rinaldi (2007) *Assassinations and Murder in Modern Italy: Transformations in Society and Culture*, New York: Palgrave Macmillan

Gurr, T. ed (1989) *Violence in America: Protest, Rebellion, Reform*, New York: Sage

Gurr, Ted (1970) *Why Men Rebel*, Princeton: Princeton University Press

Gurr, T. and C. Rutenberg (1967) The Conditions of Civil Violence: Test of a Causal Model (Princeton, N J: Princeton University Press

Habermas, Jürgen (1970) *Toward a Rational Society: Student Protest, Science and Politics*, Boston: Beacon Press

Habermas, J. (1989) *The Structural Transformation of the Public Sphere*, Cambridge, MA: Massachusetts Institute of Technology

Hall, John (2003) 'Religion and violence: social processes in comparative perspective', in Michele Dillon (ed.) *Handbook of the Sociology of Religion*, Cambridge: Cambridge University Press, pp. 359–83

Hall, John (2002) 'Mass suicide and the Branch Davidians', in David Bromley and J. Melton (eds) *Cults, Religion and Violence*, Cambridge: Cambridge University Press, pp. 149–69

Hall, Mimi (2008) 'US has Mandela on terrorist list', *USA Today*, 30 May, available at http://www.usatoday.com/news/world/2008-04-30-watchlist_N.htm?loc=inter stitialskip (accessed 1 July 2010)

Hafez, Mohammed (2006) *Manufacturing Human Bombs: Strategy, Culture, and Conflict in the Making of Palestinian Suicide Bombers*, Washington: United States Institute of Peace

Hafez, Mohammed (2007) *Suicide Bombers in Iraq: The Strategy and Ideology of Martyrdom*. New York: United States Institute of Peace Press

Hagemeister, M. (2008) 'The Protocols of the Elders of Zion: between history and fiction', *New German Critique*, 35, 1, 83–95

Haj, S. (1992) 'Palestinian women and patriarchal relations', *Signs*, 17, 4, 761–78

Hamm, M. (1997) *Apocalypse in Oklahoma: Waco and Ruby Ridge Revenged*, Boston: Northeastern University Press

Hamm, M. (2004) 'Apocalyptic violence: the seduction of terrorist subcutlures', *Theoretical Criminology*, 8, 3, 323–39

Hamm, M. (2007) *Terrorism as Crime: From Oklahoma City to Al-Qaeda*, New York: New York University Press

Hammami, R. (1990) 'Women, the Hijab and the Intifada', *Middle East Report*, 164, May–August, 24–8

Hammami, R. and S. Tamari (2001) 'The second uprising: end or new beginning?', *Journal of Palestinian Studies*, 30, 2, 5–25

Hardacre, Helen (1996) *Aum Shinrikyo and the Japanese Media*, Tokyo: Japan Policy Research Institute, Working Paper 19

Hardt, Michael and Antonio Negri (2004) *Multitude: War and Democracy in the Age of Empire*, New York: Penguin

Harub, Khalid (2000) *Hamas: Political Thought and Practice*, Washington: Institute for Palestine Studies

Haslam, S. and S. Reicher (2007) 'Debating the psychology of tyranny: fundamental issues of theory, perspective and science', *British Journal of Social Psychology*, 45, 55–64

Hasso, Frances (2005) 'Discursive and political deployments by/of the 2002 Palestinian women suicide bombers/martyrs', *Feminist Review*, 81, 23–51

Hayden, T. (1968) 'Two, three, many Columbias', *Ramparts*, 15 June, 40

Hayden, T. (2005) *The Port Huron Statement: The Visionary Call of the 1960's Revolution*, New York: Avalon Publishers

Hedges, C. (2003) *War Is a Force That Gives Us Meaning*, New York: Anchor Books

Held, D. and J. Thompson (1989) (eds) *Social Theory and Modern Societies: Anthony Giddens and His Critics*, Cambridge: Cambridge University Press

Heller, J. (1995) *The Stern Gang: Ideology, Politics and Terror 1940–1949*, London: Routledge

Henley, Jon (2003) 'Mojahedin urges calm as 17 face Paris inquiry', *The Guardian*, 23 June, available at http://www.guardian.co.uk/world/2003/jun/23/iran.france (accessed 9 January 2010)

Herbert, Ian Kin Sengupta (2005) 'The jihadist who needed no brainwashing to blow up the Aldgate train', *The Independent*, 10 September

Hill, J. (2007) 'Iranian group wins appeal over UK terrorism list', *Reuters*, 30 November, available at http://www.reuters.com/article/idUSL30888817 (accessed 9 January 2010)

Hobsbawm, E. (1989) *The Age of Empire*, 1875-1914, New York: Random House

Hoffman, Bruce (2003) 'Al Qaeda, trends in terrorism, and future potentialities: an assessment', *Studies in Conflict and Terrorism*, 26, 6, 429–42

Hoffman, Bruce (2006) *Inside Terrorism*, New York: Columbia University Press

Hoffman, Bruce (2007) *Challenges for the US Special Operations Command posed by the global terrorist threat: al-Qaeda on the run or on the march?*, Written Testimony Submitted to The House Armed Services Subcommittee on Terrorism, Unconventional Threats and Capabilities, https://www.fas.org/irp/congress/2007_hr/socom.pdf

Hoffman, Bruce (2008) 'The myth of grassroots terrorism', *Foreign Affairs*, 87, 133–38

Hoffman, B. (2011) 'The rationality of terrorism and other forms of political violence: lessons from the Jewish campaign in Palestine 1939–1947, *Small Wars and Insurgencies*, 22, 2, 258–72

Holden, R. (1986) 'The contagiousness of aircraft hijacking', *American Journal of Sociology*, 91, 4, 874–904

Holsti, K. (1991) *Peace and War: Armed Conflicts and International Order, 1648–1989,* Cambridge: Cambridge University Press

Honneth, Axel (2010) 'Liberty's entanglements: Bob Dylan and his era', *Philosophy and Social Criticism*, 36, 7, 777–83

Horgan, John (2005) *The Psychology of Terrorism*, London: Routledge

House of Commons (2006) *Report of the Official Account of the Bombings in London on 7th July 2005*, London: The Stationery Office

Hroub, Khalid (2000) *Hamas: Political Thought and Practice*, Washington: Institute for Palestinian Studies

Huggins, Martha, Mika Haritos-Fatouros and Philip Zimbardo (2002) *Violence Workers: Police Torturers and Murderers Reconstruct Brazilian Atrocities*, Berkeley: University of California Press

Hughes, J. (2011) *State Violence in the Origins of Nationalism: The British Reinvention of Irish Nationalism 1969–1972*, Paper at Nationalism and War Workshop, McGill University, March, available at http://personal.lse.ac.uk/HUGHESJ/images/StateViolenceintheOriginsofNationalism.pdf (accesssed 30 March 2012)

Hsu, Spencer and Michael Chandler (2010) 'Graduate of Va.'s Oakton High charged with trying to join terrorist group', *The Washington Post*, 22 July, available at http://www.washingtonpost.com/wp-dyn/content/article/2010/07/21/AR2010072104577.html (accessed 1 August 2010)

Hunt, Lynne (1998) 'The sacred and the French Revolution', in Jeffrey Alexander (ed.) *Durkheimian Sociology: Cultural Studies*, Cambridge: Cambridge University Press, pp. 25–43

Huntington, S. (1993) 'The clash of civilizations', *Foreign Affairs*, 72, 22–49

Huntington, S. (1996) *The Clash of Civilizations and the Remaking of World Order*, New York: Simon & Schuster

Hylland Eriksen, Thomas (2007) 'Stacking and continuity: on temporal regimes in popular culture', in Robert Hassan and Ronald Purser (eds) *24/7: Time and Temporality in the Network Society*, Stanford: Stanford University Press

Igarashi, Y. (2007) 'Dead bodies and living guns: the United Red Army and its deadly pursuit of revolution, 1971–1972', *Japanese Studies*, 27, 2, 119–37

Iida, Yumiko (2000) 'Between the technique of living an endless routine and the madness of absolute degree zero: Japanese identity and the crisis of identity in the 1900s', *Positions*, 8, 2, 423–63

Iida, Yumiko (2001) *Rethinking Identity in Modern Japan*, London: Routledge

Independent Panel to Review DoD Detention Operations (2004) *Final Report*, Arlington: Department of Defence

Introvigne, M. (2002) 'There is no place for us to go but up: new religious movements and violence', *Social Compass*, 49, 2, 213–24

Isaac, J. and J. Selby (1996) 'The Palestinian water crisis', *Natural Resources Forum*, 20, 17–26

Ito, Mizuko (2004) *Technologies of the Childhood Imagination: Media Mixes, Hypersociality, and Recombinant Cultural Form*, available at http://web.mit.edu/2.00b/www/documents/ito-childhood.pdf (accessed 10 Jan 2009)

Jackson, R. (2005) *Writing the War on Terrorism: Language, Politics and Counter-Terrorism*, Manchester: Manchester University Press

Jackson, Richard (2007) 'Constructing enemies: Islamic terrorism in political and academic discourse', *Government and Opposition*, 42, 3, 394–426

Jackson, Richard, Marie Breen Smyth and Jeroen Gunning (eds) (2009) *Critical Terrorism Studies: A New Research Agenda*, London: Routledge

Jamieson, Alison (1990) 'Entry, discipline and exit in the Italian Red Brigades', *Terrorism and Political Violence*, 2, 1, 1–20

Jarvis, L. (2009) 'The spaces and faces of critical terrorism studies', *Security Dialogue*, 20, 1, 5–27

Jean-Klein, Iris (2003) 'Into committees, out of the house? Familiar forms in the organization of Palestinian committee activism during the first Intifada', *American Ethnologist*, 30, 4, 556–77

Jenkins, Brian (1975) 'International terrorism: a new mode of conflict', in D. Carlton and C. Schaerf (eds) *International Terrorism and World Security*, London: Croom Helm, pp. 13–49

Jensen, R. (2004) 'Daggers, rifles and dynamite: anarchist terrorism in nineteenth century Europe', *Terrorism and Political Violence*, 16, 1, 116–53

Jensen, R. (2008a) 'The evolution of anarchist terrorism in Europe and the United States from the 19th century to World War One', in Brett Bowden and Michael Davis (eds) *Terror: From Tyrannicide to Terrorism*, Brisbane: University of Queensland Press, pp. 134–60

Jensen, R. (2008b) 'Nineteenth-century anarchist terrorism: how comparable to the terrorism of al-Qaeda?', *Terrorism and Political Violence*, 20, 4, 589–96

Joas, Hans (2000) *The Genesis of Values*, Cambridge: Polity Press

Joas, Hans (2003) *War and Modernity*, Cambridge: Polity Press

Jordán, Javier (2007) 'The threat of grassroots jihadi networks', *Jamestown Terrorism Monitor*, 5, 3, available at http://www.jamestown.org/programs/gta/single/?tx_ttnews[tt_news]=1013&tx_ttnews[backPid]=182&no_cache=1 (accessed 9 January 2010)

Juergensmeyer, Mark (1994) *The New Cold War? Religious Nationalism Confronts the Secular State*, Berkeley: University of California Press

Juergensmeyer, M. (1997) 'Terror mandated by God', *Terrorism and Political Violence*, 9, 2, 16–23

Juergensmeyer, M. (2003) *Terror in the Mind of God: The Global Rise of Religious Violence*, Berkeley: University of California Press

Juergensmeyer, Mark (2008) 'Martyrdom and sacrifice in a time of terror', *Social Research*, 75, 2, 417–34

Kaldor, M. (2001) *New and Old Wars: Organised Violence in a Global Era*, Cambridge: Polity Press

Kaldor, Mary (2002) *Cosmopolitanism and Organised Violence*, available at www.theglobalsite.ac.uk/press/01kaldor.htm (accessed 30 March 2010)

Kanaana, Sharif (1994) 'The Role of Women in Intifada Legends', in Annelies Moors, Toine VanTeeffelen, Sharif Kanaana and Ilham Abu Ghazaleh (eds) *Discourse and Palestine: Power, Text, and Context*, Amsterdam: Het Sphinsus, pp. 153–62

Kaplan, R. (1994) 'The coming anarchy', *The Atlantic*, February, available at http://www.theatlantic.com/magazine/archive/1994/02/the-coming-anarchy/304670/, accessed 30 March 2011

Kao, G. (2012) 'Of tragedy and its aftermath: the search for religious meaning in the shootings at Virginia Tech', in J. Carlson and J. Ebel (eds) *From Jeremiad to Jihad: Religion, Violence and America*, Berkeley: University of California Press, pp. 177–95

Kassim, Anis (1997) *The Palestine Yearbook of International Law 1995: Vol. 8, 1994/95*, Leiden: Brill

Kaufman, E. (1991) 'Prisoners of conscience: the shaping of a new human rights concept', *Human Rights Quarterly*, 13, 339–67

Keane, J. (2003) *Global Civil Society*, Cambridge: Cambridge University Press

Kellner, D. (2012) 'The dark side of the spectacle: terror in Norway and the UK riots', *Cultural Politics*, 8, 1, 1–43

Khan, Mohammed Sidique (2005) *Final Testament*, Pakistan: As-Sahab Islamic Media Production

Khondker, H. (2011) 'Role of the new media in the Arab Spring', *Globalizations*, 8, 5, 675–79

Khosrokhavar, Farhad (2005) *Suicide Bombers: Allah's New Martyrs*, trans. David Macey, London: Pluto Press

Khosrokhavar, Farhad (2009) *Inside Jihadism: Understanding Jihadi Movements Worldwide*, Boulder: Paradigm

Khosrokhavar, F. (2012) *The New Arab Revolutions that Shook the World*, Boulder: Paradigm

Khoury, Elias and Rabih Mroué (2006) 'Three posters: a performance/video', *The Drama Review*, 50, 3, 182–91

Kimhi, S. and S. Even (2004) 'Who are the Palestinian suicide bombers?', *Terrorism and Political Violence*, 16, 4, 815–40

King, Sallie (2000) 'They who burned themselves for peace: Quaker and Buddhist self-immolators during the Vietnam War', *Buddhist-Christian Studies*, 20, 127–50

Kitson, F (2011) *Low Intensity Operations: Subversion, Insurgency, Peacekeeping*, London: Faber & Faber

Kleingold, P. (ed.) (2006) *Immanuel Kant: Towards Perpetual Peace and Other Writings on Politics, Peace and History*, New Haven: Yale University Press

Knudsden, Are (2005) 'Crescent and sword: the Hamas enigma', *Third World Quarterly*, 26, 8, 1373–88

Kohlmann, E. (2004) *Al-Qaida's Jihad in Europe: The Afghan–Bosnian Network*, Oxford: Berg

Kordt Højbjerg, Christian (2005) 'Masked violence: ritual action and the perception of violence in an Upper Guinea ethnic conflict', in Neil Kastfelt (ed.) *The Role of Religion in African Civil Wars*, London: Hurst, pp. 147–71

Koschade, S. (2006) 'A social network analysis of Jemah Islamiyah', *Studies in Conflict and Terrorism*, 29, 6, 559–75

Kotef, H. and M. Amir (2007) '(En)gendering checkpoints: checkpoint watch and the repercussions of intervention', *Signs: Journal of Women in Culture and Society*, 32, 973–96

Kristiansen, W. (1999) 'Challenge and counterchallenge: Hamas's response to Oslo', *Journal of Palestinian Studies*, 28, 3, 19–36

Krueger, A. and J. Maleckova (2003) 'Education, poverty and terrorism: is there a causal connection?', *Journal of Economic Perspectives*, 17, 119–44

Kushner, H. (2003) *Encyclopedia of Terrorism*, Thousand Oaks: Sage

Lacina, B. and N. P. Gleditsch (2005) 'Monitoring trends in global combat: a new dataset of battle deaths', *European Journal of Population*, 21, 145–66

Landberg, R. (2004) 'U.K.'s Brown says poverty breeds terrorism, urges more aid', *Bloomberg*, available at http://www.bloomberg.com/apps/news?pid=newsarchive&sid=aOuhKjwmXfTo&refer=uk (accessed 10 March 2011)

Landsberger, S. (1997) *Chinese Propaganda Posters: From Revolution to Modernization*, Amsterdam: Pepin Press

Laqueur, Walter (1996) 'Postmodern terrorism', *Foreign Affairs*, 75, 5, 24–36

Laqueur, Walter (1999) *The New Terrorism: Fanaticism and the Arms of Mass Destruction*, Oxford: Oxford University Press

Larzillière, Pénélope (2004) *Être jeune en Palestine*, Paris: Balland

Law, R. (2009) *Terrorism: A History*, Cambridge: Polity Press

Lawrence, B. (2005) *Messages to the World: The Statements of Osama bin Laden*, London: Verso

Lawson, R. (1995) 'Seventh-day Adventist responses to Branch Davidian notoriety: patterns of diversity within a sect reducing tension with society', *Journal for the Scientific Study of Religion*, 34, 3, 323–41

Lavi, S. (2005) 'The use of force beyond the liberal imagination: terror and empire in palestine, 1947', *Theoretical Inquiries in Law*, 7, 198–228

Lemarachand, R. and D. Martin (1974) *Selective Genocide in Burundi*, London: Minority Reports Group

Lentini, P. (2008) 'Antipodal terrorists?' in R. Devetak and C. Hughes (eds) *The Globalization of Political Violence*, London: Routledge, pp. 181–202

Levi, Primo (1986/1989) *The Drowned and the Saved*, London: Abacus

Levy-Barzilai, Vered (2007) 'Ticking bomb', *Haretz*, 7 November, available at www.haretz.com (accessed 10 January 2009)

Lewis, Bernard (1986) 'Islamic Terrorism?', in Benjamin Netanyahu (ed.)*Terrorism: How The West Can Win*, London: Weidenfeld and Nicolson, pp. 65–9

Lewis, Bernard (1990) 'The roots of Muslim rage', *The Atlantic Monthly*, 226, 3, 47–60

Lifton, R.J. (1998) 'Reflections on Aum Shinrikyo', *Journal of Personal and Interpersonal Loss*, 3, 1, 85–97

Lifton, R.J. (1999) *Destroying the World to Save It: Aum Shinrikyo, Apocalyptic Violence and the New Global Terrorism*, New York: Henry Holt

Lifton, R.J. (2007) 'Destroying the world to save it', in B. Drozdek and J. Wilson (eds) *Voices of Trauma: Treating Survivors Across Cultures*, New York: Springer

Lind, W. (2004) 'Understanding fourth generation war', *Military Review*, Issue 845, 12–16

Locke, S. (2009) 'Conspiracy culture, blame culture, and rationalisation', *The Sociological Review*, 57, 4, 567–85

Lusky, Louis and Mary Lusky (1969) 'Columbia 1968: the wound unhealed', *Political Science Quarterly*, 84, 2, 169–288

Lybarger, Loren (2007) *Identity and Religion in Palestine: The Struggle between Islamism and Secularism in the Occupied Territories*, Princeton: Princeton University Press

Lyon, D. (2004) 'Surveillance technology and surveillance society' in T. Misa, P. Brey and A. Feenberg (eds) *Modernity and Technology*, Cambridge: MIT Press, 161–84

Lyotard, Jean-François (1990) *Heidegger and 'the Jews'*, trans. Andreas Michel and Mark S. Roberts, Minneapolis: University of Minnesota Press

Mandela, Nelson (1990) *The Struggle Is My Life*, New York: Pathfinder

MacBride, Sean, A.K. Asmal, B. Bercusson, R.A. Falk, G. de la Pradelle, S. Wild (1983) *Israel in Lebanon: The Report of International Commission to Enquire into Reported Violations of International Law by Israel During Its Invasion of the Lebanon*, London: Ithaca Press

Magloff, L. (2011) 'Munich Olympics massacre', in G. Martin (ed.) *Sage Encyclopedia of Terrorism*, (2nd edn), Los Angeles: Sage, pp. 409–11

Malešević, S. (2008) 'The sociology of new wars? Assessing the causes and objectives of contemporary violent conflicts', *International Political Sociology*, 2, 2, 97–112

Malešević, S. (2010) *The Sociology of War and Violence*, Cambridge: Cambridge University Press

Malkki, Liisa (1995) *Purity and Exile: Violence, Memory, and National Cosmology among Hutu Refugees in Tanzaina*, Chicago: University of Chicago Press

Mao, Zedong (1936) 'Problems of strategy in China's Revolutionary War', in S. Schram (ed.) (1999a) *Mao's Road to Power: Revolutionary Writings 1912–1949*, Vol. V, Armonk: Sharp

Mao, Zedong (1938) 'On protracted war', *in* S. Schram (ed.) (1999b) *Mao's Road to Power: Revolutionary Writings 1912–1949*, Vol. 1, Armonk: Sharp, pp. 319–90

Maqdsi, M. (1993) 'Charter of the Islamic Resistance Movement (Hamas) of Palestine', *Journal of Palestine Studies*, 22, 4, 122–34

Margalit, Avishai (2003) 'The suicide bombers', *The New York Review of Books*, 50, 1

Marx, K. and F. Engels (2007) *The Paris Commune*, Whitefish: Kessinger Publishing

Massumi, Brian (2007) 'Potential politics and the primacy of preemption', *Theory and Event*, 10, 2, available at http://muse.jhu.edu/journals/theory_and_event/v010/10.2massumi.html (accessed 30 March 2012)

Mauss, Marcel (1950/1990) *The Gift: Forms and Functions of Exchange in Archaic Societies*, London: Routledge

McCarthy, Rory (2009) 'Palestinian woman gets 20 years hard labour for helping Israel', *The Guardian*, 25 June

McDonald, Andrew [William Pierce] (1995) *The Turner Diaries*, Hillsboro, WV: National Vanguard Books

McDonald, Kevin (1999) *Struggles for Subjectivity: Identity, Action and Youth Experience*, Cambridge: Cambridge University Press

McDonald, Kevin (2006) *Global Movements: Action and Culture*, Oxford: Blackwell

McDonald, K. (2010) 'May's tensions today: France, then and now', in M. O'Donnell (ed.) *Sixties Radicalism and Social Movement Activism: Retreat or Resurgence*, London: Anthem Press, pp. 22–38

McDonald, K. (2011) 'Violence, the political and the religious: rethinking jihad in western societies, *Australian Religious Studies Review*, 24, 1, 80–97

McDonald, K. (2012) 'They can't do nothin' to us today', *Thesis Eleven*, 109, 17–23

McPhail, Clark and John McCarthy (2005) 'Protest mobilization, protest repression and their interaction', in Christian Davenport, Carol Mueller and Hank Johnston (eds) *Repression and Mobilization: Social Movements, Protest and Contention*, Minneapolis: University of Minnesota Press, pp. 3–32

McVeigh, Timothy (2001) *Letter to Rita Cosby*, reproduced in Vincent Burns, Kate Dempsey Peterson and James Kallstrom (eds) (2005) *Terrorism: A Documentary and Reference Guide*, New York: Greenwood, pp. 46–7

Mellor, Anne (1996) 'Immortality or monstrosity? Reflections on the sublime in Romantic literature and art', in Frederick Burwick and Jurgen Klein (eds) *The Romantic Imagination: Literature and Art in England and Germany*, Amsterdam/New York: Rodopi, pp. 225–39

Melucci, A. (1996) *Challenging Codes: Collective Action in the Information Age*, Cambridge: Cambridge University Press

MEMRI (Middle East Media Research Institute) (2006) 'American Al-Qaeda Operative Adam Gadahn, Al-Qaeda Deputy Al- Zawahiri, and London Bomber Shehzad Tanweer in New Al- Sahab/Al-Qaeda Film Marking the First Anniversary of the 7/7 London Bombings', *Special Dispatch*, 1201, 11 July

Merleau-Ponty, M. (1948/2004) *The World of Perception*, London: Routledge

Merton, R. (1968) *Social Theory and Social Structure*, New York: Free Press

Merton, Robert and Alice Rossi (1950) 'Contributions to the theory of reference group behavior', in *Continuities in Social Research*, Robert Merton and Paul Lazarsfeld (eds) New York: Free Press, pp. 40–105

Michel, L. and D. Herbeck (2001) *American Terrorist: Timothy McVeigh and the Oklahoma Bombing*, New York: Regan Books

Mickolus, Edward (2009) *The Terrorist List: the Middle East*, Westport: Praeger Security International

Milgram, Stanley (1965) 'Some conditions of obedience and disobedience to authority', *Human Relations*, 18, 57–76

Milgram, Stanley (1974) *Obedience to Authority: An Experimental View*, London: Tavistock Publications

Miller, Frederick (1999) 'The end of the SDS and the Emergence of the Weathermen: Demise through success', in Victoria Johnson and Jo Freeman (eds) *Waves of Protest: Social Movements Since the Sixties*, New York: Rowman & Littlefield, pp. 303–24

Miller, M. (1995) 'The intellectual origins of modern terrorism in Europe', in M. Crenshaw (ed.) *Terrorism in Context*, Philadelphia: Pennsylvania State University Press, pp. 27–62

Milton-Edwards, B. (1992) 'The concept of jihad and the Palestinian Islamic Movement: a comparison of ideas and techniques', *British Journal of Middle Eastern Studies*, 19, 1, 48–53

Milton-Edwards, B. (1996) 'Political Islam in Palestine in an environment of peace', *Third World Quarterly*, 17, 2, 199–226

Milton-Edwards, B. and J. Crooke (2004) 'Elusive ingredient: Hamas and the peace process', *Journal of Palestine Studies*, 33, 4, 39–52

Moghadam, A. (2006) 'Defining suicide terrorism' in Ami Pedahzur (ed.) *Root Causes of Suicide Terrorism: The Globalization of Martyrdom*, London: Routledge

Moghadam, A. (2008) *The Globalization of Martyrdom*, Baltimore: Johns Hopkins University Press

Moghadam, A. (2009) 'Motives for martyrdom', *International Security*, 33, 3, 46–78

Moretti, M. (1994) *Brigate Rosse. Una storia italiana*, Milan: Anabasi

Moss, David (1981) 'The kidnapping and murder of Aldo Moro', *European Journal of Sociology*, 22, 265–95

Mosse, George (2001) *The Nationalization of the Masses: Political Symbolism and Mass Movements in Germany from the Napoleonic Wars through the Third Reich*, New York: Howard Fertig

Mouchard, D. (2002) 'Les mobilizations des "sans" dans la France', *Revue française de science politique*, 52, 4, 425–48

Mulcahy, Aogán (1995) 'Claims-Making and the Construction of Legitimcy: Press Coverage of the 1981 Northern Irish Hunger Strike', *Social Problems*, 42, 449–67

Murakami, H. (2001) *Underground: The Tokyo Gas Attack and the Japanese Psyche*, New York: Vintage International

Negri, Antonio (1979) *Dall'operaio massa all'operaio sociale: Intervista sull'operaismo*, Milan: Multhipla

Neumann, Peter and Brooke Rogers (2007) *Recruitment and Mobilisation for the Islamist Militant Movement in Europe*, London: Kings College

New Left Notes (1969) 'You don't need a weatherman to know which way the wind blows', June 18, available at http://archive.org/stream/YouDontNeedAWeathermanToKnowWhichWayTheWindBlows_925#page/n0/mode/2up

Newport, K. (2006) *The Branch Davidians of Waco: The History and Beliefs of an Apocalyptic Sect*, Oxford: Oxford University Press

Newsinger, John (2001) *British Counterinsurgency: From Palestine to Northern Ireland*, Basingstoke: Palgrave Macmillan

New York Times, The (2007) 'Bolivia: prostitutes sew lips together in protest', 25/10, available at http://www.nytimes.com/2007/10/25/world/americas/25briefs-prostitutes.html (accessed 9 January 2010)

Nuwer, Hank (2002) *Wrongs of Passage: Fraternities, Sororities, Hazing and Binge Drinking*, Bloomington: Indiana University Press

Oberschall, Anthony (2004) 'Explaining terrorism: the contribution of collective action theory', *Sociological Theory*, 22, 1, 26–37

OECD (Organisation for Economic Co-operation and Development) (2004) *The Security Economy*, Paris: OECD

Office of the Coordinator for Counterterrorism (2004) *Patterns of Global Terrorism 2003*, Washington: US Department of State

Ohnuki-Tierney, E. (2004) 'Betrayal by idealism and aesthetics', *Anthropology Today*, 30, 1, 15–21

Olson, K. (1999) 'Aum Shinrikyo: once and future threat?', *Emerging Infectious Diseases*, 5, 4, 513–26

Orne, Martin and Charles Holland (1968) 'On the ecological validity of laboratory deceptions', *International Journal of Psychiatry*, 6, 282–93.

Palestinian Centre for Human Rights (2006) 'Extra-judicial execution of citizens suspected of collaboration', Field update, 27 February, http://www.pchrgaza.org/files/weapon /english/report9.htm (accessed 30 March 2011)

Pantucci, R. (2011) 'What have we learned about lone wolves from Anders Behring Brevik?', *Perspectives on Terrorism*, 5, 5–6

Pape, Robert (1996) *Bombing to Win: Air Power and Coercion in War*, Ithaca: Cornell University Press

Pape, Robert (2003) 'The strategic logic of suicide terrorism', *American Political Science Review*, 97, 3, 343–61

Pape, Robert (2005) *Dying to Win: The Strategic Logic of Suicide Terrorism*, New York: Random House

Passerini, Luisa (2004) *Autobiography of a Generation: Italy, 1968* (trans. Lisa Erdberg) Middletown, CT: Wesleyan University Press

Pécaut, Daniel (2000) 'Configurations of Space, Time, and Subjectivity in a Context of Terror: The Colombian Example', *International Journal of Politics, Culture and Society*, 14, 1, 129–50

Pedahzur, Ami (2005) *Suicide Terrorism*, Cambridge: Polity Press

Pedahzur, Ami and Arie Perliger (2006) 'The changing nature of suicide attacks: a social network perspective', *Social Forces*, 84, 4, 1987–2008

Pedahzur, Ami, Arie Perliger and Leonard Weinberg (2003) 'Altruism and fatalism: the characteristics of Palestinian suicide terrorists', *Deviant Behavior*, 24, 4, 405–23

Peel, M. (1997) ' Hunger strikes', *British Medical Journal*, 315, 829–30

Pigden, C. (1995) 'Popper revisited, or what is wrong with conspiracy theories?', *Philosophy of the Social Sciences*, 25, 3, 3–34

Pisano, V. (1979) 'A survey of terrorism of the Left in Italy: 1970–1978', *Studies in Conflict and Terrorism*, 2, 3–4, 171–212

Plant, S. (1992) *The Most Radical Gesture: The Situationist International in a Postmodern Age*, London: Routledge

Pressman, J. (2003) 'The Second Intifada: Background and Causes of the Israeli–Palestinian Conflict', *Journal of Conflict Studies*, 23, 2, 114–41

Quandt, W., F. Jabber and A. Lesch (1973) *The Politics of Palestinian Nationalism*, Berkeley: University of California Press

Rahnema, Ali (2000) *An Islamic Utopian: A Political Biography of Ali Shariati*, London: I.B. Tauris

Ramadan, T. (2012) 'Behind the Toulouse shootings', OnIslam, available at http://www. onislam.net/english/politics/europe/456384-behind-the-toulouse-shootings.html (accessed 25 March 2012)

Ranstorp, Magnus (2006) *Mapping Terrorism Research: State of the Art, Gaps and Future Directions*, London: Routledge

Rapoport, D. (2002) 'The four waves of rebel terror and September 11', *Anthropoetics*, 8, 1, available at http://www.anthropoetics.ucla.edu/ap0801/terror.htm (accessed 30 March 2010)

Rapoport, David (2004) 'Four waves of modern terrorism', in *Terrorism: Critical Concepts in Political Science*, London: Routledge, pp. 46–73

Ray, L. (2011) *Violence and Society*, London: Sage

Razack, S. (2010) 'A hole in the wall; a rose at a checkpoint: the spatiality of colonial encounters in occupied Palestine', *Journal of Critical Race Inquiry*, 1, 1, 90–107

Reader, Ian (1988) 'The rise of a Japanese "new new religion": themes in the development of Agonshu', *Japanese Journal of Religious Studies*, 15, 4, 235–61

Reader, Ian (2000) *Religious Violence in Contemporary Japan: The Case of Aum Shinrikyo*, Hawaii: University of Hawaii Press

Reader, Ian (2006) 'Japanese new religious movements', in M. Juergensmeyer (ed.) *The Oxford Handbook of Global Religions*, Oxford: Oxford University Press, pp. 141–54

Red Brigades (1970–80) Communiqués, available at http://www.brigaterosse.org/brigaterosse/index.htm (accessed 10 March 2010)

Red Brigades (1973) *Norme di sicurezza e stile di lavoro*, Typescript, available at http://www.rifondazione-cinecitta.org/brigaterosse25.html (accessed 10 March 2010)

Reinis, Austra (2007) *Reforming the Art of Dying: The Ars Moriendi in the German Reformation, 1519–1528*, London: Ashgate

Repsher, Brian (1999) 'Review of "Medieval Death: Ritual and Representation"', *Journal of the American Academy of Religion*, 67, 1, 100–202

Reuter, C. (2003) *My Life Is a Weapon: A Modern History of Suicide Bombing*, Princeton: Princeton University Press

Reuters (2012) 'Worker sets himself on fire to protest against unpaid wages', *The Guardian*, 30 March, http://www.guardian.co.uk/world/2012/mar/30/italy-worker-self-immolation, accessed 1 July 2012

Ricolfi, L. (2006) 'Palestinians, 1981–2003' in D. Gambetta (ed.) *Making Sense of Suicide Missions*, Oxford: Oxford University Press: 77–130

Riesman, D., N. Glazer and R. Denny (1961) *The Lonely Crowd*, New Haven: Yale University Press

Roberts L., R. Lafta, R. Garfield, J. Khudhairi and G. Burnham (2004) 'Mortality before and after the 2003 invasion of Iraq: cluster sample survey', *Lancet*, 364, 1857–64

Robespierre, M. (1794) *Rapport presenté à la Convention au nom du Comité du Salut Public*, available at www2.cndp.fr/laicite/pdf/Robespierre.pdf (accessed 30 March 2010)

Robinson, Glenn (1993) *Building a Palestinian State: The Incomplete Revolution*, Bloomington: Indiana University Press

Robinson, P. (2006) *Military Honour and the Conduct of War: From Ancient Greece to Iraq*, London: Taylor & Francis

Rorty, Richard (1989) *Contingency, Irony, Solidarity*, Cambridge: Cambridge University Press

Roux, Jacques (1997) 'Mettre son corps en cause : la grève de la faim, une forme d' engagement public', in Jacques Ion and Michel Peroni (eds) *Engagement public et exposition de la personne*, Paris: Editions de l'Aube, pp. 111–34

Roy, Olivier (1994) *The Failure of Political Islam*, London: I.B. Tauris

Roy, Olivier (2004) *Globalized Islam: The Search for a New Ummah*, New York: Columbia University Press

Roy, Olivier (2008) *La sainte ignorance: Le temps de la religion sans culture*, Paris: Seuil

Roy, Sara (1995) *The Gaza Strip: The Political Economy of De-Development*, Beirut: Institute for Palestine Studies

Roy, S. (2001) 'Palestinian society and economy: the continued denial of possibility', *Journal of Palestine Studies*, 30, 4, 5–20

Rudd, M. (2010) *Underground: My Life with SDS and the Weathermen*, New York: HarperCollins

Ruggiero, Vincenzo (2005) 'Brigate Rosse: political violence, criminology and social movement theory', *Crime, Law and Social Change*, 43, 4–5, 289–307

Russakoff, D. and S. Kovaleski (1995) 'An ordinary boy's extraordinary rage', *The Washigton
Post*, July 2, A01, available at http://www.washingtonpost.com/wp-srv/national
/longterm/oklahoma/bg/mcveigh.htm (accessed 30 March 2011)

Russell, Charles and Bowman H. Miller (1983) 'Profile of a terrorist', in L.Z. Freedman and
Y. Alexander (eds) *Perspectives on Terrorism*, Wilmington, Delaware: Scholarly Resources
Inc.: 45–60

Russell, John (2007) *Chechnya: Russia's 'War on Terror'*, London: Routledge

Sageman, M. (2004) *Understanding Terror Networks*, Philadelphia: University of Pennsylvania
Press

Sageman, M. (2008) *Leaderless Jihad: Terror Networks in the 21st Century*, Philadelphia: University
of Pennsylvania Press

Sanders, T. and H. West (2003) 'Power revealed and concealed in the new world order', in
H. West and T. Sanders (eds) *Transparency and Conspiracy: Ethnographies of Suspicion in the
New World Order*, Durham NC: Duke University Press, pp. 1–37

Sarat, A. (2001) 'Why Timothy McVeigh's execution should be televised', *FindLaw Forum*, 5 April,
available at http://archives.cnn.com/2001/LAW/04/columns/fl.sarat.mcveigh.04.05/
(accessed 10 November 2011)

Sartre, Jean-Paul (1961/2001) 'Preface', in Frantz Fannon, *The Wretched of the Earth*, Basingstoke:
Penguin, pp. 7–26

Sayigh, Yezid (1992) 'Turning defeat into opportunity: the Palestinian guerrillas after the June
1967 war', *Middle East Journal*, 46, 2, 244–65

Sayigh, Yezid (1997) *Armed Struggle and the Search for State: The Palestinian National Movement*,
Oxford: Oxford University Press

Schinkel, W. (2004) 'The will to violence', *Theoretical Criminology*, 8, 1, 5–31

Schinkel, W. (2010) *Aspects of Violence: A Critical Theory*, Basingstoke: Palgrave Macmillan

Schlatter, Evelyn (2006) *Aryan Cowboys: White Supremacists and the Search for a New Frontier,
1970–2000*, Austin: University of Texas Press

Schmeidel, John (2008) *STASI: Sword and Shield of the Party*, London: Routledge

Schmid, Alex (2004) 'Terrorism – the definitional problem', *Case Western Reserve Journal of
International Law*, 36, 2/3, pp. 375–420

Scolino, E. and S. Grey (2006) 'British terror trial traces a path to militant Islam', *The New
York Times*, 26 November, available at ftp://212.111.50.100/smo/British%20Terror%20
Trial%20Traces%20a%20Path%20to%20Militant%20Islam%20%20NYT%20%2026.11.06.
pdf (accessed 10 December 2011)

Seidman, G. (2001) 'Guerrillas in their midst: armed struggle in the South African Anti-
Apartheid movement', *Mobilization*, 6,2, 111–27

Sekules, Veronica (2001) *Medieval Art*, Oxford: Oxford University Press

Sepp, K. (2007) 'From "shock and awe" to "hearts and minds": the fall and rise of US counter-
insurgency capability in Iraq', *Third World Quarterly*, 28, 2, 217–30

Seybert, Gislinde (1995) 'The concept of virtue in literature and politics during the French
Revolution of 1789: Sade and Robespierre', in Gail Schwab and John Jeannery (eds) *The
French Revolution of 1789 and Its Impact*, New York: Greenwood, pp. 51–60

Shani, G. (2005) 'Beyond Khalistan? Sikh diasporic identify and critical international theory',
Sikh Formations: Religion, Culture, Theory, 1, 1, 57–74

Sharpe, T. (2000) 'The Identity Christian movement: ideology of domestic terrorism', *Journal
of Black Studies*, 30, 4, 604–23

Shekhar, Manisha (2009) 'Crisis management: a case study of the Mumbai terrorist attack',
European Journal of Scientific Research, 27, 3, 358–71

Shepherd, Jonathan (1998) 'The circumstances and prevention of bar-glass injury', *Addiction*, 93, 1, pp. 5–7

Silber, Mitchell (2012) *The Al Qaeda Factor: Plots against the West*, Philadelphia: University of Pennsylvania Press

Silke, A. (1998) 'Cheshire-cat logic: the recurring theme of terrorist abnormality in psychological research', *Psychology, Crime and Law*, 4, 51–69

Silke, A. (2000) 'Drink, drugs and rock'n'roll: financing loyalist terrorism in Northern Ireland Part Two', *Studies in Conflict and Terrorism*, 23, 2, 107–27

Silke, A. (2004) 'Courage in dark places: reflections on terrorist psychology', *Social Research*, 71, 1, 177–98

Silke, A (2008) 'Holy warriors: exploring the psychological processes of jihadi – radicalization', *European Journal of Criminology*, 5, 1, 99–123

Simcox, Robin, Hannah Stuart and Houriya Ahmed (2010) *Islamist Terrorism: The British Connections*, London: Centre for Social Cohesion

Siméant, Johanna (1993) 'La violence d'un répertoire: les sans-papiers en grève de la faim', in P. Braud (ed.) *La violence politique dans les démocraties occidentales*, Paris: L'Harmattan, pp. 315–38

Slotkin, R. (1973) *Regeneration through Violence: The Mythology of the American Frontier, 1600–1800*, Norman: University of Oklahoma Press

Sommier, Isabelle (2002) 'Terrorism as total violence', *International Social Science Journal*, 54, 473–481

Sommier, Isabelle (2008a) *La violence politique et son deuil*, Rennes: Presses Universitaires de Rennes

Sommier, Isabelle (2008b) *La violence révolutionaire*, Paris: Sciences Po Editions

Sommier, Isabelle (2010) 'Revolutionary groups after 1968: some lessons drawn from a comparative analysis', *Twentieth Century Communism*, 2, 1, 66–91

Sorel, G. (1908/1999) *Reflections on Violence*, ed. J. Jennings, Cambridge: Cambridge University Press

Spark, A. (2001) 'Conjuring order: the new world order and conspiracy theories of globalization', in J. Parish and M. Parker (eds) *The Age of Anxiety: Conspiracy Theory and the Human Sciences*, Oxford: Blackwell, pp. 46–62

Stanger, Cary David (1988) 'A haunting legacy: the assassination of Count Bernadotte', *Middle East Journal*, 42, 2, 260–72

Statera, G. (1979) 'Student politics in Italy: from utopia to terrorism', *Higher Education*, 8, 6, 657–67

Steinhoff, P. (1989) 'Hijackers, bombers and bank robbers: managerial style in the Japanese Red Army', *Journal of Asian Studies*, 48, 724–40

Steinhoff, P. (1992) 'Death by defeatism and other fables: the social dynamics of the Rengo Sekigun purge', in T. Lebra (ed.) *Japanese Social Organization*, Hawaii: University of Hawaii Press, pp. 195–224

Stern, Jessica (2003) *Terror in the Name of God*, New York: HarperCollins

Stern, S. (2007) *With the Weathermen: The Personal Journey of a Revolutionary Woman*, New York: Rutgers University Press

Stewart, Kathleen (1999) 'Conspiracy theory's worlds', in George Marcus (ed.) *Paranoia Within Reason: Casebook on Conspiracy as Explanation*, Chicago: University of Chicago Press, pp. 12–19

Stockholm International Peace Research Institute (2010) *SIPRI Yearbook 2010*, Oxford: Oxford University Press

Stockton, Ronald (1990) 'Intifada deaths', *Journal of Palestine Studies*, 19, 4, 86–95

Stolberg, S.G. (2004) 'Prisoner abuse scandal puts McCain in spotlight once again', *New York Times*, 10 May, p. A 19

Stolow, Jeremy (2004) 'On the spiritual telegraph in the nineteenth century', *Slought Foundation Online Content*, http://slought.org/content/11220 (accessed 5 May 2009)

Stone, R. (2001) 'At 100, Alfred Nobel's legacy retains its luster', *Science Magazine*, 294, 288–91

Swedenburg, Ted (1990) 'The Palestinian peasant as national signifier: tendentious revisions of the past in the construction of community', *Anthropological Quarterly*, 63, 1, 18–30

Tanweer, Shehzad (2006) *The Martyr Shehzad Tanweer*, Pakistan: As-Sahab Foundation for Islamic Media Production

Tarrow, Sidney (1989) *Democracy and Disorder: Protest and Politics in Italy, 1965–1975*, Oxford: Oxford University Press

Tarrow, S. (2005) *The New Transnational Activism*, Cambridge: Cambridge University Press

Taylor, C. (2011) *Dilemmas and Connections: Selected Essays*, Harvard: Harvard University Press

Thoburn, N. (2008) 'What is a militant?', in I. Buchanan and N. Thoburn, *Deleuze and Politics*, Edinburgh: Edinburgh University Press, pp. 98–120

Thompson, A.K. (2010) *Black Block, White Riot: Antiglobalization and the Genealogy of Dissent*, Baltimore: AK Press

Thrift, N. (2011) 'Lifeworld Inc – and what to do about it', *Environment and Planning D: Society and Space*, 29, 1, 5–26

Tilly, C. (2002) 'Violence, terror, and politics as usual', *Boston Review*, available at http://www.bostonreview.net/BR27.3/tilly.html (accessed 30 March 2010)

Tilly, Charles (2003) *The Politics of Collective Violence*, Cambridge: Cambridge University Press

Tilly, Charles (2005) 'Terror as strategy and relational process', *International Journal of Comparative Sociology*, 46, 1, 11–33

Tomsen, Stephen (1997) 'A top night: social protest, masculinity and the culture of drinking violence', *British Journal of Criminology*, 7, 90, 1–2

Tonkin, Elizabeth (1979) 'Masks and powers', *Man*, 14, 2, 237–48

Toufic, Jalal (2002) 'I am the Martyr Sanâ' Yûsif Muhaydlî', *Discourse*, 24, 1, 76–84

Touraine, Alain (1988) *Return of the Actor: Social Theory in Postindustrial Society*, University of Minnesota Press

Transportation Research Board (2006) *Transportation Security: Making Transportation Tunnels Safe and Secure*, Washington: Federal Transit Administration

Trinh, Sylvaine (1998) 'Aum Shinrikyô: secte et violence (Part 2)', *Cultures et Conflits*, 29–30, Autumn–Winter 1998, available at http://www.conflits.org/index720.html (accessed 8 September 2009)

Tu, A. (1999) 'Overview of Sarin terrorist attacks in Japan', in A. Tu and W. Gaffield (eds) *Natural and Selected Synthetic Toxins: Biological Implications*, American Chemical Society, pp. 304–17

Tumlin, K. (2004) 'Suspect first: how terrorism policy is reshaping immigration policy', *California Law Review*, 92, 4, 1173–239

Turk, A. (2004) 'The sociology of terrorism', *Annual Review of Sociology*, 30, 271–86

Ullman, H. and P. Wade (1996) *Shock and Awe: Achieving Rapid Dominance*, Washington DC: National Defence University

United Nations, Department of Economic and Social Affairs, Population Division (2009) *World Marriage Data 2008*, available at http://www.un.org/esa/population/publications /WMD2008/Main.html, consulted 30 March 2012

United States Department of State (2003) *Patterns of Global Terrorism*, Washington, DC: Department of State

United States District Court, Southern District of New York (2010) *United States of America v. Faisal Shahzad*, Plea, New York: Southern District Reporters

Urban, B. (2000) 'The devil at heaven's gate: rethinking the study of religion in the age of cyber-space', *Nova Religio: The Journal of Alternative and Emergent Religions*, 3, 2, 268–302

Uribe, M. (1990) *Matar, rematar y contramatar: las masacres de la violencia en el Tolima, 1948–1964*, Bogota: Centro de Investigación y Educación Popular

Uribe, Maria Victoria (2004) 'Dismembering and expelling: semantics of political terror in Colombia', *Public Culture*, 16, 1, 79–96

Urry, John (2005) 'The complexities of the global', *Theory, Culture and Society*, 22, 5, 235–54

Usher, G. (1996) 'The politics of internal security: the PA's new intelligence services', *Journal of Palestinian Studies*, 25, 2, 21–34

Van der Veer, P. (2000) 'Religious nationalism in India and global fundamentalism', in J. Guidry, M. Kennedy and M. Zald (eds) *Globalizations and Social Movements*, Ann Arbor: University of Michigan Press

Van Krieken, R. (1990) 'Social discipline and state formation: Weber and Oesterich on the historical sociology of subjectivity', *Amsterdams Sociologisch Tijdschrift*, 17, 1, 3–28

Varon, Jeremy (2004) *Bringing the War Home: The Weather Underground, the Red Army Faction, and Revolutionary Violence in the Sixties and Seventies*, Berkeley: University of California Press

Varzi, Roxanne (2006) *Warring Souls: Youth, Media, and Martyrdom in Post-Revolution Iran*, Durham, NC: Duke University Press

Venkatraman, Amritha (2007) 'Religious basis for Islamic terrorism: the Quran and its interpretations', *Studies in Conflict and Terrorism*, 30, 3, 229–48

Vetlesen, J.A. (2005) *Evil and Human Agency: Understanding Collective Evildoing*, Cambridge: Cambridge University Press

Wagner-Pacifici, Robin (1986) *The Moro Morality Play: Terrorism as Social Drama*, Chicago: University of Chicago Press

Waldmann, Peter (2007) *Guerra civil, terrorismo y anomia social: el caso colombiano en un contexto globalizado*, Bogota: Normal

Walmsley, R. (2010) *World Prison Population List*, 9th edn), Institute for Democracy and Conflict Resolution, University of Essex

Watanabe, Manabu (1998) 'Religion and violence in contemporary Japan', *Terrorism and Political Violence*, 10, 4, 80–100

Weber, Max (1978) 'The structure of social action', in W. Runciman (ed.) *Max Weber: Selections in Translation*, Cambridge: Cambridge University Press

Weber, Max (1918/2008) 'Politics as a vocation', in *Max Weber's Complete Writings on Academic and Political Vocations*, New York: Algora

Weber, M. (1978a) *Economy and Society*, Vol. 1, ed. Gunther Roth and Claus Wittich, Berkeley: University of California Press

Weisbrod, Bernd (2002) 'Fundamentalist violence: political violence and political religion in modern conflict', *International Social Science Journal*, 54, 174, 499–508

Weisburd, A. (2009) 'Comparison of visual motifs in Jihadi and Cholo videos on YouTube', *Studies in Conflict and Terrorism*, 32, 1066–74

Weiskel, Thomas (1976) *The Romantic Sublime: Studies in the Structure and Psychology of Transcendence*, Baltimore: Johns Hopkins University Press

Wieviorka, Michel (1993) *The Making of Terrorism*, Chicago: University of Chicago Press

Wieviorka, M. (1995) *The Arena of Racism*, London: Sage

Wieviorka, Michel (2009) *Violence: A New Approach*, London: Sage

Wojick, Daniel (1999) *The End of the World As We Know It*, New York: New York University Press

Wolin, Richard (2004) *The Seduction of Unreason*, Princeton: Princeton University Press

Wolin, R. (2010) *The Wind from the East: French Intellectuals, the Cultural Revolution and the Legacy of the 1960s*, Princeton: Princeton University Press

Wood, J. (2003) 'Hells Angels and the illusion of counterculture', *Journal of Popular Culture*, 37, 2, 336–51

Wright, S. (ed.) (1995) *Armageddon in Waco: Critical Perspectives on the Branch Davidian Conflict*, Chicago: University of Chicago Press

Wright, S. (2009) 'Reframing religious violence after 9/11: analysis of the ACM campaign to exploit the threat of terrorism', *Nova Religio: The Journal of Alternative and Emergent Religions*, 12, 4, 5–27

Voll, John and Michael Voll (2010) 'Muslim activism and social movement theory for the 21st century', APSA 2010 Annual Meeting Paper, available at SSRN: http://ssrn.com /abstract=1642611 (accessed 30 March 2011)

Yom, S. and B. Saleh (2004) 'Palestinian suicide bombers: a statistical analysis', *Economists Allied for Arms Reduction Newsletter*, 16, 8–11

Zedner, L. (2007) 'Pre-crime and post-criminology', *Theoretical Criminology*, 11, 2, 261–81

Zimbardo, Philip (1972) *The Psychology of Imprisonment: Privation, Power and Pathology*, Stanford: Stanford University Press

Zimbardo, P. (2008) *The Lucifer Effect: How Good People Turn Evil*, New York: Random House

Žižek, S. (1989) *The Sublime Object of Ideology*, London: Verso

Žižek, S. (2008) *Violence*, London: Profile Books

Zwerman, G., P. Steinhoff and D. della Porta (2000) 'Disappearing social movements: clandestinity in the cycle of new left protest in the U.S., Japan, Germany and Italy', *Mobilization*, 5, 1, 85–104

Index

211